D0237971

"*This is a well-argued and compelling defence of religious belief in the face of apparent challenges from neuroscience, psychology, and genetics.*"
Russell Stannard, Professor Emeritus of Physics, The Open University and author on science and religion

"'*Modern neuroscience raises challenges for many of our most basic ethical and religious beliefs*' writes neuroscientist Peter Clarke in the introduction to All in the Mind. *In this honest, clearly written, and wide-ranging book, he describes how the brain works and discusses the relationship between brain mechanisms, mind, consciousness, free/conscious will, morality, and a range of spiritual/religious beliefs and experiences. The breadth of scholarship is impressive, giving rise to a very informative text with a large amount of material packed economically into its pages. It is a much-needed and welcome addition to the Science-Religion literature.*"
John Bryant, Emeritus Professor, University of Exeter

"*Peter Clarke gives a wide-ranging critique of the view that there is a threat to human responsibility and dignity from modern neuroscience. He writes as an expert on how and why brain cells live and die, and a practising Christian. He urges us to take seriously the observations and experiments that show that wherever it has been possible to devise a means of testing the issue, all our cognitive abilities, including making judgments and ethical decisions, depend on the integrity of brain circuits. On the other hand he shows that it does not follow that we are nothing but automata: you need your brain but you aren't its slave. There is careful discussion of a number of the arguments often presented as knocking down one view or another, such as whether the Libet experiment undermines free will, and whether 'near-death experiences' prove that materialism is false. Contrary to the common view that modern neuroscience leaves no room for the soul, Clarke argues that it leaves plenty of room for an Aristotelean-Thomist view of the soul and there are theological reasons for preferring this to the Platonic concept. He reviews the claim that modern neuroscience presents fundamental challenges to key notions of criminal responsibility and finds it wanting. A demanding but rewarding read.*"
Dr Stuart Judge, neuroscientist, Emeritus Reader in Physiology, University of Oxford

"*Reports of exciting discoveries by neuroscientists are frequently followed by speculation about what these discoveries may mean for traditional beliefs about human nature, including our religious beliefs. The links between mind and brain seem to tighten with every new discovery so we wonder are we really nothing more than a machine without free will, and is there any longer room for the soul? And, given the discoveries of rudimentary aspects of religious behaviour in animals, what is special, if anything, about our religious beliefs and practices?*

This book, written by someone with a lifetime career in neuroscience, gives a concise, evenhanded, fair-minded, well-informed and balanced account of how some of our cherished religious beliefs look in light of what neuroscience tells us. Peter Clarke does not offer slick, dogmatic, simplistic answers to difficult problems but makes accessible to the nonspecialist the relevant evidence necessary to reach meaningful conclusions. He argues for an attitude of open but not empty-minded assessment. This excellent book is up-to-date, clearly written, helpful in thinking through pressing issues and is thoroughly permeated by a secure Christian faith solidly based on historical biblical foundations. I commend it most warmly."
Malcolm Jeeves, Emeritus Professor, CBE, F.Med.Sci, FRSE, past President of the Royal Society of Edinburgh, School of Psychology and Neurosciences, St Andrews University

ALL IN
THE MIND?

CHALLENGES OF
NEUROSCIENCE TO
FAITH AND ETHICS

Peter G. H. Clarke

LION

Published by Lion Books
an imprint of
Lion Hudson plc
Wilkinson House, Jordan Hill Road,
Oxford OX2 8DR, England
www.lionhudson.com/lion

ISBN 978 0 7459 5675 6
e-ISBN 978 0 7459 5676 3

First edition 2015

Acknowledgments
Scripture quotations taken from the Holy Bible, New International
Version Anglicised. Copyright © 1979, 1984, 2011 Biblica, formerly
International Bible Society. Used by permission of Hodder &
Stoughton Ltd, an Hachette UK company. All rights reserved. "NIV"
is a registered trademark of Biblica. UK trademark number 1448790.
p. 24: Extract from *English Literature in the Sixteen Century, Excluding
Drama* by C. S. Lewis copyright © 1954 C. S. Lewis. Reprinted by
permission of Oxford University Press.
p. 143: Extract from *The Problem of Pain* by C. S. Lewis copyright ©
C. S. Lewis Pte. Ltd. 1940. Extract reprinted by permission.
p. 236: Extract from de Duve, Christian, "Mysteries of Life: Is there
'Something Else'?", *Perspectives in Biology and Medicine* 45:1 (2002),
1. © 2002 The Johns Hopkins University Press. Reprinted with
permission of Johns Hopkins University Press.

A catalogue record for this book is available from
the British Library

Printed and bound in the UK, April 2015, LH36

To

STEPHANIE CLARKE
medical doctor, neuropsychologist, friend, and spouse

LYDIA LEHMANN
medical doctor and daughter

and in memory of
CHRISTINE CLARKE (1979–2014)
daughter, neurobiologist, "Lady Slamenco"

Contents

Acknowledgments

I am grateful to the late Professor Donald MacKay, who supervised my doctoral research 40 years ago and stimulated my interest in the philosophical and theological implications of neuroscience. I thank Stephanie Clarke, John Clarke, Martyn Frame, John and Lella Futcher, Stuart Judge, and Cara Wall-Scheffler for their invaluable comments on the manuscript. I am indebted also to Alison Hull of Lion Hudson for her help and insightful guidance at every stage of the preparation of this book.

Introduction

Modern neuroscience raises challenges for many of our most basic ethical and religious beliefs. Numerous authors including new atheist Sam Harris have used neuroscience to call into question free will and to attack religion-based ethics, and neuroscience professor José Musacchio went so far as to write an entire book trying to show that neuroscience contradicts all religion, as is implied in the book's title: *Contradictions: Neuroscience and Religion.*[1] I am far from convinced by the arguments of these authors, but it remains true that neuroscience raises deep questions about both ethics and religion. It casts the dangerous cold light of analytical science on almost everything about us that is supremely human. It challenges our basic humanity by insinuating that we may be nothing more than complicated physico-chemical machines. Its *determinism*[*2] challenges our free will. By studying the brain events involved in ethical decision-making, neuroscience gets uncomfortably close to the roots of moral responsibility. By revealing the brain activity associated with religious experience, brain-imaging techniques raise questions about its reality. Some people have gone even further, arguing on neuroscientific grounds that religious faith is a delusion, even a mental disease. The brain has been called the seat of the *soul*[*], but in the light of advancing science many writers have argued that the very notion of soul should be abandoned – and with it, the associated Christian (or Jewish, or Muslim, etc.) worldview.

At the same time, less materialistic voices have taken an opposite approach that can be almost as disturbing to Christians such as myself. The occurrence of unique brain activation patterns during meditation has been claimed to support oriental religious approaches. And "near-death experiences" by cardiac patients and others who have returned from the brink of death may (perhaps!) support belief in life after death, but in many cases the details of the experiences do not match well with what would be expected on the basis of Christian doctrine.

The aim of this book is to face up to these challenges. Having worked as a neuroscientist throughout my entire career, my approach is not to reject the findings of neuroscience, but to consider their implications with due caution, because I believe that the greatest threat to human values and to religious faith comes not from the neuroscientific facts themselves, but from their misinterpretation or their distortion. The book is divided into five sections, as follows.

Section 1, a single chapter, looks back into history to examine how, in the wake of the scientific revolution, the "mechanical philosophy" (as it was then called) became the predominant worldview of Christendom. I review how the unstoppable advance of this approach caused the machine metaphor to be extended first to nonhuman animals and then to human beings. At the same time, accumulating evidence has made it difficult to believe in any additional non-physical element – a special vital force or a non-physical soul – interacting with the "machine". The question to be faced, then, is whether we are just machines. Are we just complicated lumps of matter? This major question lies at the root of virtually all the themes of this book. To answer it will require the entire book.

Section 2 leaves history behind and gets to grips with the data of modern neuroscience. Chapter 2 ("Brain Makes Mind") summarizes recent evidence showing that brain activity underlies every aspect of our mental world – our thoughts, desires, emotions, actions, and even our moral judgments, love, and religious experience. Many questions about the brain–mind relationship are still currently unresolved, but it is already clear that the interaction is causal. Brain activity does not merely *correlate* with mental processes, it actually *causes* them. Then Chapter 3 ("How the Brain Works") gets down to the nuts and bolts of how the brain's neuronal circuits actually perform *cognitive** tasks (i.e. thinking tasks) that used to be attributed to a non-physical soul, taking as examples the brain mechanisms for visual identification of objects and for storing and recovering memories.

Section 3 moves on to the related themes of free will, responsibility, and ethics. Chapter 4 addresses the question of *reductionism**, the view that we are the sum of our parts: are we "nothing but a pack of neurons" (to quote Francis Crick[3])? I shall emphasize the key notions of *complementarity* and *levels of description*, arguing that low-level descriptions (in terms of molecules or *neurons**) do not invalidate higher levels (emotions, decision-making, meaning, belief). Then come three chapters on the challenges of neuroscience and psychology to free will. This is a controversial area, and outspoken popular authors such as new atheist Sam Harris use the results of neuroscience to argue that free will does not exist.[4] The first of my free will chapters (Chapter 5: "Are We Robots Without

Free Will?") tackles the classical question of brain determinism and its implications. If the interacting neurons in our brains work according to the laws of physics and chemistry, thus (almost) deterministically, does this undermine free will? This is a difficult subject, where even the leading experts on free will can be in blatant disagreement with each other, but most nevertheless accept that free will can be defended and I shall explain why. Then Chapters 6 and 7 deal with notorious claims, based on data from electrophysiology and psychology, that conscious will plays no causal role in behaviour. I shall refute these extreme claims.

The final chapters of Section 3 (Chapters 8 and 9) show that ethics is rooted in brain activity and face up to some of the ethical questions that are raised by modern neuroscience (including neurogenetics). Should "bad genes" or brain abnormalities revealed by modern brain-imaging techniques be accepted in law courts as evidence for diminished responsibility? Or does the combined determinism of genes-plus-environment rule out the very notion of responsibility anyway? This debate has merged with a second one about the validity of the principle of retribution in the punishment of criminals, and I shall argue for a moderate position here.

Section 4 is concerned with questions of the soul and religion. Chapter 10 addresses the *soul*. Critics often assume that Christianity is wedded to Descartes' notion of a separate, non-physical soul interacting with the brain, and they argue that modern neuroscience makes such a view difficult to accept. Descartes, the founder of modern (Western) philosophy, maintained that animals (and plants) are mere machines but that humans are different, being non-physical rational souls that interact with the physical machine. I agree that neuroscience raises major difficulties for this idea, but the point that many of these critics (including José Musacchio and Owen Flanagan[5]) fail to appreciate is that Descartes' notion of a non-physical soul interacting with the brain is by no means the only notion of soul in Christianity (or in Judaism), and modern biblical scholarship tends to reject this particular conception. This chapter summarizes the different notions of soul within Christianity and Judaism, and favours the concept of a soul that is embodied within the brain, not disembodied and external to the brain. Such a view seems to me fully compatible with the results of modern neuroscience.

But despite the neuroscientific critique of the *Cartesian** soul, intriguing support for a rather similar conception comes from a different direction. Particularly over the last 40 years, extraordinary experiences

– especially near-death experiences (NDEs) – have been interpreted by many people as proving the existence of a separate soul.[6] Debate on this subject tends to be very polarized, but I attempt (in Chapter 11) to address it neutrally, considering both neurobiological critiques and counterarguments by NDE "believers".

The remainder of Section 4 deals with other areas where neuroscience has implications for religion. Chapter 12 ("God in the Brain?") refutes claims that some people are genetically programmed to believe in God and discusses the implications of studies on the brain activity underlying religious experience. It also counters the claim that religious experiences are inherently pathological, resulting from abnormal brain events such as temporal lobe epilepsy. Then Chapter 13 considers the claim of several secularists (Dawkins, Dennett, etc.) that religion is just an illusory side effect of evolution. I argue that evolution may perhaps help to explain *religiosity**, our psychological tendency to be religious, although this is still uncertain, but that a religion is more than the religiosity of its adherents. Religions have to be evaluated on a much broader basis, including the evidence for their truth claims.

Finally, in Section 5 (Chapter 14), I draw the threads together and discuss how to approach the onward march of science, which will inevitably bring surprises and may even lead to further changes in worldview.

1

History

1

How We Came to Think of Humans as Complex Machines

Summary

This chapter looks at the history of how humans and our brains came to be thought of as complex machines, made from interacting parts. As a reaction to this approach, many attempts were made to explain the differences between living beings and machines by postulating the existence of special elements or forces present only in living matter, but belief in these has been completely abandoned since the first quarter of the twentieth century. The remarkable properties of living matter are now explained in terms of special *organization*, not special forces. A different approach, adopted by Descartes, was to accept that *animals* were machines, but to postulate that humans are more than machines because we have a non-physical soul, separate from the brain and interacting with it. This view became very popular, but now has few supporters in academia. The modern "mechanistic" approach raises numerous challenges for our conception of what it is to be human and these are the subject of this book.

Oh the nerves, the nerves; the mysteries of this machine called man!
Charles Dickens, *The Chimes*, 1844

In our age, when people look for explanations, the tendency more and more is to conceive of any and every situation by analogy with a machine... There is all the difference in the

world between describing and analysing a particular system
as a mechanism, and claiming that the "real" explanation,
the only objective or worthwhile explanation to be had of
the situation, is the explanation you get in terms of machine
analogies.
Donald M. MacKay, *The Clockwork Image*, 1974

The Notion of Mechanism

If there is one characteristic more than any other that distinguishes our
way of thinking from that of the Middle Ages or the ancient Greeks and
Romans, or the biblical writers, it is the modern tendency to conceive of
everything and everyone by analogy with machines. Applied to our brains,
this "mechanistic" approach challenges fundamental notions of what it
is to be human, including the soul, free will, moral responsibility, and the
validity of religious experience. The whole of this book is devoted to these
challenges. In this first chapter, we take a hard look at this fundamental
concept of *mechanism** and how it came to play such a dominant role.

Throughout most of history, a mechanism was a mechanical
contrivance with moving parts such as levers and gears. Over the last
100 years or so, this same term has been co-opted into the language
of biology. It is nowadays used very commonly to speak of organisms,
or parts of organisms, though in a more abstract sense, because the
interactions between biological molecules cannot be understood in terms
of simple pushing and pulling. But there is still the same underlying idea
that ultimately, if we take to pieces the cells of which we are composed,
we will find only inanimate things – electrons, atoms, molecules, etc.
To a modern biologist, then, we are mechanisms made of inanimate
interacting parts.

This *mechanistic* approach is very widespread in biology. We speak,
for example, of the *mechanisms* of cell division or the *mechanisms* of brain
function. Philosophers of science sometimes describe biology as a kind
of *reverse engineering*. Whereas an engineer may put components together
to make a machine that works, a biologist takes to pieces a cell, organ,
or organism to try to understand the parts and how they interact. The
mechanistic approach is applied in every branch of biology, including
brain research. In the early twentieth century it spread into psychology
as well. It is now common, for example, to speak of psychological

defence *mechanisms* or psychological *mechanisms* of depression. Clinicians even speak about *spiritual mechanisms* when referring to the contribution of spirituality to a patient's ability to cope with ill health and suffering. The word "mechanism" is here being used in a still more abstract sense, referring to networks of causal interactions rather than interacting physical parts, but ultimately the interactions are assumed to have a physical basis. Thus, mechanistic thinking dominates biology and psychology, and influences profoundly the way we think about ourselves.

From Holistic Teleology to Mechanism

This profound change has its origins in the scientific revolution. It altered the way people (at least, Westerners) thought, not just about science, but about literature and religion as well. The machine image became predominant in physics in the sixteenth and seventeenth centuries, and took root in biology in the eighteenth and nineteenth centuries. Throughout the classical period and the Middle Ages, the predominant metaphor was not *machine* or *mechanism* but *organism*. Plato and Aristotle and many of their followers considered the cosmos (the universe) to be alive and even conscious. Their thought was *holistic*, which means that they emphasized the whole more than the interaction between its parts. It was also *teleological*, by which I mean that they thought things (even inorganic objects) all had a *purpose* (*teleology**) or natural condition. For example, a stone fell to the ground because it was made of the element *earth* (one of the four elements in classical thought) and therefore wanted to be as close to the centre of the earth as possible. The ancients sought to explain *why* the stone fell to the ground, in contrast to the modern approach of describing the regularity of its fall by mathematical laws.

This holistic and teleological approach was almost universal until the scientific revolution (sixteenth and seventeenth centuries), when it was replaced by the mathematical, experimental, and mechanistic approach of modern science. The mechanistic approach was not, however, totally new in the sixteenth century. For example, the fourth-century theologian Gregory of Nazianzus thought of the universe as a musical instrument that was both made and played by God. But the machine metaphor really took hold at the time of the scientific revolution, whose leading figures conceived of the universe as an intricate mechanism that had been designed by God for our benefit. For example, Nicolaus Copernicus

(1473–1543) wrote in his major work, *On the Revolution of the Celestial Spheres*: "… the machine of the world… was built for us by the best and most orderly Artificer of all things." Much of the emphasis at this time was on understanding the movements of the stars and planets. These had been assumed to behave according to principles completely different from earthly events, but the heavens and the earth were united by the publication of Isaac Newton's *Principia* in 1687, showing that the same law of gravity accounted for the fall of apples on the earth and the movement of planets in the sky. These discoveries ultimately changed the way people thought about almost everything.

Mechanism Enters Biology

Descartes and Mechanism

The discoveries in physics led to changes in the understanding of biology. Plants and animals, and finally man, came to be thought of as machines. As early as the thirteenth century, Thomas Aquinas compared animals with mechanical clocks, and the sixteenth-century Spanish physician Gomez Pereira proposed that animals were mere machines, but it was the French philosopher René Descartes (1596–1650) who gave wide currency to this idea. He had been impressed by seeing automated statues that were moved by hydraulics, and he came to the conclusion that animals were machines operating according to a similar principle. He thought the driving fluids of these machines were the so-called *animal spirits*, which had been invoked by many classical and medieval thinkers as being a kind of gas or volatile liquid that flowed along the nerves, considered (wrongly, of course) to be hollow tubes.

Descartes attempted to explain how the flow of animal spirits could produce reflex movements. External stimuli would move the skin that would pull on the filaments and hence open valvules to release the flow of the animal spirits, ultimately affecting the muscles and producing movement. He also tried to account for sensation as being due to the flow of animal spirits from the periphery to the brain ventricles.

But Descartes made one important exception to his mechanistic explanation of living beings. He thought that man was more than a machine, possessing a *rational soul**, as is discussed in some detail in Chapter 10.

Vitalism

Subsequent debate about Descartes' mechanistic approach to animals and plants focused on the question of *vitalism**, which was the claim (by Descartes' opponents) that living organisms must possess some vital element or force not present in inanimate matter. Vitalism certainly seemed a reasonable position in the eighteenth and early nineteenth centuries. To a naïve observer, living organisms do seem very different from machines in numerous ways. These include their capacities to self-replicate and to develop reliably so as to take on the characteristics of their species. And, of course, higher animals can move with great skill and apparently can think and feel. At that time nobody had the slightest idea of how any of these processes could occur, so even eminent physiologists of the calibre of Johannes Müller (1801–1858) felt it necessary to postulate that living organisms were animated by special vital forces, entirely different from those in dead matter. The debate went on until the early years of the twentieth century, when vitalism was still supported by such leading figures as Hans Driesch and Henri Bergson, but tremendous advances in many areas of biology have since transformed the subject so much that nobody any longer argues for the existence of any mysterious vital force. It is now universally accepted that the special properties of living matter result, not from special *forces*, but from special *organization*.

In short, Descartes was – in a sense – right about animals and plants being machines. They are, of course, far more complicated than the simple hydraulic (or pneumatic) machines that Descartes thought them to be, and the subtle biochemical mechanisms at work inside cells bear no resemblance to the simple push-and-pull kinds of machines that Descartes had in mind. But the mechanistic approach that he championed is now universally considered to be applicable to living organisms, and even to human beings.

Nowadays, the only thing resembling a vital force that has any supporters at all is Descartes' notion of a non-physical soul. Writing in the middle of the seventeenth century, he maintained that *man*, unlike the animals, was more than a machine. He thought that man's intelligence and conscious thought could not be explained mechanistically and must result from a separate, non-physical soul that was conscious and intelligent and could interact with the brain. This view, known as *Cartesian dualism**, became very famous because of Descartes' status as the founder of modern philosophy, but it was controversial from the start and was subjected to strong attacks in the eighteenth century, as we shall see below. I here discuss Cartesian dualism only very briefly, because it is a major theme of Chapter 10. It currently has a few supporters but is a minority view.

Eighteenth-Century Reactions to Cartesian Dualism

The revolution in thought launched by Newton and Descartes led to the vast movement of critical reasoning known as the *Age of Reason* or the *Enlightenment*, which dominated the eighteenth century. In France, where the Catholic Church attempted to control philosophy and morals rather strictly, the eighteenth century was characterized by an anti-religious backlash, and most of the leading French thinkers were either deists (believing in an impersonal creator God who had set the universe in motion but had then abandoned it) or atheists. Many were also materialists, very happy to accept Descartes' ideas of animals being machines, but opposed to his notion of the soul.

Among these was the French medical doctor Julien Offray de La Mettrie, who reacted strongly against Cartesian interactionism in his two books *Natural History of the Soul* (1745), and then in his shorter and more polemical *L'Homme Machine* (1747). He made no distinction between humans and other animals, and argued from the limited physiological evidence available in the 1740s that the Cartesian "rational soul" did not exist. His arguments were not particularly strong, being concerned largely with semi-relevant facts such as the ability of muscles to contract even when removed from the body, but his writings became famous because of his vigorous statement of his conclusion. Toward the end of *L'Homme Machine* he writes, "Let us then conclude boldly that man is a machine." This was considered scandalous, and La Mettrie's works were officially condemned by the Paris parliament.

But so far as the debate about *dualism** is concerned, the debate was not atheists against Christians. It was more complex. Many Roman Catholic authors opposed Descartes' views. So did English nonconformist minister Joseph Priestley (1733–1804), who assured his place in the annals of science by isolating "dephlogisticated air" (oxygen). He complained that body–mind dualism was due to a contamination of Christianity by Platonism, and objected to the idea of an immortal soul, because it rendered the doctrine of the Resurrection superfluous.

Despite all the assaults on Cartesian dualism, it retained a prominent place in academia until the middle of the twentieth century, as is discussed in Chapter 9. Even today it still seems to be a common view among non-academics, and popular books attacking belief in a soul usually consider only the Cartesian conception.

The Triumph of Mechanistic Thinking and its Limits

The important point for the present chapter is that the mechanistic approach to biology and psychology ultimately triumphed. Few if any modern scientists have any qualms about analysing living organisms, including humans and our psychology, in mechanistic terms. In a sense, then, La Mettrie has been vindicated. In saying that man is a machine he was speaking loosely, but the point he wished to make, that the human brain–mind can be considered without invoking a Cartesian soul, is now the mainstream view. This is reflected in the titles of several books about neuroscience and psychology: *The Mind Machine* by Colin Blakemore, *The Brain Machine* by Marc Jeannerod, *The Mind's Machine* by Neil V. Watson and S. Marc Breedlove, *The Brain Machine* by Chris Turner, and *Mind as Machine* by Margaret Boden. This is not a matter of anti-religious presuppositions (for example, Blakemore is indeed an atheist but Jeannerod was a practising Roman Catholic). Whatever their religious (or anti-religious) commitments, almost all neuroscientists and most philosophers of mind (or of biology) accept a mechanistic approach, even to the human brain.

That does not, however, mean that there are no problems with the mechanistic approach. It is useful, but it does have some serious limitations. Here are just a few.

The Limits of Mechanistic Thinking as a Style of Thinking

Many thinkers have been disturbed by the idea that mechanistic science should address human brain function and psychology. For example, the Christian philosopher–theologian Francis Schaeffer wrote:

> *The modern scientists insist on a total unity of the downstairs and the upstairs, and the upstairs disappears. Neither God nor freedom are there any more – everything is in the machine... We find they include in their naturalism no longer physics only; now psychology and social science are also in the machine.*[1]

By "upstairs" Schaeffer meant the spiritual and the aesthetic, the human; by "downstairs", he meant science, logic, and reason. He was thus concerned that the rise of mechanistic (and analytical) thinking over the last few hundred years has distorted our way of thinking about human beings.

The great Christian apologist C. S. Lewis had similar concerns. Lewis was an expert on late medieval literature and was very much aware of the ways in which the rise of mechanistic thought in philosophy and science first led to abstract thinking and dualism, and ultimately affected artistic sensitivity:

> *By reducing Nature to her mathematical elements it substituted a mechanical for a genial or animistic conception of the universe. The world was emptied, first of her indwelling spirits, then of her occult sympathies and antipathies, finally of her colours, smells, and tastes. (Kepler at the beginning of his career explained the motion of the planets by their anima motrices; before he died, he explained it mechanically.) The result was dualism rather than materialism*. The mind, on whose ideal constructions the whole method depended, stood over against its object in ever sharper dissimilarity. Man with his new powers became rich like Midas but all that he touched had gone dead and cold.[2]*

A well-known exaggeration that contains a grain of truth refers to culture wars between scientific left-brainers and artistic right-brainers. In such conversations, religion and spirituality – along with intuition, holistic thinking, artistic appreciation, and creativity – are often assumed to belong to the right brain (or right cerebral hemisphere), whereas abstract reasoning and speech depend more on the left cerebral hemisphere. As a broad generalization there is some truth in this view, but in saying this I do not mean to imply that our different psychological faculties can be totally separated, or that we use each one individually. They are all linked and intertwined. The parts of our brains that perform rational thought need input from other parts dealing with our emotions, as Antonio Damasio has argued so convincingly.[3]

Purpose in Biology

As is explained above, the adoption of a mechanistic approach in science involved expelling teleological (purposive) presuppositions. This is however paradoxical, because it is impossible to fully understand a machine without understanding what it was made for. Thus, even for understanding mechanisms, a mechanistic approach is insufficient! A mechanic who unravelled in every detail the workings of a car engine would have missed the essential if he failed to appreciate that the car was *for* something: for transport. The machine analogy implies teleology.

This has led to considerable debate in the philosophy of biology. For example, the great eighteenth-century philosopher Immanuel Kant maintained that the peculiar nature of human understanding compels us to view organisms teleologically. Most people would agree that you can't understand a body without realizing that the heart is for pumping the blood and the legs are for walking and running, but various philosophers have objected to such language because it gives the impression that we are bringing back the old Aristotelian worldview that had been thrown out in the seventeenth century.

There is still debate about how to deal with this problem, but the most popular solution is just to sidestep it by using the word *teleonomy** instead of *teleology*. Teleonomy means *apparent* teleology. Atheist Nobel Prize-winner Jacques Monod insisted that living beings are objects endowed with a purpose and continued:

> *Rather than reject this idea [purpose or project] (as certain biologists have tried to do) it is indispensable to recognize that it is essential to the very definition of living beings. We shall maintain that the latter are distinct from all other structures or systems present in the universe through this characteristic property, which we shall call teleonomy.[4]*

In other words, biologists still need and use the concept of purpose, even though it was thrown out during the scientific revolution.

The Need for Global Approaches in Biology

To understand the purposive behaviour of an organism you need to study it as a whole, not analyse it into parts as the mechanistic approach requires. Few would deny that the mechanistic–analytical approach is an important part of biology (including neurobiology), but we also need global approaches to understand the overall operation of the organism. Over the last 30 years or so, "global biology" has become increasingly recognized, often linked with "complexity theory". Global biology does not contradict analytic biology; the two are complementary. We will come back to the relationship between analytical and global approaches in the context of reductionism (Chapter 4).

Conclusions

- The mechanistic approach of modern biology is founded on concepts that were established during the scientific revolution and the Enlightenment, leading to La Mettrie's claim that man is a machine.
- Few modern biologists would deny that this is in a sense true, but complementary, non-mechanistic approaches are needed as well to provide a valid statement about the nature of humanity.
- The mechanistic approach raises many fundamental questions about human identity and value, and about the validity of religious and humanistic concepts such as the soul, the self, free will, and responsibility. These are the subjects of this book.

II

Modern
Neuroscience

2

Brain Makes Mind

Summary

Few today would doubt that our thoughts, desires, emotions, and actions are somehow linked to our brain activity. This chapter confirms that this is true for every aspect of our mental world – even moral judgments and religious experience. Moreover, the brain–mind connection is *causal*, not merely correlational.

> **Men ought to know that from the brain, and from the brain only, arise our pleasures, joy, laughter and jests, as well as our sorrows, pains, griefs and tears. Through it, in particular, we think, see, hear, and distinguish the ugly from the beautiful, the bad from the good...**
>
> **Hippocrates, *On the Sacred Disease*, fifth century BC**

> **The great regions of the mind correspond to the great regions of the brain.**
>
> **Paul Broca, 1861[1]**

Brain Activity Underlies Our Thoughts, Desires, Emotions, and Actions

Early Studies of People with Brain Damage

The notion that the brain is the main organ of sensation and thought is not new. It goes back to Alcmaeon (about 500 BC). Soon afterwards,

Hippocrates (460–377 BC), or perhaps one of his associates, came to a similar conclusion, arguing in *On the Sacred Disease* (400 BC) that epilepsy was a brain disease and not a result of demonic possession. He went so far as to assert that the brain is the "messenger to consciousness", the "interpreter of consciousness", and the organ that "tells the limbs how to act". But the evidence for these insights was limited, and many of the ancients rejected them, preferring the heart as seat of mental activity. Others attributed mental function to the brain ventricles (large liquid-filled cavities in the brain), and the central role of the brain tissue was finally established only in the latter half of the seventeenth century, thanks to the anatomical dissections and clinical observations of people with brain lesions, by Thomas Willis (1621–1675) and his contemporaries.

But it was not until the nineteenth century that detailed descriptions of the mind–brain relationship began to be made, including considerable evidence that particular aspects of behaviour and thought were related to corresponding brain areas.

Much of the data came from humans who had suffered brain damage. A particularly famous case is that of Vermont railway construction worker Phineas Gage, who in 1848 suffered serious damage to his frontal lobes when an iron bar that he was using to compact an explosive charge provoked an accidental explosion. The bar was blown through Gage's left eye socket and out of the top of his head, causing severe damage to the left *prefrontal cortex** (the part of the frontal lobe in front of the motor regions – Figure 2.1) and more moderate damage to the right prefrontal cortex. Physically, he recovered remarkably well within a few days, apart from direct damage to his left eye and face. Also, his general intelligence appears not to have been greatly affected. In contrast, the brain lesion had serious effects on his *personality*. Prior to the accident he had been a man of admirable character, capable, reliable, well organized, and responsible. But afterwards, and for the rest of his life, he was capricious and vacillating, socially inappropriate, short-tempered, and irresponsible.

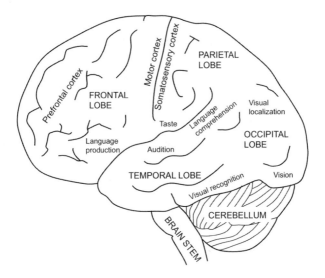

Fig. 2.1. *View of the left side of the brain. The amygdala and the hippocampus lie in the temporal lobe, but below the surface, with the amygdala further to the front.*

The *cerebral localization* of cognitive (thinking) skills was an important subject of investigation in the nineteenth century. This endeavour suffered from a false start because of the exaggerated claims of phrenology in the period 1820–1850, and the French physiologist Marie-Jean-Pierre Flourens (1794–1867) claimed on the basis of lesion experiments on animals that mental functions were not localized to particular cortical regions. However, the tide turned in the 1860s and 1870s because of observations of language deficits in human patients. Following initial work by Jean-Baptiste Bouillaud and others, Paul Broca (1824–1880) famously reported in the early 1860s the results of autopsies showing that aphasic (speech-impaired) patients had suffered damage to an area of the left frontal lobe that is now called *Broca's area*. This indicated that the *production* of speech depends on Broca's area, in the left frontal lobe. Then, in 1874, German neurologist Karl Wernicke provided evidence that the *understanding* of speech depends on a different area (now called *Wernicke's area*), in the left temporal lobe. Subsequently, David Ferrier and others obtained a wealth of further evidence for the specialization of cortical areas for particular brain functions using a combination of brain stimulation and lesion studies in animals. Thus, by the end of the nineteenth century there was no doubt about the principle of cortical localization, although a major debate about the cortical localization of *memory* was still to come in the period 1920–1950 because of the failure of Karl Lashley's behavioural experiments to identify a single cortical locus of memory storage in rats. We shall come back to the question of memory storage in Chapter 3.

Modern Studies of the Brain–mind Relationship

The study of the human brain has been revolutionized in recent years by the development of new techniques for localizing where in the brains of humans or animals the activity changes as a result of some task or stimulus. For more than half a century, techniques have been available for recording such changes in brain activity with electrodes on the scalp, but it is not easy to localize where the activity is coming from in this way. In recent years, the use of many electrodes coupled with computer analysis has permitted moderately good localization, but still more precise localization is now possible by several new techniques, of which I mention just the two most widely used. (1) *Positron emission tomography (PET)** can be used to detect the incorporation of radioactive materials into the more active regions of the brain. (2) *Functional magnetic resonance imaging (fMRI)** estimates changes in brain activity from local differences in the oxygen level in the blood.

By these methods one can compare the distribution of brain activity in an experimental condition, for example, looking at a small red spot while a green light flashes in the lower visual field, with a control condition, just looking at the red spot. The computer subtracts the second result from the first and prints out a series of virtual "sections" through the brain showing where the green light had affected the activity. By a similar approach, scientists have found different regions of the brain that are activated during particular tasks: performing a movement, or just imagining the movement, or performing mental arithmetic, or playing chess, or understanding language, or suffering pain. Many thousands of such studies have been performed, and I can only give a few examples.

Emotional experiences have likewise been studied by fMRI. These have included the experience of pain as well as empathy elicited by observing others suffering pain, which both involved activation of largely the same areas.[2] Still other studies have indicated particular cortical networks associated with passionate love or with other types of love.[3]

Other fMRI studies have focused on *ethical decision-making*. In one such study on volunteers, ethical decision-making was shown to involve activity mainly in two areas of the cerebral cortex: the posterior superior temporal sulcus (part of the temporal lobe) and the ventromedial prefrontal cortex (part of the frontal lobe).[4] In another fMRI study, volunteers were faced with moral dilemmas as to whether they would (in principle) be willing to kill one person to save the lives of five others. By comparing two different situations involving different degrees of empathy and moral conflict, the authors were able to draw conclusions about which brain regions are involved in the coldly rational aspect of the decision (better to kill one than five) and which are involved in the empathic, more emotional aspect (to kill anyone seems utterly repulsive).[5]

Other studies have focused on *religious experience*. Carmelite nuns underwent fMRI imaging while trying to relive their mystical experience of union with God. This increased the activation of many different brain regions including the lower part of the parietal lobe, the visual cortex, the caudate nucleus, and part of the brain stem.[6] In another study, using a different imaging technique, glossolalia (speaking in tongues) was found to be associated with decreases in activity in several brain regions including both prefrontal cortices, the front part of the left temporal lobe, and the upper part of the left parietal lobe.[7]

Such studies tell us *where* in the brain the activity is changing during a particular experience, but they do not address the causal relationships between mind and brain. Nor do they tell us whether the religious experiences involved inspiration by the Holy Spirit. But they do provide striking evidence that everything we do and think and experience involves changes in the activation of particular brain regions, supporting the link between brain and mind.

Brain Stimulation Shows a Causal Relationship Between Brain and Mind

The above evidence all supports the view that brain activity is *correlated* with mental activity, but does not show that brain activity *causes* it. Evidence for this stronger claim has, however, long been available from the fact that stimulating the brain, damaging it, or modifying it with drugs affects mental activity. A dualist may wish to remind us that the converse is also true: that our thoughts, feelings, and actions affect brain activity.

Some of the earliest evidence from brain stimulation was provided by the "brilliant but ghoulish" experiments of a German military physician, Eduard Hitzig, shortly before 1870. He studied patients who had had parts of their skulls blown away in battle leaving the surfaces of their brains exposed. He stimulated the uncovered parts with shocks from a battery, and observed that stimulation near the back of the brain caused a patient's eyes to move. To follow up this result, Hitzig collaborated with Gustav Fritsch, stimulating the brains of live dogs. Since they did not have a laboratory, they performed the experiments at Hitzig's home on his wife's dressing table! The classic conclusion of these experiments was that certain well-defined regions of the cerebral cortex are specifically involved in the control of movements, including what is now described as the *motor cortex*. Stimulating this area caused movements of muscles on the opposite side of the body. The equivalent area in man is at the back of the frontal lobe (Figure 2.1). Stimulation of its most medial part causes movement of the legs and perineal muscles; when the electrode is moved more laterally, the muscle movements occur progressively higher in the body, and very lateral stimulation causes movement of the facial muscles. The movements seem involuntary to the patient, who is surprised when suddenly his leg moves or one of his fingers twitches.

Since these initial experiments on motor regions, electrical stimulation has been used in a wide range of situations, by many researchers, extending the results to virtually every aspect of mental life. Some fascinating results were obtained in the 1920s and early 1930s by the Swiss physiologist Walter Hess. He explored the effects of stimulating deep parts of the brains of awake cats with fine wire electrodes that had been implanted previously under anaesthesia, and thereby discovered the control centres for some of life's most basic functions. These were situated in the *hypothalamus**, which lies close to the pituitary gland at the underside of the brain (Figure 2.2). In one small part of the hypothalamus, stimulation made the animal aggressive; its pupils would dilate, its hairs would bristle, it would start to spit, and when approached it would launch a well-aimed attack. In another region only a few millimetres away, stimulation would evoke friendly submission. In still others, it would evoke sleep, or feeding, or bladder evacuation accompanied by the characteristic posture, or changes in respiration. Hess's most important paper was published in 1932. At first, it attracted little attention, but later it became very influential and led to him receiving the Nobel Prize in Physiology or Medicine in 1949.

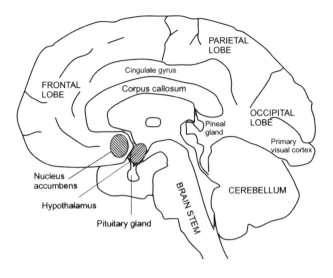

Fig. 2.2. *View of the inside of the right half of the brain, as it can be seen after sectioning all the structures that cross the mid-line (corpus callosum, cerebellum, brainstem, etc.).*

Another famous series of experiments on brain stimulation was performed by the experimental animals themselves! James Olds, working in the 1950s, implanted electrodes into the brains of rats and connected the electrodes to stimulators controlled by push-buttons in the cages. When the electrodes were in certain brain regions that came to be called "pleasure centres", the rats would press the buttons endlessly, as though they were receiving pleasure from the stimulation. In some experiments, the rats would even cross electrified grids in order to be able to press the switch. The "pleasure centres" were found in many regions of the brain, including a part at the base of the forebrain called the *nucleus accumbens**, which I shall refer to later.

Brain Stimulation in Humans

But it is stimulation of the *human* brain that provides the most direct evidence concerning the relation of brain activity to conscious states. Since Hitzig's first observations on wounded soldiers, an immense amount of information has thus been obtained, mostly from locally anaesthetized patients in whose brains electrodes had been implanted for diagnostic purposes. In humans, just as in rats, emotions can be elicited by the electrical stimulation of specific areas, although the hypothalamus is not often tested because of technical difficulties. Pleasure has been elicited from the septal region (in the frontal lobe, but near the hypothalamus), among others; fear from the *amygdala** and *hippocampus** (both in the temporal lobe); occasionally rage from the amygdala.[8]

By contrast, stimulation of sensory regions of the human brain gives relatively simple subjective effects. For example, stimulating the somatosensory region, just behind the motor cortex, gives pricking sensations in a small part of the skin on the opposite side of the body. There is a "sensory map" of the body in this cortex, corresponding roughly to the motor map in the motor cortex: medial stimulation causes sensations in the legs and genital region, whereas lateral stimulation affects the face. Likewise, stimulating the visual cortex, at the back of the brain, causes flashes of light in limited parts of the opposite field. Again, there is a map of the retinas onto the visual cortex, and there have been successful attempts at restoring a modicum of sight to blind patients by stimulating the visual cortex with an array of electrodes activated by a matched array of optic sensors worn on the front of the head.

It was the Canadian neurosurgeon Wilder Penfield who did much of the classic work establishing the sensory and motor maps in epileptic patients, mainly between 1930 and 1950, but his most surprising observations resulted from stimulation of the cortex of the temporal lobe. Up to that time, neurologists had been unable to ascribe any function to it, but it is now known to be involved in vision, audition, and memory. In about 40 (8 per cent) of Penfield's patients, the temporal lobe stimulation evoked a vivid experience (memory?) causing a strange doubling of consciousness: the patient was aware of being in the operating room, but at the same time had the strong impression of being elsewhere, for example riding in a forest or working in an office.

The first of these hallucinations was evoked when Penfield passed electric current through an electrode in the right temporal lobe of a middle-aged woman (who was epileptic, as were all of these patients). Suddenly, she exclaimed: "I seem to be the way I was when I was giving birth to my baby girl." Several years later, in 1938, Penfield was operating on the brain of a 14-year-old girl who suffered from frightening epileptic seizures. He exposed the right temporal lobe and found signs of brain damage due to a haemorrhage some years before. As he stimulated different parts of the damaged area, he evoked complex auditory or visual hallucinations. For example, upon stimulation of one point in what is now known to be a visually related region, she suddenly cried, "Oh, I can see something come at me! Don't let them come at me!" Upon successive stimulation of two adjacent points in an auditory part of the temporal lobe, she said: "They are yelling at me for doing something wrong," then, "I imagine I hear a lot of people shouting at me." From the complex, organized effects of this stimulation, Penfield deduced that he was stimulating an abnormal area that tended to produce epileptic discharges. He removed it, and the epilepsy was cured.[9]

In many other patients, Penfield's electrodes evoked similarly complex hallucinations from the temporal lobe. "Music, a familiar air", in one patient. Another exclaimed, "I had the same very, very familiar memory, – in an office somewhere. I could see the desks. I was there and someone was calling to me, a man leaning on a desk with a pencil in his hand." A woman under stimulation suddenly felt as if she was at home in her kitchen and could hear from outside the voice of her young son against a familiar background of noises. Ten days after surgery, she denied that the illusion was only a memory, insisting that it was more real than a mere memory. In most cases, repeated stimulation of the same site evoked the same hallucination.[10]

Brain Lesions and Consciousness

Studying the effects of brain lesions on mental function has produced a wealth of data showing not only that the brain is necessary for consciousness and voluntary behaviour, but that different parts of the brain are necessary for different aspects of our mental life. The systematic study of the effects of brain lesions goes back to Galen (c. 129–200 AD), who made careful observations of the consequences of brain damage in head-injured gladiators in Pergamum, and did parallel experimental studies in animals. I have also mentioned above some nineteenth-century cases involving lesions, notably the changed personality of Phineas Gage following severe damage to his prefrontal cortex, and the degradation of speech production or speech comprehension following lesions of certain parts of the left frontal or temporal lobe. I shall also describe (in Chapter 8) the effects of brain lesions on ethical behaviour, and evidence is available showing the effects of lesions in different parts of the brain on virtually every aspect of our thought, emotivity, and behaviour. For brevity, I shall focus here on just one of these: vision.

Effect of Brain Lesions on Vision

Some fascinating examples of the effects of brain lesions on mental life, including vision, are presented to the general public in Oliver Sacks's very readable books, including *The Man Who Mistook His Wife for a Hat*.[11] The man responsible for the title of this book was a distinguished musician, Dr P. It was while teaching music that his problems were first observed. He failed to recognize his students' faces. Then he began to see faces where there were no faces to see, patting the tops of water hydrants and parking meters that he took to be the heads of children. His disability became so great that he could not even tell that a head was a head, let alone recognize its face, and on one occasion Dr Sacks saw him reach out his hand and take hold of his wife's head, apparently believing that it was his hat. In the case of Dr P., the recognition of all kinds of objects was defective, but especially of living things, and most of all of faces. In other patients, there is sometimes a specific loss of face recognition, even though the other aspects of vision are virtually normal. This usually concerns the recognition of *human* faces, but in one famous case a farmer lost the ability to recognize the faces of his cows. The lesions that have such an effect are always in a particular region of the brain, the cortex of the inferior part of the temporal lobe. Interestingly, electrophysiological recordings from the equivalent area in the brains of awake monkeys have revealed the presence of neurons that respond specifically to faces.

Lesions in other parts of the occipital or parietal or temporal lobe can have quite different, but still specific, effects on vision. According to the position of the lesion, there may be a loss of the ability to recognize colours, or to perceive movement, or to appreciate the three-dimensional quality of the visual world known as *stereoscopic depth*. In each case, there is evidence from electrophysiological recording in monkeys, and from *functional brain imaging** in humans, that neurons in the affected area respond most readily to the corresponding quality – colour, movement, or depth. There is debate about the details – whether there is one colour area or two, whether the specificity is as great as some have claimed, etc. – but there is no doubt that particular regions of the cerebral cortex tend to specialize, and that the separate efforts of these regions are somehow combined to produce the multifaceted wholeness of our vision.

Pharmacological Effects on Mind and Mood

The effects of drugs provide further evidence that modifying brain activity can affect many aspects of consciousness, and in the case of alcohol this observation is so mundane as to be banal.

A well-studied case is that of cocaine. Cocaine works by enhancing the action of the *neurotransmitter** dopamine. One of the important sites of dopamine release is the *nucleus accumbens* (Figure 2.2). As was mentioned above, this is a "pleasure centre" and rats are enthusiastic to stimulate it if an electrode is implanted in their own nucleus accumbens. In a slightly different experiment, button-pushing by the rat caused the release of dopamine or cocaine into the nucleus accumbens from a tiny pipette, and this too evoked powerful self-stimulation. This supports the view that pleasurable effects of cocaine are due to its enhancing the effects of dopamine in "pleasure centres" such as the nucleus accumbens.

This view was based mainly on animal studies, but there is plenty of evidence that it applies to humans too. The nucleus accumbens is known to be involved in pleasure and motivation in humans; for example, neuroimaging studies show that it is selectively activated during the perception of pleasant, emotionally arousing pictures or even during mental imagery (imagination) of pleasant, emotional scenes.[12] There have been studies in which neurosurgeons made lesions in the nucleus accumbens in drug-addicted patients, and this helped to relieve the addiction. There is also evidence that most drugs, including opium, heroin, and alcohol, cause dopamine release in the nucleus accumbens in humans as in animals,[13] and the pleasure from the drugs is believed to depend on this.

We Need to Understand Much More About the Mind–Brain Relationship

The admittedly brief sketch above provides strong evidence for two important claims:

1. Brain processes underlie our mental functions. This claim is undoubtedly true, but it is rather vague, because it leaves unanswered many fundamental questions about the nature of the brain–mind relationship, as is pointed out below.

2. The brain–mind relationship is *causal*, in the sense that interference with the brain (by electrical or magnetic stimulation, drugs, or brain damage) causes changes at the level of mental function. The converse is also true to the extent that a mind event (e.g. imagining a movement) causes changes at the level of brain activity.

I have so far emphasized what we *do* understand, but there is much about the brain–mind relationship that is still a mystery. It is easy to reel off a whole string of questions about consciousness that we can't answer. Here are eight such questions.

Eight Unanswered Questions About Consciousness

1. Which creatures are conscious? Opinions range from the claim that only humans are conscious (Descartes in at least some of his writings) to the view that all things have some degree of consciousness, even stones and dead leaves (panpsychism, the view of many philosophers throughout history, including Plato, Leibniz, and William James, and in the modern world, Galen Strawson). Like most people, I would place my bets somewhere between the two extremes: I suspect that apes and dolphins and dogs are conscious (although perhaps only the higher apes are *self-conscious*), and that bacteria, trees, and stones are not conscious in any sense of the word. I'm not sure about fish, insects, and worms. But this is guesswork, and my point is that nobody really knows the answer.

2. At what age do human babies (or foetuses) become conscious? The occurrence of a strong hormonal stress response to a needle prick in foetuses has led some authors to conclude that human foetuses are conscious well before birth and need anaesthesia for prenatal operations, perhaps even in the second trimester,[14] but others have argued that babies are unconscious even in the first months after birth. The observation of sophisticated behaviours in very young babies does not prove that they are conscious, because unconscious behaviour can be complex. Based on a search for the patterns of electroencephalographic activity in babies that would reflect consciousness in adults, a 2013 paper in the journal *Science* provided evidence that the earliest glimmers of consciousness may begin as late as five months after birth.[15] The difference between the second

prenatal semester and five months after birth is enormous, and the question is far from being settled.

3. How precise is the relationship between mind and brain? Some philosophers go so far as to speak of *mind–brain identity*, implying a one-to-one correlation between physical states of the brain and mind states. Others (called *functionalists*) deny the identity claim, but argue that *functional* (not physical) brain states are responsible for mental states. Just as many different computer hardware configurations can be responsible for a particular computation, so many different physical states of the brain may correspond to a particular brain function, and hence to the corresponding mental state. I tend to favour the functionalist view, and there is evidence in favour of it. For example, a change in perceived brightness can be produced by cortical neurons in more than one way. But we are still a long way from having a detailed understanding of the relationship between mind and brain.

4. If two human brains were *exactly* identical, down to the finest details, would their thoughts and experiences be identical? Along with most neuroscientists I assume they would, but this raises a further question. Would the two brains with identical thoughts and experiences be two people or just one? Nobody knows.

5. If the electrical activity of a human brain were to be simulated in great detail on a computer, would the computer become conscious? This is widely believed to be a serious possibility, and the research field known as "machine consciousness" or "artificial consciousness" is growing.[16] But if we accept that machine consciousness is a possibility (as I cautiously do), this leads to yet another difficult question: how detailed would the simulation of a conscious brain have to be to reproduce its consciousness? Nobody knows.

6. In "split-brain patients", whose main communication link between their two cerebral hemispheres, the *corpus callosum*, has been sectioned, are the two hemispheres individually conscious like two separate human beings? There is support for this view, but the patients do not claim to experience any dual consciousness. Should one then conclude that the non-dominant hemisphere (the one without speech) is unconscious? The latter view might be deduced

from the fact that the patient is apparently unaware of sensory information that is received only by the non-dominant hemisphere and has been supported by some leading philosophers and neurobiologists, notably Karl Popper and Sir John Eccles in their book *The Self and Its Brain*.[17] Soon after the publication of this book (in 1977), the Popper–Eccles view was contested on the grounds of experiments on split-brain patients showing that the non-dominant hemisphere can mediate self-recognition and social awareness.[18] There is a considerable literature on this subject, by neurobiologists, psychologists, and philosophers, and a whole range of views have their advocates. The Popper–Eccles view tends to be rejected as too extreme, but there is no consensus.

7. What aspects of the brain's electrical activity are required for consciousness? Our understanding of this is very limited. We know that activity in some regions (notably certain areas of the cerebral cortex) are very important for consciousness, whereas other regions are not (e.g. the cerebellum), and we know that some patterns of electrical activity in the cerebral cortex are associated with consciousness, whereas others are not, but we are still a long way from understanding this in detail. Francis Crick (of double helix fame) and Christoff Koch have led the way in addressing questions such as these,[19] but there is still a long, long way to go.

8. How is it that a physical object such as the brain could ever give rise to consciousness at all? This is the greatest mystery of all. Some philosophers (e.g. Daniel Dennett) think we may be on the way to solving it, whereas others (e.g. David Chalmers) think it is fundamentally unsolvable.

Conclusions

- The above survey has touched only briefly on a vast subject, but it should be sufficient to show that our mental functions are not only paralleled by the physical events occurring in the brain, but are in some sense caused by them.
- Many fundamental questions remain to be answered about the brain–mind relationship, but it remains undeniable that our mental life depends on brain processes.

- The implications of this are dealt with in Chapters 4–12, but first we need to look more closely at how the brain's different components cooperate together to perform the brain's different tasks, and this is the subject of the next chapter.

3

How the Brain Works

Summary

Following the demonstration in the previous chapter that brain activity parallels mental activity and causes it, we now take the brain-machine to bits to see how its main working parts, the neurons, interact to perform its different tasks. In a few cases, such as visual form analysis and memory, we understand in considerable detail how these tasks are performed.

> **There are billions of neurons in our brains, but what are neurons? Just cells. The brain has no knowledge until connections are made between neurons. All that we know, all that we are, comes from the way our neurons are connected.**
> **Tim Berners-Lee, *Weaving The Web*, 1999**

The previous chapter showed that "brain makes mind". In other words, our different mental functions depend on the brain. Our feeling, our understanding, and our planning depend on events that happen in the brain. The present chapter goes further. We now take the brain-machine to pieces, so as to try to understand *how* the brain performs these different tasks.

This is of course a complicated subject and, despite my efforts to simplify it, some readers may wish to skip some of the details. The important thing is to keep in sight the main message that despite the brain's enormous complexity, we have a reasonably good understanding of how it works. We know how its neurons function, and we understand fairly well how they interact together to perform complex cognitive tasks such as visual form analysis and memory. This will be important for our discussion in Chapter 10 on the soul, where I shall argue that Descartes' notion of a separate, non-physical soul interacting with the brain becomes redundant since it is clear that at least some of the roles that Descartes attributed to the soul are performed by the neural circuits of the brain.

Neurons and How They Interact

The brain works electrically, and the cells most involved in its electrical information processing are the neurons. These are by no means the only cells in the brain; most of the others are called *glial cells* (or *neuroglia*, or just *glia* from the Greek word *glia*, which means glue). Some of the glial cells (*oligodendrocytes*) insulate the neuronal output wires, others (*astrocytes*) regulate the nutrition of the neurons, and yet others (*microglia*) clear away rubbish. Recent research shows that astrocytes can also play a role in neural computing operations, but in the account that follows I shall focus on the functioning of neurons. My purpose is not to give all the details, but to show that as research advances we are getting to understand how the neurons interact so as to perform the many different tasks that the brain performs.

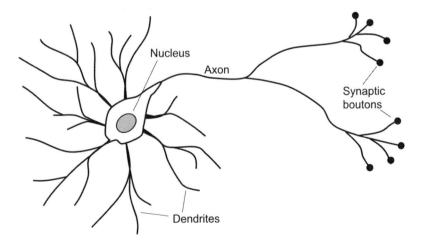

Fig. 3.1. *A typical neuron.*

Like all cells, neurons are surrounded by an electrically resistant external membrane called the *plasma membrane*. From the cell body of a typical neuron (Figure 3.1) sprout numerous branched protrusions, called *dendrites** (from the Greek word *dendron*, a tree), which receive inputs from other neurons, and a single output wire called the *axon** (a Greek word meaning axle or axis), which usually sends off hundreds or thousands of branches that end in *synaptic boutons**, button-shaped swellings that contact other neurons. Thus, the neurons are connected together in complex networks (Figure 3.2).

The contents of a neuron (as of any cell) are many and various, but these are held in a relatively simple salt solution that is particularly rich in potassium and chloride *ions** but poor in sodium. Outside the cells, there is a different salt solution, rich in sodium and chloride ions but poor in potassium. This difference between the internal and external salt solutions causes there to be a steady difference in electrical potential (or voltage) between the inside and the outside of the cell, the inside being more negative by about 70 millivolts in inactive neurons.

At this potential, the membrane is impermeable to most of the surrounding ions, but potassium ions can cross it through special pores in the membrane called "channels" – in this case, *potassium channels*. Since the concentration of potassium is 20 times higher inside the cell than outside, the potassium would normally diffuse out, but this tendency is counterbalanced by the negative resting potential, which attracts the positive potassium ions inwards. The potential at which this occurs can be calculated by means of an equation derived by Walther Nernst at the end of the nineteenth century for understanding how batteries work. The relevant point is that the electrical potential across a neuron's membrane can be determined by a simple equation that is not something unique to living organisms.

When a neuron is activated (or "excited"), its internal potential changes suddenly and transiently from the -70 millivolt resting potential to about +55 millivolts. The reasons for this are well understood biophysically. The transient change is called the *action potential**. It travels from the cell body down the axon, at a speed (usually between 0.5 and 100 metres per second) that can be calculated from a complicated set of equations named after Alan Hodgkin and Andrew Huxley, who received a Nobel Prize in 1963 for the research that led to these equations.

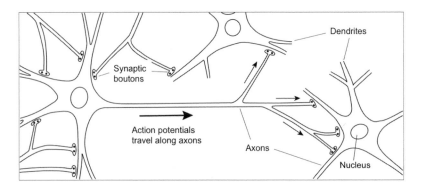

Fig. 3.2. *The neurons in the brain communicate with each other by means of bursts of electricity ("action potentials") that travel along axons toward the receiving neurons. The axons form numerous branches that finish in "synaptic boutons", from which the neurotransmitter molecules are released when an action potential arrives. The synaptic boutons are usually juxtaposed to neuronal branches called dendrites, but are sometimes on neuronal cell bodies and even occasionally on other synaptic boutons.*

Neurotransmission

When the action potential arrives at the axon terminals, it causes the release of a particular chemical substance, the *neurotransmitter,* which provokes a small potential change in the receiving neuron. Positive changes tend to excite the neuron, and negative changes tend to inhibit it (i.e. prevent it from being excited). This occurs at special junctions, known as *synapses** (from the Greek verb for "to clasp"), between the terminal branches of axons and the receiving cell. Thus, communication between neurons is not (usually) just electrical, but involves a chemical step. This whole process is called *neurotransmission.*

The mechanisms of neurotransmission are very complicated, but the essence of the process is illustrated in Figure 3.3. The neurotransmitter molecules produced by the presynaptic neuron are contained in the synaptic boutons in small bags called *synaptic vesicles**. Each vesicle contains several thousand neurotransmitter molecules. Some of the vesicles are "tethered" by various protein molecules, which hold them close to the cell membrane of the synaptic bouton. When an action potential arrives, this causes them to release their neurotransmitter molecules into the *synaptic cleft,* which is the narrow space between the terminal and the neuron to be excited or inhibited (Figure 3.3).

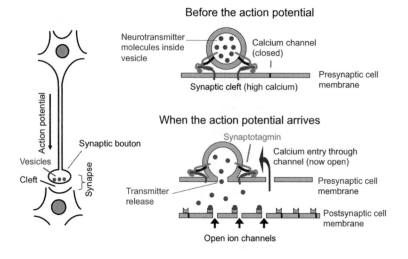

Fig. 3.3. *Mechanism of neurotransmitter release, showing that the arrival of an action potential in the synaptic bouton causes calcium ions to enter the synaptic bouton through a channel. Some of them bind to a calcium-sensitive protein (synaptotagmin), which therefore changes shape and pulls the vesicle against the cell membrane. This causes it to fuse to the membrane and release its neurotransmitter molecules. These diffuse across the synaptic cleft and bind to receptors on the postsynaptic membrane, causing ion channels to open.*

The release mechanism is triggered by calcium ions, which are much more abundant outside neurons than inside. When the action potential arrives in the axon terminal, the voltage change opens *voltage-sensitive calcium channels* in the membrane that open or close depending on the voltage. These allow calcium ions to diffuse into the terminal, where they interact with various specialized proteins including molecules of *synaptotagmin**, which are attached both to synaptic vesicles and to the cell membrane. The binding of calcium changes the shape of the synaptotagmin, causing it to pull the vesicle against the membrane so that they fuse together and the neurotransmitter molecules in the vesicle spill out into the synaptic cleft.

Once in the synaptic cleft, these molecules diffuse across it and bind to special "receptors" on the outside of the receiving neuron. These are complexes of proteins in the neuronal membrane whose particular shapes ensure that they are bound only by the appropriate transmitter. They are particularly abundant in the region of the synapse. The binding process affects the next ("postsynaptic") neuron in one of two ways. In some cases, it triggers a cascade of biochemical reactions (these are well understood, but I shall not explain the details). In other cases, it causes the opening of *ion channels**, which allow a particular kind of ion* to pass: usually sodium or potassium or chloride or calcium (and sodium). From now on, I shall discuss only this latter kind of transmission, which is called "ionotropic".

Neurotransmitter receptors are of two sorts, excitatory or inhibitory, depending on whether they increase the level of activity in the next neuron (excitation) or decrease it (inhibition). The effect of a neurotransmitter molecule binding to a given kind of receptor is either excitatory or inhibitory, never both. In the case of ionotropic receptors, the channels of excitatory receptors allow sodium and in some cases calcium ions to pass through, but not potassium or chloride ions. Since there is much more sodium outside the neuron than inside, the opening causes the positively charged sodium ions to enter, thereby depolarizing the neuron (i.e. making it less negative). On the other hand, the channels of inhibitory receptors allow only potassium or chloride to pass through; negatively charged chloride flows in or positively charged potassium flows out, so in this case channel opening hyperpolarizes the neuron (i.e. makes it even more negative than before). The balance of excitation and inhibition will determine whether and when an action potential is produced.

There are many types of neurotransmitter molecule, but only a few need be mentioned here. The most abundant one in the brain is the amino acid *glutamate*, which can act on several different types of receptor. In the brain, glutamate is always excitatory. The brain's most abundant *inhibitory* transmitter is another amino acid, gamma-aminobutyric acid (GABA). Other neurotransmitters include dopamine (mentioned in Chapter 2 because of its involvement in pleasure), serotonin (involved in mood, appetite, and sleep), noradrenaline (also called norepinephrine), and acetylcholine.

From Neuron to Circuit

From what has been said above, it should be clear that a neuron's functioning would be predictable if we had a detailed knowledge of the electrical properties of the neuron, the strengths of all the inputs from other neurons, and the time of arrival of all the action potentials arriving along the input axons. Such detailed information is rarely available in practice, especially in complex situations such as the cerebral cortex where each neuron has inputs from thousands of other neurons. But, even with incomplete and approximate information, some remarkable understanding has been obtained of the conditions that make individual neurons fire and the way that the different neurons cooperate to perform particular sensory or cognitive tasks – tasks that were traditionally attributed to a non-physical soul.

The Brain Performs Tasks That Descartes Attributed to the Soul

The question arises, therefore, whether modern understanding of how neural circuits work is sufficient to understand human cognition. Such detailed understanding is only available in a few cases, and we shall look at just two of these: visual form analysis, and the storage and retrieval of memories.

The Neural Basis of Visual Form Analysis

When Descartes claimed that sensation, including vision, could be dealt with mechanistically without intervention from the soul, he was referring only to the transfer of sensory data (to use modern terminology) to the brain ventricles, from where they would be communicated via the pineal gland to the soul. It was the soul's job to understand the data. But the job of understanding a visual scene can now be broken down into steps, and we know quite a lot about how these are achieved in the brain.

The basic neuroanatomy of the human visual system is shown in Figure 3.4. In the initial stages of vision, the formation of an image on the retina leads to electrical changes there in special light-sensitive neurons called photoreceptors, which pass the information on to other retinal neurons, leading to the excitation or inhibition of the *retinal output neurons* (officially called *retinal ganglion neurons*), which are the ones that project their axons to the brain. The most important retinal projection to the brain terminates in the *lateral geniculate body** (there is one on each side), and its neurons project up to the primary visual cortex. We shall focus on the progressive analysis of visual information at these three levels: retina, lateral geniculate body, and primary visual cortex.

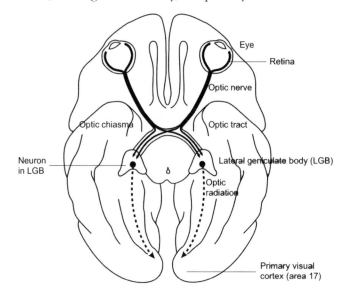

Fig. 3.4. *Diagram showing the eyes and underside of the human brain, including the first three stages of visual processing. Axons of retinal neurons extend through the optic nerve, chiasma, and optic tract to the lateral geniculate body, where they form synapses on neurons that project through the optic radiation to the primary visual cortex.*

An important advance in the history of neuroscience was the realization that neurons at all levels in the visual system beyond the photoreceptors do not respond to light shone diffusely onto the retina, but only to the presentation of a particular light stimulus that is appropriate for the individual neuron in question. The first evidence for this was obtained in the 1950s from electrophysiological recordings in frogs by Horace Barlow at the University of Cambridge, England, and by the group of Warren McCulloch, at the Massachusetts Institute of Technology, in the other Cambridge (near Boston, USA). However, I shall here concentrate on the Nobel Prize-winning experiments of David Hubel and Torsten Wiesel on the visual systems of cats and macaque monkeys, performed mainly between 1960 and 1980 at Harvard University. The visual systems of macaques are organized very much in the same way as our own, and they have similar visual capacities. Cats have a much lower visual acuity (capacity to see small objects) and very little colour vision, but the overall organization of their visual systems is along the same lines as those of monkeys and humans.

Hubel and Wiesel's Research on the Visual Cortex

Prior to the work of Hubel and Wiesel, it was already known that retinal output neurons do not simply signal the presence of diffuse light. Some are excited by light falling in a small region of the retina, and are inhibited by light falling in a surrounding annular (ring-shaped) region. These two regions of retina taken together are called the *receptive field* of the retinal ganglion neuron, and the separate parts are called the *centre* and the *surround*. For other retinal output neurons the arrangement is the opposite, in that the neuron is inhibited by light in the centre region, but excited by light in the annular surround (Figure 3.5A). A consequence of this arrangement is that diffuse light both excites and inhibits the neurons, and these two effects can cancel each other out, making the retinal output neurons rather insensitive to changes in the overall level of illumination. In contrast, retinal output neurons respond vigorously to small bright spots or to small dark spots when their images fall in the centre of the neuron's receptive field. This information is sent from the retina to the brain.

In the next stage of the visual pathway – the lateral geniculate nucleus (near the middle of the brain) – Hubel and Wiesel found that the neurons responded in virtually the same way as the retinal output neurons. But in the visual cortex (which contains many subregions called V1, V2, V3, etc.) the response requirements were strikingly different. A key discovery was that most neurons in the visual cortex respond only to edges or lines of a particular orientation, moving across a particular part of the retina in a particular direction. Oblique or horizontal lines fail to stimulate a vertical-preferring neuron. In many cases, the direction of movement matters too; a neuron may respond when the line moves right-to-left, but not when it moves left-to-right. Some neurons are still more choosy, responding to short lines but not to long ones. Most are also choosy about the width of the line. Some are very choosy about binocular interaction relevant to the depth (distance away) of the stimulus; they respond only to objects at a particular distance. Such depth-selective neurons are believed to provide the neural basis for stereoscopic (three-dimensional) vision.

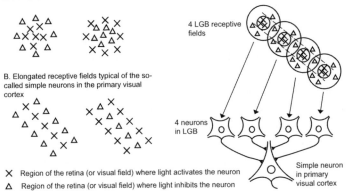

A. Concentric receptive fields typical of neurons in the retina or LGB

B. Elongated receptive fields typical of the so-called simple neurons in the primary visual cortex

C. Wiring diagram to explain the properties of simple neurons

4 LGB receptive fields

4 neurons in LGB

Simple neuron in primary visual cortex

X   Region of the retina (or visual field) where light activates the neuron

△   Region of the retina (or visual field) where light inhibits the neuron

Fig. 3.5. *A. Retinal ganglion neurons and neurons of the lateral geniculate body (LGB) usually have concentric receptive fields composed of a centre and a surround. The effects of light falling on the centre or on the surround are opposite. B. The receptive fields of simple neurons, which occur almost exclusively in the primary visual cortex, are usually composed of 2 or 3 elongated subregions. C. Wiring diagram proposed by Hubel and Wiesel in 1962 to explain the response characteristics of simple neurons. They receive connections from many LGB neurons (here only 4 are shown) with receptive fields that are arranged in a straight line. (Adapted from D. H. Hubel and T. N. Wiesel, "Receptive Fields, Binocular Interaction and Functional Architecture in the Cat's Visual Cortex",* Journal of Physiology *160 (1962): 106–54 (p. 142).)*

Hubel and Wiesel and many others confirmed that the initial results from cats could be duplicated in anaesthetized or awake monkeys, and even in awake humans, apart from some differences of detail. One of the differences is that neurons in monkeys and humans are even choosier than those in cats, because monkeys and humans have much better colour vision, and colour adds a further characteristic for the neurons to be choosy about.

An important point in the present context is that the visual response properties of the cortical neurons were simple enough for Hubel and Wiesel to be able to suggest wiring diagrams to explain them, yet sufficiently "high-level" to help explain certain aspects of the psychology of vision. Different wiring diagrams were proposed for different kinds of neuron. Hubel and Wiesel distinguished three main kinds of line-detecting neurons in the visual cortex: *simple neurons*, responding to a line of a given orientation in a given position; *complex neurons*, responding with the same selectivity to line orientation, but less selective to the position on the retina; and *hypercomplex neurons*, resembling *complex neurons* but responding better to short lines than to long ones.

Figure 3.5 explains a famous wiring diagram proposed by Hubel and Wiesel in 1962 for *simple neurons*. The receptive fields of these neurons are divided into about three elongated regions, in each of which light either excites or inhibits the neuron but not both. Hence, a flashing slit of light correctly positioned and oriented on an "excitatory" (or "on") region will cause the neuron to fire when the light goes on, but will reduce its firing rate when the light goes off. A slit of light on an "inhibitory" (or "off") region will do the opposite (Figure 3.5B). It is easy to see that a correctly oriented moving slit of light of approximately the right width will excite the neuron strongly when it leaves an "off" region (one cause of excitation) to enter an "on" region (a second cause of excitation). On the other hand, a slit oriented perpendicularly to the receptive field subregions will simultaneously excite and inhibit small parts of the "on" and "off" subregions, leading to a mixture of weak excitation and weak inhibition that will tend to cancel out, so the neuron will not respond. The illustrated wiring diagram (Figure 3.5C) proposes that many lateral geniculate neurons (only four are shown), with "on" centres lined up along the "on" region of the cortical simple neuron, all project onto the latter, forming excitatory synapses. This would explain the response of the simple neuron. Even when Hubel and Wiesel first proposed this scheme in 1962, they realized that it was an oversimplification, and indeed it was. After substantial experimentation and considerable debate over the last half century, the details are still being worked out, but the consensus is that the basic idea behind this wiring scheme is largely correct.[1]

Similar wiring diagrams have been proposed by Hubel and Wiesel, and by others, to explain the visual response properties of many other kinds of neuron in the visual system, including the retinal output neurons, the lateral geniculate neurons, and the complex and hypercomplex neurons in the visual cortex.

Wiring diagrams have also been proposed for neurons in many brain regions outside the visual system. In mammals and higher vertebrates these are always simplified and approximate, but they continue to be refined in the light of new experimental data and computer simulation.

From Visually Responsive Neurons to Conscious Perception

But what about the links with psychology? Even at the retinal level, the arrangement of the ganglion neuron receptive fields in separate "centre" and "surround" regions with opposing effects helps to explain one well-known characteristic of visual perception: our much greater sensitivity to visual contrast than to the overall level of illumination. If you start reading a book in the garden at noon and continue till the evening, the light intensity may diminish by a factor of more than a thousand, but this will not prevent you from reading and you may hardly notice the change (if the book is fascinating!). And yet we can detect contrast differences of less than 1 per cent. Our insensitivity to the level of illumination is partly because the light-sensitive cells in our retinas increase their sensitivity as the level of light decreases, but the contrast-enhancing centre-surround arrangement of the retinal output neurons' receptive fields is the main cause of our greater sensitivity to contrast than to illumination level.

The fact that most neurons in the visual cortex are line detectors has numerous implications for perception, and I mention just two. First, they are used for analysing the contours around objects. Clearly any contour can be split up into a number of short, straight lines. The line-detecting neurons detect these lines, and this is the first stage of contour analysis, which probably explains why we are much more sensitive to the contours of an object than to other aspects, and have no trouble recognizing an object from a drawing showing its contours alone. Second, the presence of such neurons can explain a number of visual after-effects and illusions. For example, if you stare for about 20 seconds at a high-contrast pattern made of alternating white and black bars, this reduces your ability to see another pattern that is similar but at very low contrast (i.e. the bars are in two different shades of grey that are difficult to distinguish). But this after-effect only occurs if the high- and low-contrast patterns are at the same orientation (say, both vertical). If the orientations are different (say, vertical and oblique), the after-effect does not occur. Recordings from the visual cortices of cats and monkeys indicate that orientation-sensitive adaptation effects such as this are due to the fatiguing of cortical neurons sensitive to the orientation of the high-contrast grating.

For the vision of colour and of movement, there are similar links between perceptual psychology and neurophysiology. Following initial analysis by the line-detector neurons in the first three visual areas (V1, V2, and V3), the visual information is sent to additional visual areas for further analysis. Different areas analyse different aspects of the stimulus.

For example, neurons in area V4 of monkeys are particularly sensitive to the colour of the stimulus and seem to be involved in colour analysis, whereas those in area V5 (also called MT for *middle temporal area*) are more sensitive to the speed and direction of motion of the stimulus and seem to be involved in the vision of movement. In humans, brain-imaging techniques indicate that the same is true: V4 is activated during vision of a coloured object (or during a coloured hallucination). Moreover, human patients with lesions (e.g. from stroke or head injury) that have destroyed their V4 area suffer from *achromatopsia*, the inability to distinguish colours, while other aspects of their vision seem almost normal.[2] Likewise, patients with lesions that include V5 on both sides of the brain suffer from *akinotopsia*, the inability to experience visual motion. They have lost, for example, the ability that seems so natural to us of seeing that a car is moving fast toward them, and they have to deduce this from the fact that its position has changed.

A natural interpretation of the results on visual movement would be that neurons in early-stage visual areas such as V1 are serving as preliminary analysers and encoders of object movement, and that they send this encoded information to V5 for a more complete analysis of the movement. Thus, the destruction of the V5 neurons deprives the rest of the brain, and the person, of this movement information, making movement perception impossible. One would predict, moreover, that stimulating neurons responding to a particular direction (say, motion to the left) would tend to evoke the corresponding movement sensation. Since neurons in area V5 tend to be grouped according to their preferred direction of motion, it is indeed possible (although difficult!) to stimulate a group of V5 neurons all responding to the same direction. This was done in awake monkeys by Newsome and colleagues who had first trained the monkeys to indicate the direction of motion they saw by making a corresponding eye movement. The result was as predicted: if neurons that encoded motion to the left were stimulated, this tended to evoke the illusory sensation of motion to the left.[3]

Brains and Pattern Recognition Programs

This work of Hubel and Wiesel and their successors is only one example, albeit a classic one, of the increasing ability of neuroscience to fill the gap between the biophysics of single neurons and the overall performance of the brain and mind. Its profound implications have influenced not only neurobiology and psychology, but also computer science. For example, some computer programs for recognizing objects from digitized images have incorporated elements for detecting lines of different orientations. And elements within other pattern recognition programs have been found to reorganize spontaneously to become line detectors, without this being explicitly programmed. Thus, the strategies for analysing visual patterns seem to be similar in the biological neural networks of the human brain and in artificial pattern analysis machines.

The more advanced stages of object recognition are less well understood, but we know that they depend on analysis by circuits in the inferior and posterior parts of the temporal lobe, using partially processed visual signals supplied by the visual areas in the occipital lobe. Current research aims to understand in detail how these temporal lobe circuits produce our remarkable ability to recognize objects despite substantial variations in their retinal images due to differences in the angle of view or of lighting. Research on this difficult subject involves bringing together a whole range of different approaches including electrophysiological recording of the responses to visual stimuli of individual neurons in monkeys or of neuronal populations in humans, detailed anatomical analysis of neural circuitry, testing of visual behaviour, and computational models. There is a long way to go, but progress continues to be made.[4]

People who believe that a non-physical soul interacts with the brain may object that, since we do not *completely* understand the neural analysis of visual form recognition, there may still be a role for a separate soul. Perhaps. But this would not be the soul that Descartes proposed. His soul was supposed to do the whole job, but in the light of current neuroscientific knowledge we know that a great deal of the analysis is performed by the neural circuits, so the soul's role would have to be subsidiary.

Memory Storage

My second example is that of how memories are stored. As in the case of visual form analysis, the challenge once again is to understand memory storage at many different levels, from molecules to conscious experience, and to link the different accounts together.

I have chosen this example because even though neurobiologists all accept that memories are stored in the brain, this is occasionally contested by philosophers, as in a book published in 2010 that drew on old data showing that it was difficult to eliminate memories by deleting particular parts of the brain.[5] It is indeed true that Karl Lashley's famous behavioural experiments on rats, mainly between 1930 and 1950, failed to reveal particular parts of the brain whose deletion would eliminate complex learned behaviours such as finding the way in mazes. But an immense amount of research performed since the 1970s makes it absolutely clear that different kinds of memories are stored in particular brain regions.

I am here talking about long-term memories, which can last for days or years or a whole lifetime. Remembering things for a few seconds, such as someone's telephone number while I write it down, is probably achieved by reverberating neural activity, but long-term memories require molecular and structural changes in neurons. Experiments on animals show that establishing a long-term memory requires new proteins to be made, and once this has occurred the memory storage no longer requires neural activity, although its retrieval – the act of remembering – does require neural activity. There are different kinds of memories, for motor skills, for emotions, for events, and so on, and these are stored in different parts of the brain, but for all these different types of memory the best understood storage mechanism is the long-term changing of *synaptic strengths** (i.e. the powers of the synapses to affect the postsynaptic neuron). This long-term change is called *long-term potentiation* (LTP)* when the synapse is strengthened and *long-term depression* (LTD) when the synapse is weakened. Changes in the strengths of existing synapses may not be the only mechanism of memory storage, because there is evidence that the production of new synapses or even of new neurons may also contribute to memory, and there may be still other mechanisms, but we shall here focus on LTP and LTD because their underlying molecular events and their roles in memory have been particularly well studied.

LTP and LTD in Different Kinds of Memory

Even though different parts of the brain are involved in different memories, similar mechanisms are involved at the cellular level, and in all cases, LTP and/or LTD is involved. Many motor memories, such as the ability to ride a bicycle, are stored mainly in the cerebellum, and the details of how these memories are stored and retrieved have been studied in considerable detail.[6] On the other hand, the detailed memory of *events* is stored in the hippocampus, deep in the temporal lobe, and the memories of the *emotions* associated with those events are stored in parts of the amygdala, in the anterior part of the temporal lobe in front of the hippocampus. Thus, if you see a frightening snake, the memory of the fear is stored in the amygdala, whereas the memory of the details (colour, shape, and size of the snake etc.) is stored in other regions, notably the hippocampus. The hippocampus is the brain region where LTP was first discovered and has been the most intensively studied, and so I shall focus on this. I shall have to simplify, because the detailed mechanisms of LTP are extremely complicated, and more than 6,000 papers have been published on hippocampal LTP.

Hippocampal Memory

The hippocampus (so named because of its supposed resemblance to a sea horse – *hippocampus* in Latin) is a curved structure that in humans is about 5 cm long and lies deep in each temporal lobe. Its importance in the memory of events first became apparent because of the consequences of hippocampal damage in humans. Bilateral damage to the hippocampus in humans causes severe defects in the ability to remember events (*episodic memory*) and general concepts and facts (*semantic memory*). Memory for places (*spatial memory*) is also affected.

The most famous case involved a patient known as H. M. (for Henry Molaison) who in 1953 underwent a surgical removal of the hippocampus and adjacent regions of the temporal cortex on both sides of the brain as a last-resort attempt to control epileptic seizures that had resisted all other treatments. The surgery was successful to the extent that the epileptic seizures ceased, and there was no detectable impairment of the patient's motor functions, language, or general cognitive ability. But the surgery had two disastrous consequences for his memory. H. M. lost his memory of most events that had occurred in the two years preceding the surgery as well as some events occurring a few years earlier, and he completely lost the ability to memorize new events. Till his death in 2008, H. M. was convinced that he was living shortly before 1953. Yet his *short-term memory* (e.g. for lists of numbers remembered for a few seconds) and his *procedural memory* (which includes motor learning) were intact.

Why were H. M.'s old memories, occurring several years before his brain operation, not affected? Several lines of evidence, in both humans and lower animals, indicate that memories stored initially in the hippocampus are subsequently transferred to regions of the cerebral cortex including the frontal lobe.[7]

There have been numerous subsequent studies in humans, and these have fully confirmed the importance of the hippocampus in memory tasks.

Electrophysiology of Hippocampal Neurons

Still further evidence has come from electrophysiological recording from hippocampal neurons in rats and other species that were learning where to find food in an artificial maze. In this case, the kind of memory involved is not event memory but *spatial memory*. Some neurons, called "place cells", fire selectively when the rat is in a particular part of the maze.[8] Detailed analysis has subsequently shown that this place-specific neuronal firing does not occur on initial exposure to a new environment, but that the pattern is established within a few minutes and is then stable. These place cells, as well as other neurons called "grid cells" in a region of cerebral cortex overlying the hippocampus, are believed to be involved as the rat forms a mental map of its environment.[9] This system for making mental maps has been described as an "inner GPS", as many members of the general public recently learned from the media when the 2014 Nobel Prize in Physiology or Medicine was awarded to John O'Keefe and Edvard and May-Britt Moser for their research on place cells and grid cells. A similar system may occur in the brains of humans, because functional imaging studies show that parts of the human hippocampus and overlying cerebral cortex become very active during spatial learning or navigation.[10]

Even though most of these studies have focused on hippocampal activity during spatial learning, electrophysiological recording has also been used to study how hippocampal neurons behave in other kinds of memory. I here mention just one rather intriguing study in humans.

Quian Quiroga and his colleagues managed to record from single neurons in the hippocampus of epilepsy patients and found neurons, now called "concept cells", that responded to general concepts but ignored particular details. For example, one neuron fired in response to any representation of Oprah Winfrey, be it various pictures of her, or her name written on a screen or spoken by a computer-synthesized voice, but to nothing else. Another neuron responded to pictures of Jennifer Aniston, firing when the patient was shown each of seven different images of this actress – including front views and side views – but did not respond to photos of animals, or people, not even most other actresses. This neuron did, however, respond to pictures of Lisa Kudrow, Jennifer Aniston's co-star in the TV series *Friends*. Another neuron responded to pictures of the *Star Wars* character Luke Skywalker, and to his spoken and written name, but to almost nothing else; but it did also respond to another *Star Wars* character, Yoda. The neurons did not all encode people. Some fired to representations of well-known objects. For example, one was activated by various different pictures of the Tower of Pisa, but not by ones of other buildings. I mention these results because they indicate that the human hippocampus is involved in dealing with high-level concepts that have had to be learned. Theoretical considerations suggest that these neurons play an important role in the conceptual learning underlying memory,[11] but we cannot be sure whether the memory storage was in this case in the hippocampus, or elsewhere in the brain (or in both).

But we do know that LTP does occur in the hippocampus, and we know which synapses are involved, so we now come back to LTP and to whether it is involved in memory storage.

LTP as a Hebbian Mechanism in the Hippocampus

Since the discovery of LTP in the late 1960s,[12] experiments on animals have provided abundant evidence that its occurrence in hippocampal synapses is important for the storage of new memories. LTD is involved as well, but I shall focus on LTP. The main form of LTP is triggered by the activation of a particular type of glutamate receptor, the NMDA (for N-methyl-D-aspartate) receptor. This receptor lies in the postsynaptic membrane and controls an ion channel that allows calcium (and sodium) to enter into the postsynaptic cell. This leads to changes in the postsynaptic part of the synapse, and later in the presynaptic part as well, causing the synapse to become "stronger" (i.e. the excitatory effect of its activation is greater).

About 75 years before the discovery of LTP, the Spanish neuroanatomist Santiago Ramón y Cajal had already suggested that the strengthening of connections between neurons might be a brain mechanism for learning,[13] and in 1949 Donald Hebb extended this idea, proposing that the synapses would be strengthened when they were successful in exciting the receiving neuron.[14] This is now called the *Hebbian learning rule*, and synapses that so respond are known as *Hebbian synapses**. The first suggestion that Hebbian synapses might actually be useful for learning came from the emerging field of artificial intelligence in the late 1950s, when Frank Rosenblatt invented a learning algorithm, called the *perceptron*, which employed the computational equivalent of Hebbian synapses.[15]

This link between artificial intelligence and the neurobiology of Hebbian learning has become very strong. The perceptron algorithm, and its subsequent variations, became important tools in artificial intelligence, and by the 1980s were being used for many different tasks including speech recognition, image recognition, and machine translation. Almost all models of learning mechanisms in the brain have postulated Hebbian learning, and several have been based on the perceptron algorithm. Early models based on the perceptron focused on the cerebellar cortex,[16] but subsequently several models of the hippocampus[17] and cerebral cortex[18] incorporated modified versions of the perceptron.

All known Hebbian synapses are excitatory, use glutamate as neurotransmitter, and are formed on small protrusions from dendrites known as "dendritic spines". Hebbian synapses are not limited to the hippocampus, but occur on many neurons in the cerebral and cerebellar cortices and in other brain regions. In all these regions their change in synaptic strength is believed to be a major mechanism underlying memory.

The Molecular Mechanisms of LTP

Much of the research on LTP has focused on unravelling the molecular mechanisms by which the increase in synaptic strength occurs. Without going into the details, I would like to make two main points.

First, the "Hebbian" nature of LTP results from the very first stage of the mechanism, the inflow of calcium through channels controlled by NMDA receptors. These channels have the special property of being "Hebbian" by their very nature. This is because they are normally blocked by a magnesium ion, which needs to be chased away by the occurrence of an action potential in the postsynaptic cell. Thus, the inflow of calcium through the channel requires *both* the binding of a glutamate molecule to the NMDA receptor *and* the firing of the postsynaptic neuron. This is precisely the Hebbian condition.

Second, the synaptic potentiation (strengthening) results from a complex series of events that is all set in motion by the calcium entry (Figure 3.6). Unlike the other ions that flow in and out of cells, calcium has the special property of being able to activate certain enzymes (proteins that control chemical reactions in cells). The next step in LTP after the initial calcium inflow is that the calcium activates various enzymes. Among these, the two most important for LTP are called calcium/calmodulin-dependent protein kinase II (CaMKII) and protein kinase C (PKC). Their activation by calcium leads to two key changes, both of which involve a class of glutamate receptors called AMPA receptors. CaMKII and PKC increase the *number* of AMPA receptors in the postsynaptic membrane by causing ones that were lying below it to move into the membrane, where they need to be to get activated by glutamate released from the synaptic bouton. CaMKII and PKC also increase the *activity* of AMPA receptors that are already in the membrane, by sticking phosphate molecules onto them. These increases in the number and activity of AMPA receptors make the synapse stronger, more effective in activating the postsynaptic cell.

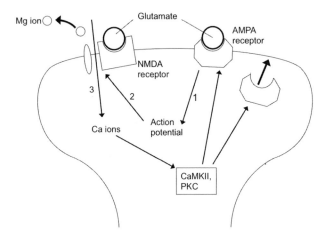

Fig. 3.6. *Events occurring in a dendritic spine leading to the initial synaptic enhancement in LTP. 1. The binding of glutamate to AMPA-receptors causes an action potential. 2. This chases away the magnesium (Mg) ion that had been blocking the NMDA-channel. 3. Now that the NMDA-receptor is both bound by glutamate and freed from its magnesium ion, calcium ions flow in through its channel. 4. Calcium (Ca) ions activate the enzymes calcium/calmodulin-dependent protein kinase II (CaMKII) and protein kinase C (PKC). 5. These enzymes cause AMPA-receptors to move into the synaptic membrane and sensitize those that are already in the membrane.*

This effect is only temporary, however, and many further changes are involved in making the synaptic enhancement long lasting. These include changes in gene expression and protein synthesis in the postsynaptic neuron, and signals are even sent back to the presynaptic bouton to enhance transmitter release. The overall effect of all these changes is that the synaptic enhancement can last a very long time.[19]

Tests of LTP's Role in Hippocampal Memory Storage

Can we be sure that the LTP is involved in memory storage? This is supported by the facts that LTP is long-lasting and occurs in regions that are involved in memory. Also, the usefulness of Hebbian synapses in computer programs for artificial learning confirms that LTP can provide a useful mechanism for the storage of retrievable memories.

But, despite this, during the 1980s scientists who were perfectly convinced about the physiology and cell biology of LTP felt uncertain whether it was really the basis of memory storage. The first clear evidence for this came in 1986 from a study on rats that were learning to find a platform hidden below the surface in a water maze. It was already known that pharmacological inhibition of NMDA receptors prevents most LTP. In the 1986 study, such inhibition was obtained by infusing an NMDA receptor inhibitor into the brains of the rats so that it entered the hippocampus (and other regions), and this severely impaired their spatial learning.[20] Further experimentation in the subsequent decades confirmed this finding and ruled out certain alternative explanations, but a more *region-specific* test was needed, because the inhibitor probably affected other brain regions as well as the hippocampus.

Region-specific inactivation of NMDA receptors was finally achieved by means of genetic engineering. These receptors are made up of several different protein subunits, of which the one called "NR1" is indispensable for the receptor to function. The group of Susumu Tonegawa at the Massachusetts Institute of Technology used genetically engineered mice in which the NR1 subunit was deleted selectively from a part of the hippocampus called CA1, believed to be involved in spatial memory. As expected, the CA1 region lacked NMDA receptor-mediated synaptic currents and LTP. The spatial learning of these mice, as tested in a water maze, was severely impaired whereas other learning tasks believed not to depend on the CA1 region were unaffected.[21] This confirmed the importance of NMDA receptors in memory storage, and made it clear that NMDA receptors in CA1 are crucial for spatial memory.

The above account shows that the storage of certain kinds of memory depends on LTP in hippocampal synapses.

Test of LTP's Role in Memory Retrieval

But what about memory *retrieval?* To be really confident that the LTP is involved in memory, it would be comforting if someone could show that the memories stored by LTP can actually be retrieved. This is very difficult to test, but by some extraordinary technical mastery Tonegawa's group managed to provide a convincing demonstration in mice that learned to be afraid of a specific context (a box with particular lighting and a particular smell). Some unfortunate mice received electric shocks when they were in this context, so they learned to associate the context with the shocks, and thereafter the mere fact of being in the box caused them to be afraid, as was manifested by their "freezing" (stopping all movement). Previous research indicated that the memory of the context (but not of the fear) would be encoded in a small percentage of synapses contacting a scattered population of neurons in a hippocampal region called the *dentate gyrus*. If this is true, excitation of the neurons involved in the memory, and just those neurons, should be enough to reactivate the memory. The researchers managed to excite these neurons selectively by using the elegant technique of optogenetics, which involves using molecular trickery to make neurons sensitive to light. They managed to do this just to the neurons excited during the fear-learning task. Subsequently, they tested the effect of shining light (via an optic fibre) onto the dentate gyrus, to see whether it would produce behaviour suggestive of fear. It did! The mice "froze", showing that they were frightened.[22] This technical tour de force provided the strongest evidence so far that activating the specific sub-population of neurons involved in storing a memory is sufficient to evoke that memory.

Summary of LTP in Memory

We have seen that there is a vast array of experimental evidence showing that hippocampal LTP is an important mechanism of memory storage, and that there is recent evidence that memories stored by LTP can be retrieved. Data from many different levels – molecular biology, cell biology, morphology, electrophysiology, and behavioural analysis – combine to provide a coherent understanding of LTP-based memory. While most of the evidence comes from rats and mice, results from monkeys and humans indicate that the same principles apply in us. Furthermore, computer models confirm that the "Hebbian" condition for the occurrence of most LTP is indeed appropriate and effective for many kinds of memory storage. In short, there is little doubt that LTP in hippocampal circuits mediates memory storage.

Conclusions

- The brain is, in a sense, a biological machine, and we understand the principles according to which its working parts – the neurons and glial cells – interact in the brain's neural circuits.
- One of the major aims of neuroscience is to understand how these neuronal circuits perform cognitive tasks, including those that used to be attributed to a non-physical soul.
- In several cases this aim is being achieved, as in visual form analysis and in memory. Thus, we understand in some detail how the brain performs tasks that were traditionally attributed to a non-physical soul.

III

Free Will, Responsibility, and Ethics

4

Nothing but a Pack of Neurons?

Summary

This chapter focuses on the question of *reductionism*, which is the view that complex entities (including human beings) can be understood as the summed behaviour of their parts. I refute extreme forms of reductionism by arguing that different levels of description – physical, chemical, neurobiological, etc. – are all necessary and valid. Low-level accounts (at the levels of physics, chemistry, or cellular neuroscience) do not replace or debunk higher-level accounts (at the levels of system neuroscience, psychology, ethics, or religion).[1]

The whole is more than the sum of its parts.
Aristotle, *Metaphysics*

Reductionism

One reason why neuroscience has sometimes been considered a threat to religious and "human" concepts of man is that much of neuroscience attempts to explain the *whole person* (her psychology, religious belief, decision-making, etc.) in terms of the parts (neurons and their interactions), and this has been seen as devaluing us. My daughter seems to become a mere conglomeration of cells. Your love for God, or your boyfriend, is reduced to the impersonal activity of neurons in certain parts of your brain. Because of misunderstandings such as this, opponents of science decry its *reductionism*, whereas some opponents of religion go to the other extreme and try to explain it away in terms of mechanistic science.

There are different types of *reductionism* (sometimes called simply *reduction*), but a standard definition in the context of science and philosophy is *the analysis of a complex entity into its component parts*; or, in more functional terms, *the understanding of the workings of the entity in terms of its interacting components*.

The question of reductionism is subtle and complex. The web is replete with slanging matches between reductionists, who affirm with gusto that the whole is nothing but the sum of its parts, and holists who deny this claim. But we need to go deeper, because there are different types of reductionism, and each type can be approached in different ways.

The Good, the Bad, and the Nothing But

Most people agree that at least some types of reductionism are invalid. At the simplest level, some authors make a straightforward distinction between good and bad reductionism. Thus, psychologist Steven Pinker writes:

> *Reductionism, like cholesterol, comes in good and bad forms. Bad reductionism – also called "greedy reductionism" or "destructive reductionism" – consists of trying to explain a phenomenon in terms of its smallest or simplest constituents. Greedy reductionism is not a straw man. I know several scientists who believe (or at least say to granting agencies) that we will make breakthroughs in education, conflict resolution, and other social concerns by studying the biophysics of neural membranes or the molecular structure of the synapse.*[2]

In extreme cases, bad (or greedy etc.) reductionism is easy to identify, as in the following fiction. We are admiring a painting of a beautiful woman, when your mad-scientist brother walks in. "What's that?" he asks, somewhat aggressively. "A woman", you reply. "Wrong!" he thunders. "It's just molecules, *nothing but* molecules." We start to object, but he interrupts triumphantly: "Take away the molecules, and you'll be left with nothing at all!" He is, of course, denying what you never wished to assert. He is insisting that there is not a nonmaterial principle hiding mysteriously between the molecules of paint. Of course not!

It might seem implausible that intelligent people could ever make such a mistake, but no less than the great Francis Crick came close to it in the following notorious words with which he begins a popular book about the brain entitled *The Astonishing Hypothesis*:

> *The Astonishing Hypothesis is that "you", your joys and your sorrows, your memories and your ambitions, your sense of identity and free will, are in fact no more than the behaviour of a vast assembly of nerve cells and their associated molecules. As Lewis Carroll's Alice might have phrased it: "You're nothing but a pack of neurons."*[5]

To be fair, I should mention that Crick was writing light-heartedly, and was alluding to a passage in *Alice in Wonderland* where Alice replied to the Queen and others that they were "nothing but a pack of cards". By his words "no more than" and "nothing but", he may have meant merely to exclude the notion of a separate, non-physical soul of the kind that Descartes proposed (see Chapter 10), but his wording did not make this clear. At all events, this is a blatant example of what neuropsychologist–philosopher Donald MacKay called "*the fallacy of nothing-buttery*", and we shall come back to this below.

In most cases, however, confusion related to reductionism is more subtle. We will therefore need to distinguish between different types of reductionism, and for this I must first introduce the key concept of *levels of description*.

Levels of Description

When we discuss anything at all complex, we have to choose the *level* at which we are going to talk. For example, when confronted with the message "LECTURE CANCELLED OWING TO BUBONIC PLAGUE" on the blackboard, we might start to describe the spatial positions of the grains of chalk. Let us call this level A. Or we might make a list of all the letters (level B). But we would probably be more concerned about the *meaning of the message* (level C). Level A is the lowest of the three, and level C is the highest. The criterion for deciding which of any two levels is the higher is that you can change the lower of the two without changing the higher, but not vice versa. You could obviously move some of the grains of chalk without changing the string of letters or the meaning, but you could not change the meaning without changing the letters or the grain positions.

Clearly a description can be complete in its own terms without excluding other ones at different levels. The different descriptions are said to be *complementary*. (Two descriptions at the same level can also be complementary – for example, two pictorial representations of an object from distinct viewpoints; but complementarity between *different* levels is the key issue in the present context.) Although in our example of a blackboard message the highest-level description was obviously the most relevant, this is not always the case. For example, we need to understand a car at several different levels – what the individual parts are, how they interact, what the car is for, etc. And the same is true for understanding human beings.

Figure 4.1 shows a hierarchy of levels at which a human being might be considered. The first point to be made is that descriptions at the different levels are complementary. One does not exclude another.

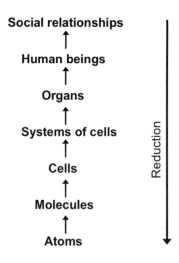

Fig. 4.1. *Levels and reduction. Many levels are needed to describe people or groups of people. Reduction means analysing the upper levels in terms of the lower.*

The second point is that the *significance* of low-level entities is to be found with reference to the higher levels. For example, the significance of the protein molecules making up a neurotransmitter receptor is to be found in the functioning of the receptor during synaptic transmission; and, still higher, at the levels of neural circuit function and the behaving human being. Why should anybody care about the protein molecules apart from the fact that they play an important part in the overall functioning? The significance of a human being is to be found at still higher levels, in social relationships, for example. But where do these get their significance? To avoid being provocative, I have not added to Figure 4.1 any levels higher than that of social relationships, although I personally believe that the highest of all is that of God's eternal purpose for us and for the universe. Whether this belief is true is beyond the scope of the present text, but it should at least be clear from the above remarks that looking for higher-level interpretations to give meaning and significance to lower-level phenomena is not a strange hobby for a few weird mystics, but is a standard part of scientific endeavour.

My third point is that although descriptions at all the levels may be valid, and need not be rivals, different levels can still make contact, in at least two ways. First, low-level descriptions can *set constraints* on what is possible (or likely) at a higher level and vice versa. There can thus be tension between theories that focus on different levels, and major debates in science (including medicine) sometimes involve clashes between theories that work at different levels. Second, descriptions from different levels often need to be integrated in order to obtain a satisfactory understanding. To take a famous example, during much of the twentieth century, different psychiatrists attributed schizophrenia to problems at one of at least three different levels. Family therapists maintained that the patient's symptoms were provoked by "schizogenic" interactions within the family. Psychoanalysts and other psychodynamic therapists attributed the disease to unconscious or subconscious conflicts within the patient's psyche. And biological psychiatrists and neurobiologists provided evidence for the disease being caused by a combination of genetic factors and different prenatal stresses on brain development. There is still debate about this, but the dominant view is now that changes in brain development caused by genetic factors and prenatal stresses create vulnerability to subsequent psychological stresses occurring many years later. Thus, a full understanding will probably involve an integration of low-level (neurobiological) and higher-level (psychological) understanding. My point is that in situations where the truth is uncertain, hypotheses at different levels can sometimes conflict, but even when a low-level (in this case, neurobiological) approach gains acceptance, higher levels (in this case, psychological) may still be needed for an adequate understanding. In any case, there is no inherent reason why low-level descriptions should discredit high-level ones, nor vice versa. Why then, are low-level scientific accounts sometimes thought of as discrediting higher-level religious ones? Part of the answer may lie in confusions about the nature of *reduction*, a notion that we now examine.

Types of Reduction

As is mentioned above, "reduction(ism)" (in the context of science and philosophy) means *the analysis of a complex entity into its component parts.*

Is the whole then just the sum of its parts or is it more? It depends what you mean by "more". Can the workings of my brain be reduced to the functioning of its component neurons? It depends on the sense in which you use the word "reduced".

Most philosophers of science agree that we must distinguish between different types of reduction. For example, Karl Popper distinguished between "reduction as a method", which, he said, all scientists must welcome, and "philosophical reductionism", for which he considered there are no good arguments.[4] Others have proposed more types of reduction, and Murphy and Brown distinguish no fewer than five.[5] Here, for relative simplicity, I shall follow the geneticist Francisco Ayala in proposing a threefold typology.[6]

First of all there is *ontological reduction*. This is essentially the question of whether life and consciousness can be understood purely in terms of physico-chemical events, or whether we need to invoke some kind of nonmaterial principle that interacts with the physico-chemical components, such as a non-physical soul, or a "vital force". Ontological reduction means getting rid of such a principle. This is dealt with in Chapters 1 and 10, where I explain that the notion of a special vital force in living matter was abandoned long ago for good reasons, and that a non-physical soul of the Cartesian variety is becoming increasingly difficult to defend. I thus consider that ontological reduction can be perfectly valid. But beware! This is not always the case. As Nancey Murphy and Warren Brown point out,[7] ontological reduction is sometimes extended invalidly to the extreme claim that only the entities at the lowest level are *truly real*. On this view, higher-level entities – be they molecules, cells, or people – are dismissed as mere aggregates. Murphy and Brown's book shows convincingly that this exaggerated conception of ontological reduction is untenable.

74

Second, there is *methodological reduction* (also called *scientific reduction*), which is about research strategy. It is about analysing a complex entity in terms of its parts. An example of this is the analysis of how neural circuits behave as a result of the behaviour of the individual neurons and their anatomical connections (see Chapter 3). Everybody agrees that this is a useful approach, but is it the *only* valid approach? To quote Ayala, "Should we always seek explanations by investigating the underlying processes at lower levels of complexity... or must we seek understanding from the study of higher as well as lower levels of organization?"[8] He concludes that we need to seek understanding in both the bottom-up and the top-down senses. I agree. Descent to a lower level is not always the best approach. I was once a member of the examining board for a postgraduate scholarship at University of Oxford. The winning student, a biochemist, declared during her interview that "Everything boils down to biochemistry in the end." "As in the biochemistry of bird song?" asked one of the examiners, who happened to be a specialist in bird song. "Yes" was the confident reply. But this was obviously to miss the point, as all the examiners agreed, although we still awarded her the scholarship. Even though biochemical processes do underlie the functioning of the neurons that control bird song, and few would want to deny this, we need to ask other kinds of questions as well: about the connections between the neurons involved in bird song, about the temporal patterns of their action potentials, about how they control the bird equivalent of vocal cords, about the meaning for the birds of the sounds produced, and so on. These latter questions are not optional extras; they are essential. Most scientists agree on this. Many levels of question need to be asked, and one of our most interesting and challenging tasks is to fit together the results from the various levels into a coherent multilevel picture. The necessity of including a particular lower or intermediate level – for example, the ion channels in neurons involved in bird song – may perhaps be debated. But clearly the level involving the meaning of the song for the birds is indispensable.

The third type of reduction, *epistemological reduction*, is about whether a theory is a special case of a more general theory. If so, the former theory is said to have been *reduced* to the latter. A classic example is the way the *kinetic theory of gases* reduces the macroscopic behaviours of gases (their pressures, temperatures, and volumes, and the relationships between these) to the averaged behaviour of the individual molecules. If you know the number of gas molecules and their molecular weights and speeds, you can do calculations to predict the ideal gas law about the relationship between pressure, temperature, and volume ($PV = RT$). The ideal gas law is no longer needed, in principle at least, because its predictions can be derived from kinetic theory. That is not to say that the former field (macroscopical physics) becomes worthless, because, as Popper and others have pointed out, the reduction is never absolutely complete. Although its laws and theories are no longer needed for prediction, its concepts and its data are still needed. And, in practice, it is usually still much more convenient to make predictions using the higher-level theory. But, with these qualifications in mind, we must agree that many of the greatest achievements in science have involved epistemological reduction. During the last century, several branches of physics have been unified by their reduction to a few theories of great generality, notably quantum physics and relativity. Likewise, much of chemistry was reduced to physics by the discovery that the valence of an atom (i.e. its combining power with other atoms) can be explained in terms of the number of electrons in its outer orbit.

Confused Reduction and Nothing-buttery

The reason why I discuss these different types of reduction is to make the point that reduction (or reductionism) is not necessarily wrong or bad. The problem comes when people confuse different types of reduction or exaggerate their implications.

For example, failure to distinguish between the first two sorts of reduction can lead to "the fallacy of nothing-buttery" that we discussed above, and the quotation by Francis Crick about our being "nothing but a pack of neurons" illustrates this. He may perhaps have meant merely that the neurons are not being influenced by a mysterious, nonmaterial force; if so, he may be right, as I argue in Chapter 10. But the danger is that this plausible ontological reduction may be confused with methodological reduction, leading to the false idea that neurobiological accounts of humans are somehow more fundamental or more true than higher-level psychological ones. They are not.

Global and Analytical Approaches

My point so far in this chapter has been that the danger is not so much reductionism as its misuse. The enterprise of trying to understand how neural activity contributes to our psychology (or religiosity etc.), or how molecular interactions underlie neuronal functioning can be perfectly valid provided we do not confuse different types of reduction, exaggerate the implications of the reduction, or gratuitously insert words like "*nothing but*" or "*no more than*" as in the above citation from Francis Crick.

But even among experts there can still be quite a lot of chauvinism for a particular level of explanation. I was once a member of a committee whose task was to organize a large biology meeting (in Switzerland) that brought together several specialized Swiss societies for research in different branches of biology. It so happened that most of the members of the committee were experts in the area of cellular and molecular biology. In other words, their research focused on understanding how the interactions between molecules in a cell contribute to the behaviour of the cell. We were planning symposia (special interest sessions), and I noticed that all the proposals were for different areas of cell biology. I therefore suggested that we should also include some symposia focusing on higher levels (in the sense of Figure 4.1) such as systems physiology (understanding the functioning of a whole physiological system, e.g. the visual system in the brain). "Oh no," replied the president, "that would lower the standard!" – and several members of the committee agreed with him. Even when I proposed the names of two Nobel Prize-winning visual physiologists (Hubel and Wiesel) as possible speakers, several members of the committee were still reluctant to accept that systems physiology could match the scientific excellence of cellular and molecular biology, but in the end they accepted my arguments. They were cellular-molecular chauvinists because they were so totally involved in their own kind of research that they failed to appreciate the importance of other approaches. It is in fact quite common in research for scientists to think that their own particular area is more novel, more exciting, more worthy of grant money or promotion, and so on. But I have never heard a scientist say that the other levels of explanation are *not real*. That would be absurd! Almost all accept that different levels are needed.

Neuroscience is in fact an area where the integration of different levels of explanation is particularly important. Let's take as an example the neural basis of episodic memory (memory of events and experiences), which we considered in some detail in Chapter 3. We discussed there in some detail how this kind of memory depends on long-term potentiation (LTP) of synapses in the hippocampus, and how the required condition for the LTP to occur there is for the pre- and postsynaptic parts of the synapse to be activated at about the same moment. This condition is called the *Hebbian condition* or the *Hebb rule*. The approach here might be called reductionistic, because many neurobiologists studying memory have tried to understand it at increasingly lower levels. First they showed the importance of the hippocampus in episodic memory. Then they showed the occurrence and importance for memory of LTP. Then they tried to understand the molecular events underlying LTP. And so on. This was fine as far as it went, but it left some important questions unanswered, such as the following: Would such a system, based on LTP, be useful for memory storage? If so, why? How can isolated events at individual synapses be integrated into the temporally ordered seamless whole of our remembered past? And how are the memories recovered? To answer these more holistic questions, the analytic, reductionistic approach is of only limited use, and most of our understanding has come from computational approaches (mathematical modelling and computer simulation). These have shown very clearly the value of the Hebb rule in artificial learning algorithms, and have made progress toward answering the other questions. The depth and robustness of our understanding of memory depends on a combination of the reductionistic and holistic approaches. Thus, reductionistic understanding does not undermine holistic (or global) understanding. Both are important, and they complement each other.

Emergence

No discussion of reduction would be complete without a mention of *emergence**. The very notion of reduction depends, as we have seen, on the existence of multiple levels of explanation, which are essential for understanding complex entities such as human beings (but also molecules, snowflakes, ants, or economic structures). If there were not multiple levels, we could not descend from the upper ones to the lower. But we can also attempt to do the opposite, to climb from the lower layers to the upper ones. This is called emergence.

The notion of emergence has been around since the time of Aristotle, but it has become an increasingly important subject in the philosophy of science over the last 30 years. The science and philosophy of emergence is now a flourishing field of research, with a vast literature that I cannot review here. For brevity, I would emphasize just a single point, namely that entirely new properties arise at the higher levels of explanation requiring concepts that were not even present at the lower levels. In the words of physics Nobel Prize-winner Philip W. Anderson in his seminal paper "More Is Different":

> *The ability to reduce everything to simple fundamental laws does not imply the ability to start from those laws and reconstruct the universe... The constructionist hypothesis breaks down when confronted with the twin difficulties of scale and complexity... At each level of complexity entirely new properties appear... Psychology is not applied biology, nor is biology applied chemistry... We can now see that the whole becomes not merely more, but very different from the sum of its parts.[9]*

There are of course plenty of controversies in the research field of emergence, as in every field at the cutting edge of knowledge, but its overall emphasis fully confirms the point that I have been making: that the whole is more than, and different from, the sum of the parts. It is untrue to say that we are "nothing but a pack of neurons".

Conclusions

- This chapter has focused on the important question of reductionism, which has to be understood in the light of there being different levels of explanation.
- Even though some biologists may have a chauvinistic preference for their own particular level of investigation, most admit that all levels are needed.
- The different levels are complementary, not contradictory, and the upper levels involve concepts not even present at the lower ones. The need for multilevel analysis and for integration of the different levels is particularly important in neuroscience and in its relationship to psychology and the humanities.
- Human values, ethics, and religion have nothing to fear from valid reduction. The apparent threats of reductionism to our humanity and (for some of us) to our faith are due to confused reduction and nothing-buttery.

5

Are We Robots Without Free Will?

Summary

This chapter focuses on the question of whether the almost deterministic functioning of the brain makes free will impossible. It discusses the current debate between compatibilists, who believe that brain determinism is compatible with free will, and incompatibilists, who deny this. It considers the possible contributions of quantum theory to providing a possible basis for incompatibilist free will. My main point is that we do indeed have free will, provided that it is defined in a moderate and realistic way.

Is what goes on inside our heads just a deterministic physical process? If so, are we all, no matter how idiosyncratic and sparkly, nothing but slaves to rigid laws governing the invisible particles out of which our brains are built?
Douglas Hofstadter, *I Am a Strange Loop*, 2007

It is our choices, Harry, that show what we truly are, far more than our abilities.
Dumbledore in *Harry Potter and the Chamber of Secrets*, 1998

Recent Attacks on Free Will in the Name of Neuroscience

There are many senses of the term *free will*, and there is plenty of debate about its definition as we shall see, but if we didn't have at least *some sort of free will*, the implications would be disastrous. Our lives would be futile and concepts like morality, ethics, and progress would be mere illusions.

In this chapter we are concerned with the implications for free will of *physical* determinism, the determinism that results from the fact that the laws of physics are deterministic, apart from slight indeterminism at the quantum level – see below. Our purpose is to examine whether this makes free will impossible. In this chapter we focus on this question alone and do not attempt to deal with other major questions that might be asked about free will. The most ancient of these other questions is the one of whether divine predestination is compatible with free will; interesting though this is, its relation to neuroscience is unclear, so I shall leave it aside. However, the biblical texts certainly treat humans as free in the sense of being responsible for our acts and worthy of praise or blame. Other free will debates do relate to neuroscience, but to different questions, notably ones about particular aspects of neurophysiology or psychology, or about abnormal brain function, or about determinism by a combination of genes-plus-environment. These are dealt with in Chapters 6–9. Our present focus is the question of physical determinism and free will.

This has always been a subject of debate at the level of philosophy, but in recent years those who deny free will have become particularly outspoken, and tend more and more to use *neuroscience* to support their arguments. It has become highly fashionable – among a few experts and large numbers of bloggers and journalists – to claim that neuroscience shows free will to be an illusion. If I type "free will is an illusion" into Google I get nearly a million hits.

Most of the anti-free will propagandists base their claim on a mixture of philosophy and neuroscience. Some of them are neuroscientists and many are secularists of the "new atheist" strain, including neuroscientist Sam Harris and physicist Victor Stenger. The secularists often go beyond mere theorizing, because many of them deny moral responsibility and claim that nobody should be held responsible for their crimes (we shall look at this question of criminal responsibility in Chapter 9). Their anti-free will position puts them in disagreement with their new atheist colleague Daniel Dennett, a leading authority on the philosophy of free will, who has long been a committed defender of the reality of free will.

The neuroscience-refutes-free-will contenders propose two main arguments. There is a *general argument* that, irrespective of the details of brain functioning, the general principle that the brain's neural circuits obey the (almost) deterministic laws of physics rules out free will. And then there is a *specific argument* based on Benjamin Libet's experiments on the timing of conscious decisions with respect to the relevant neural events. I deal with the general argument in this chapter and the specific argument in the next.

The debate concerning physical determinism has little to do with the detailed results of neuroscientific research, because it is more concerned with the general principle that all neurons, whatever their role, work according to the laws of physics, and hence almost deterministically. The debate is therefore more the province of philosophers than of neuroscientists such as myself. Indeed, it has long been a major subject in the philosophy of mind, and is still highly controversial even among the world's leading specialists on the philosophy of free will. My aim here is not to settle the controversy, but to give a balanced survey of the main philosophical positions and arguments. I hope also to show up the emptiness of some of the more populist neuroscience-refutes-free will declarations.

The Standard Argument Against Free Will

The general argument that I alluded to above is in fact more complicated than I implied, because determinism and indeterminism can *both* raise problems for free will. In his eminently readable and informative monograph on free will,[1] Bob Doyle, author of the *Information Philosopher* website, calls this the *standard argument against free will*. This argument has two parts:

1. The determinism objection: if the brain functions deterministically, the will is not free.

2. The randomness objection: if the brain functions indeterministically, our decisions are random, so they are not caused by us and we are not responsible for them.

Before dealing with these twin objections, we need to consider the nature of determinism.

Physical Determinism

Determinism is the view that every event is determined by previous events. There are various kinds of determinism because it can be considered at different levels: genetic determinism (I'm the slave of my genes), social determinism (I'm who I am because of my social background), and so on. Everybody agrees that our range of possible behaviour is limited by our genetics and social background and so on, but that is not our concern in this chapter. Our focus here is on *physical determinism*, the view that we are determined – completely, in every detail – by the laws of physics. This is also called *Laplacian determinism* after the French mathematician and astronomer Pierre-Simon, marquis de Laplace, who argued that the universe was physically determined. This problem of *physical* determinism has always been the focus of the classical philosophical debate about determinism and free will, which still rages today.

Physical determinism is in principle stronger than other kinds because it is at the lowest level. We discussed the relation between levels in Chapter 4, using the example of a message written in chalk on a blackboard. In this case, the lowest level (a list of the precise positions of the grains of chalk) determines the message completely. You cannot change the message without moving the grains. You can, however, move the grains without changing the message; for example, you could increase the sizes of the individual letters. Thus, determinism at the lowest level is the strongest. This distinction works in biology as well. For example, genetics influences many aspects of what goes on in our bodies, but exerts no control at all on some events – for example, the diffusion of molecules in cells. Granted that our freedom is limited by many factors (genetic, environmental, etc.), the question is whether descending to the level of physical determinism rules it out completely.

Before addressing the problems posed by physical determinism for free will, it is worth pausing for a moment to consider how our status as thinking, responsible human beings depends on the ordered functioning of our brains. If our neurons did not behave in well-controlled and orderly ways, according to causal rules – thus deterministically, or almost so – their firing patterns would be completely unreliable. The information coming in from our senses would be lost in a random haze of meaningless anarchy, and so would every aspect of our brain function. Our decisions would be haphazard, and free will would be impossible. It would thus be wrong to consider determinism as the arch-enemy of free will. Determinism, or something very close to it, is needed for free will.

Some readers may want to chip in at this point to remind me that physical determinism is not total, because it breaks down at the level of the very small (electrons, atoms, etc.) since quantum physics is not entirely deterministic. It includes a stochastic (random) component. That's true, and it's why I referred above to the laws of physics and chemistry as being *almost* deterministic. We shall come back to this.

This is not the only objection to determinism, however. Quite apart from quantum physics, anti-determinist philosophers argue that:

1. to provide rigorous proof that determinism is always exactly true we would need to have an unlimited amount of perfectly accurate data, which is impossible;

2. even if we accepted determinism as a working assumption for scientific purposes (as I do, at least for neuroscience), that would not justify making it into a metaphysical (philosophical) principle;

3. thoroughgoing determinism would undermine the notion of rationality, which would in turn undermine our grounds for believing in determinism.

Of course determinists attempt to answer these objections,[2] and the debate continues. It would be beyond my scope to pursue these questions further here, but it is worth bearing in mind that the claim of physical determinism remains controversial even today. In the following pages, I shall take physical determinism to be a reasonable first approximation for trying to understand brain function, but this is not meant to be an absolutist dogma.

The Definition of Free Will

Problems of definition have always been important in discussions of free will. A literal interpretation of the term as meaning the freedom to *will* something would be almost nonsensical as Einstein pointed out:

Honestly I cannot understand what people mean by the freedom of the human will. I have a feeling, for instance, that I will something or other; but what relation this has with freedom I cannot understand at all. I feel that I will to light my pipe and I do it; but how can I connect this up with the idea of freedom? What is behind the act of willing to light the pipe? Another act of willing?[3]

Einstein was influenced by Arthur Schopenhauer, and quoted his words: "Man is free to do what he wills, but he cannot will what he wills."

But, at least in English, free will does *not* mean the freedom to will (wish) something. It rather means the *freedom to exercise our wills*, which implies the freedom: (1) to make choices; (2) to act on one's choices. Some philosophers reserve the term "free will" for the former and speak of "free action" for the latter, but others speak of free will for both, and still others sidestep the problem by using just the single word "freedom". All agree that free will implies responsibility, and this is where the debate about brain determinism and free will becomes particularly important. The crucial question is whether brain determinism undermines moral responsibility.

A further important problem for defining free will is that the two major positions of *compatibilism** and *libertarianism** (see below) are characterized by different definitions. *Compatibilists* define free will as freedom from *external* constraints, but libertarians argue that it should be defined as freedom from *all* constraints. If you search in dictionaries for a definition of free will, you will sometimes find a definition that is heavily loaded one way or the other, as in the following two examples, of which the first is compatibilist and the second libertarian.

> *Free will: The power of making free choices that are unconstrained by external circumstances or by an agency such as fate or divine will.*[4]

> *Free will: The choices which are said to have no necessary determination from the nervous system or from any other physical cause.*[5]

We need to discuss the differences between compatibilists and libertarians in much more detail.

Three Main Positions in the Free Will Debate

To some people it seems obvious that physical determinism of brain function must be incompatible with free will. If our brains work deterministically, then our behaviour must be predetermined, so how can we be free? How can we be responsible for our choices if they were determined before we made them? How can we be responsible for our behaviour if it was determined not by ourselves, but by the impersonal laws of physics and chemistry? This approach is called *incompatibilism*; it is conventionally subdivided into two radically opposed positions: *libertarianism*, which affirms free will and denies determinism, and *hard determinism*, which denies free will and affirms determinism. But many (probably most) philosophers disagree with incompatibilism, adopting the contrary view of *compatibilism*, the view that free will and determinism are compatible. Thus we have three classical positions.

1. *Compatibilism:* Determinism is compatible with free will and human responsibility (e.g. Spinoza, Hobbes, Hume, Austin Farrer, Peter Strawson, Donald MacKay, Daniel Dennett). I personally favour compatibilism, although I am open to some versions of libertarianism.

2. *Libertarianism:* We do have free will, and this is incompatible with determinism, so determinism cannot be total (e.g. Thomas Reid, Kant, William James, Isaiah Berlin, Peter van Inwagen, Carl Ginet, Robert Kane).

3. *Hard determinism:* Determinism is true even for our own brains. Free will is therefore an illusion (e.g. Holbach, Nietzsche). Neuroscientists Joshua Greene and Jonathan Cohen are among the few modern authors who explicitly self-designate as hard determinists (see Chapter 9). Few modern philosophers accept this label, but Ted Honderich and Derk Pereboom both reject free will and come close to hard determinism.[6] At a more popular level, Sam Harris might be called a hard determinist, in the sense that he is a determinist who denies free will, but he nevertheless accepts human responsibility.

Compatibilism

Compatibilism is the belief that free will is compatible with determinism. In practice, compatibilists accept physical determinism; they may be strict determinists, but more often they accept the possibility of slight indeterminism such as that due to the fuzziness of quantum physics (see section below on quantum libertarianism), while maintaining that this is not important for brain function.

The definition of free will is absolutely central to the debate between compatibilists and incompatibilists.[7] As is mentioned above, compatibilists define free will as the ability to make choices or perform actions free from *external* constraints.[8] A key insight of compatibilism is that internal causality and order are essential for human responsibility. David Hume, who was one of the first compatibilists, emphasized this point, writing:

> *Actions are, by their very nature, temporary and perishing; and where they proceed not from some cause in the character and disposition of the person who performed them, they can neither redound to his honour, if good; nor infamy, if evil.*[9]

Thus, compatibilists think that the intuitive attraction of many people to incompatibilism results from linguistic confusion. Freedom is the opposite of constraint, not of determinism. We are free and responsible, *not in spite of* the deterministic behaviour of the brain, but *because of it*.

Are Compatibilists Cheats?

Incompatibilists complain that by restricting the definition to external constraints compatibilists are cheating (Kant called compatibilism a "wretched subterfuge"), but if we look at the ordinary use of words, at least in English, we find that free will is in fact usually used in the compatibilist sense. If I say that I cleaned the bathroom "by my own free will", I am not talking about freedom from brain determinism. I simply mean that I chose to do the job and nobody forced me to do it. This is not a dishonest new-speak designed to escape from the implications of modern neuroscience, because it was already standard usage in English long before debates about brain determinism and free will began in the eighteenth century. As early as the fourteenth–sixteenth centuries, the term (written "fre wille" or "frewill") was already used generally in the sense that we now call compatibilist. The earliest examples that I have been able to find are in the Wycliffe translation of the Bible (1388), which frequently refers to offerings or actions performed by "fre wille", meaning gifts that people made or actions that they performed because they wanted to, without any obligation.

Even though ordinary usage accords with the compatibilist definition of free will, incompatibilists claim that the compatibilist definition is inappropriate in the context of discussions about brain determinism and free will. The question therefore arises whether the beliefs of ordinary people fit in with compatibilism in this particular context. Several groups have done research on this, but the conclusions were somewhat contradictory. Some researchers (e.g. Eddy Nahmias) found that people mostly thought free will was compatible with determinism, but other researchers found the contrary. Thus, studying the beliefs of ordinary people has not so far resolved the debate about definition.

Let us therefore look a bit more closely at the key point of the compatibilist definition, the distinction between internal and external constraints. Suppose that two children, Jim and Jane, are scolded for swimming in the canal without permission. "It's not my fault," says Jane, "Jim made me do it. He pushed me in." "It's not my fault either," says Jim, "my brain made me jump into the canal." It should be obvious that Jim is using the words "made me" in a very unorthodox way. If his brain *hadn't* "made him" jump into the canal, Jim's action would not have been willed, so he would not be responsible. It therefore seems strange to use "my brain made me jump" as an excuse.

Nevertheless, several neuroscientists have expressed disapproval of the compatibilist definition. One of these is eminent neuropsychologist Michael Gazzaniga, who is well known for his experiments on the behaviour of split-brain patients (i.e. people who have had most of the nerve connections between the two halves of their brain sectioned surgically). In a book on free will and brain science,[10] Gazzaniga mentions compatibilist arguments that we don't want to be free from our experience or our temperament because we need these for our decisions, and that we don't want to be free from causation because we need that for predictions. And then he provides as counterargument the question "What do we want to be free from?" That's his sole argument, and he seems to think that a compatibilist will be stymied by it. His book is well referenced as far as neuroscience is concerned, but I cannot find in it a single mention of any philosopher more recent than Hume (eighteenth century). Gazzaniga seems to be unaware that the compatibilist reply is very clear and well articulated, that we want to be *free from external constraints*. In other words, he seems not to understand the compatibilist position. This is perhaps an extreme case, but the tendency to ignore modern philosophy is not unusual among neuroscientists writing on free will.

The Consequence Argument Against Compatibilism

At this point incompatibilists bring in their heavy artillery, the so-called *consequence argument*. This argument played an important role in the rehabilitation of incompatibilism in the 1970s and 1980s, when compatibilism was almost universally accepted among philosophers. It was developed independently in the 1970s by several different philosophers, including notably Peter van Inwagen, whose monograph *An Essay on Free Will* includes the following concise summary of the argument:

> *If determinism is true, then our acts are the consequences of the laws of nature and events in the remote past. But it is not up to us what went on before we were born, and neither is it up to us what the laws of nature are. Therefore, the consequences of these things (including our present acts) are not up to us.*[11]

Van Inwagen goes on to argue that if determinism is true, we *cannot now do otherwise than we actually do*, and deduces that determinism is incompatible with freedom. Many philosophers have found this argument convincing because it deduces incompatibilism from premises that are universally accepted.

Nevertheless, compatibilists have found counterarguments, although these are often rather technical. Some of them focus on van Inwagen's words "up to us" and "cannot now do otherwise", which refer to our *power* or *ability* to do something. They argue that *power* and *ability* normally refer not to a freedom from internal determinism of neuronal function but to an absence of external impediments preventing us from performing an act. They further argue that these words refer implicitly to the ability to perform the act *if we so wished*. If somebody chose tea rather than coffee because she was predetermined to dislike coffee, this would not deny her free will (in the normal sense of the word) because she was doing what she wanted to do.

Moreover, even if the consequence argument is valid, I would point out that it assumes a very strong form of determinism, as is clear from the citation above, which refers to "consequences of... events in the remote past" and "what went on before we were born". Even though I think determinism is a reasonable working hypothesis for attempts at analysing brain function, including processes of decision-making, I shall argue below that there are reasons to doubt whether our decisions of today are *completely and precisely determined* by chains of cause and effect continuing over long periods (years or decades).

The debate between leading philosophers continues, and I would not presume to have got anywhere near settling it, but my personal view is that it is reasonable (and not cheating) to define free will in the compatibilist sense and that this kind of free will provides sufficient leeway for moral responsibility. To borrow the subtitle of Daniel Dennett's book *Elbow Room*, the *varieties of free will worth wanting* are compatible with determinism (or near-determinism).

Nevertheless, since the debate is still raging,[12] we need to consider incompatibilism and the question of whether free will can be supported within an incompatibilist framework.

Incompatibilism

As is mentioned above, incompatibilists deny that free will – or at least free will in the fullest and noblest sense (which some of them call *libertarian free will*) – is compatible with determinism. For hard determinists such as Sam Harris, this leads to a simple conclusion. Determinism is (almost) true; therefore free will does not exist.

In order to reply to the hard determinists, libertarians (incompatibilists who believe in free will) need to propose a way of resolving the tension between free will and brain determinism. Several ideas have been proposed, but for simplicity I shall ignore the Kantian notion of noumenal selves and other theories of "agent-causation" by agents not embodied in brain events, and I here mention only two positions: *Cartesian dualism* and *event-causal libertarianism*.

Cartesian dualism is the view proposed by Descartes that a separate, non-physical soul (or mind) interacts with the brain. To Descartes and his followers, this soul–brain interaction enables the soul (considered a free agent) to cause free behaviour. The question of Cartesian dualism is broader than the question of free will, however, and I deal with it in Chapter 10, where I argue against it. Therefore, I shall not consider it in detail here. Cartesian dualism is currently a minority view, although no less a philosopher than Richard Swinburne supports a view of free will based on it.[13]

Event-causal libertarianism. Most libertarian philosophers consider Cartesian dualism to be implausible and even unhelpful to their cause, because the soul might itself be determined.[14] Therefore, they argue simply for indeterministic events in the brain without invoking a Cartesian soul. But the question arises as to what kind of indeterministic brain events might contribute to libertarian free will without undermining it by introducing excessive randomness into the decision processes, and this has led event-causal libertarians to speculate as to how this might be possible. They have therefore developed models of free will with the aim of showing how the unwanted effects of randomness could be avoided.

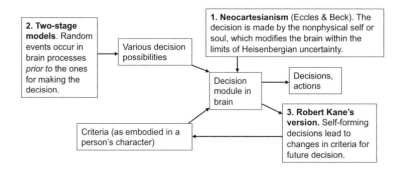

Fig. 5.1. *Three ways in which libertarians propose that indeterminism could break the bonds of determinism without introducing excessive randomness into decision-making.*

Two-Stage Models of Free Will

Two-stage models go back to William James, and several versions have been proposed. Their essence is that they separate the process of decision-making into two stages. In the first, a variety of possibilities is generated, in part indeterministically. In the second stage, a deterministic will evaluates the options and makes a choice in the light of reasons, values, preferences, and current desires. Advocates of two-stage models such as Bob Doyle argue that they provide just the kind of free will that libertarians need, by avoiding strict determinism, invoking randomness where it might be useful for generating multiple ideas, and avoiding the arbitrariness of random decisions. And, importantly, the indeterminism that these models invoke is sufficient for our acts and choices not to be determined by events "in the remote past", to quote van Inwagen's summary of the consequence argument.

I personally find the two-stage approach attractive, but libertarians such as Kane maintain that they are insufficient to provide libertarian free will in the fullest sense, and argue that indeterminism is required *in the decision process itself.*

Kane's Model Involving "Self-Forming Actions" and "Ultimate Responsibility"

For this reason, Robert Kane developed a libertarian model in which the indeterminism occurs in the decision process, but is sufficiently moderate so as not to lead to random or irrational decision-making. It is one of the most highly regarded models among free will specialists. Kane's position is founded on two key concepts.[15]

First, along with most libertarians, Kane argues that free will requires the existence of *alternative possibilities.* In other words, to be free, an agent must have the power to do otherwise than what he actually does. Kane considers that this requirement is incompatible with determinism, but he nevertheless agrees with compatibilists that indeterminism alone is not sufficient for free will. Randomness in the brain would not in itself provide free will and could vitiate it.

Kane's second key concept is *ultimate responsibility.* He accepts the point made by compatibilists that our (moral and other) decisions are normally determined by our characters, and therefore argues that for us to be responsible agents we need to be responsible for the formation of our own characters, a view that goes back to Aristotle. Kane argues that it is our responsibility for the formation of our own characters that gives us *ultimate responsibility* for our decisions. This is achieved by what Kane calls "self-forming actions" (and self-forming decisions and "willings"), which occur during moments of indecision when we experience conflicting wills ("torn decisions") (Figure 5.1). It is these decisions that Kane considers to be undetermined. Normally, randomness would compromise our control and hence our responsibility, but in the case of *torn decisions* we might have excellent reasons for choosing either way. The advantages seem "fifty-fifty" so we might even have decided by tossing a coin, yet still take responsibility for our decision. Thus, ultimate responsibility does not require every "free" act or decision to be undetermined, but only the few that are self-forming. The important point is that these form our character, which is in turn decisive for our future choices and actions. If a person has had the opportunity to make such character-forming decisions, he is responsible for the actions that result from his character.

Various conceptual criticisms of these incompatibilist models have been advanced by philosophers, but discussion of these would be beyond our present scope. I here focus on the crucial *neuroscientific* question of whether the postulated indeterministic events actually occur in the brain.

Neurobiological Realization of Libertarian Models

The first thing to bear in mind is that we have no neurobiological data providing positive support for these models. To me, as a neuroscientist, that's a problem. Libertarians reply that our subjective experience shows we have free will, and they argue that this has to be of the libertarian variety. While agreeing that we will have to wait many years before neurobiological techniques become adequate for investigating the postulated indeterminism at the level of neural functioning, they say that it is valid in the meantime for philosophers to do some hard thinking about what neurobiologists might one day be able to identify.

Second, there is the question of what kind of indeterminism might be involved. Libertarians need to make specific proposals about what could be the basis of the proposed indeterminism, and they usually bring in quantum physics.

Quantum Libertarianism

They invoke quantum physics because of its inherent indeterminacy, by which I mean that the predictions of quantum physics are slightly "uncertain" at the level of submicroscopic entities such as electrons. Many physicists think that this uncertainty is not just a problem of imprecise prediction, but reflects the fact that nature itself is fundamentally fuzzy. A problem with this *quantum libertarianism* (as it has been called[16]) is that the uncertainty (known as Heisenbergian uncertainty) is very small indeed, and probably too small to affect the functioning of neurons (see Appendix 1 if you don't mind a few calculations). For this reason, libertarians often propose that the initial Heisenbergian uncertainty might somehow be amplified – for example, by cellular events with "chaotic" dynamics. This is a difficult subject that we cannot here analyse in detail, but I have argued elsewhere that the amplification hypothesis is problematic for several reasons.[17] Here I mention just one of these, which involves a very different kind of random event: *thermal noise.*

In the warm environment of the brain (or any part of the body), everything is moving, because heat is in fact the movement of atoms and molecules. Thus, small molecules are constantly moving and large ones such as proteins are constantly changing shape. This is called *thermal noise*. These movements are not controlled biologically, so they are often described as random. In a sense this is true, but they are not *indeterministic* in the sense of quantum indeterminacy. The moving atoms and molecules are much larger than electrons, and can be described to a good approximation by classical physics (i.e. deterministically). The effects of the thermal noise have been studied in considerable detail over the last decade, and they are known to be important in many cellular events, for example in the opening and closing of ion channels and in the process by which proteins are made from DNA (via an RNA intermediate). I won't go into the details here, but in 2012 I published an academic review on the subject, where I pointed out that the brain (and other organs) have powerful noise-resistance mechanisms that enable them to cope with the thermal noise.[18] The key point for my present argument is that the potential disruptive effect of the thermal noise is about a thousand million times greater than that of Heisenbergian quantum fuzziness. Since brain function is resistant to the comparatively enormous effect of the thermal noise, it seems unlikely that it would be influenced significantly by the quantum fuzziness.

Inevitably, the issue is a bit more complicated than my brief summary above. One complication is the recent discovery that quantum effects much greater than Heisenbergian uncertainty can in special situations influence the functioning of cells.[19] But such effects have not so far been found in neural circuits.

Indeterminism without Quantum Physics

I have so far argued that quantum physics appears not to provide the indeterminism required for libertarian models. I thus consider that cerebral determinism is probably true, at least over periods of a few seconds or perhaps hours. But I also expressed doubts about strict cerebral determinism of the kind mentioned by van Inwagen in the citation above summarizing the *consequence argument*, assumed to be precise over very long periods and even from before we were born. Let us now examine why.

Even with classical (deterministic) physics, it is not clear to me that total brain determinism can be assumed over long periods. For example, a paper by Lewis and MacGregor, assuming only classical physics, analyses simple models of colliding particles and asks what would be the limit of initial error in the specification of their positions for us to be able to predict their trajectories of the particles after about 9 (or 12) collisions.[20] The answer turns out to be the fantastically small distance of about 1×10^{-35} m (i.e. 1 divided by 1 followed by 35 zeroes). This raises problems for determinism because this tiny number is of the same order as the Planck length, and physicists are currently uncertain whether distances as small as this can have any meaning. Lewis and MacGregor argue that their calculations apply also to neuronal functioning, and deduce that strict determinism cannot be assumed in brain function.

Thus, even though I favour compatibilism, it seems to me that determinist positions that assume strict determinism from "before we were born" are not supported by current science.

Conclusion on Libertarian Models

Heisenbergian uncertainty is probably too small to provide the indeterminism required by libertarians. Amplification (by chaos etc.) seems not to solve this problem. Quantum effects much greater than Heisenbergian uncertainty might solve it, but these have not so far been demonstrated in neurons. However, even on the assumption of classical physics, there is no convincing reason to accept strict brain determinism over long time periods, so minimal forms of libertarianism remain tenable.

Hard Determinism and its Implications

The main thrust of this chapter has been to defend free will against the challenge of physical determinism. My approach has not been to prove that we have free will, but to maintain that current arguments *against* free will are insufficient. Even hard determinists admit that we intuitively feel we have free will, so the burden must surely be on them to show that this fundamental intuition is illusory. And they fail, as I argued above, for at least two reasons. First, the incompatibilist critique of compatibilism fails to refute it. Second, strict brain determinism over long periods cannot be demonstrated.

Nevertheless, some people reject free will and accept hard determinism, so what difference does this make to their behaviour and to their worldview?

There is experimental evidence that what we believe about free will does make a difference to our behaviour. Roy Baumeister, Kathleen Vohs, and others tested the effects of telling people that free will is an illusion and found that this led them to cheat more, help others less, and behave more aggressively.[21] How exactly these experiments should be interpreted is still a matter of debate, but there is little doubt that beliefs about free will really do make a difference to the way people behave.

However, the logical implications of the anti-free will arguments are not always as serious as the rhetoric implies, as we shall now see.

The Vacuousness of Some Recent Attacks on Free Will

The above, admittedly brief and simplified, discussion of the determinism versus free will debate should be enough to show that the subject is subtle and difficult, and attempts to settle the matter in a few pages should be viewed with suspicion. And yet the anti-free will propagandists of the last few years claim to show, once and for all, that neuroscience shows free will to be an illusion. End of story, they claim! As an example, we shall consider Sam Harris's short book *Free Will*.[22] This easy-to-read mini-book is probably the best (or least bad) of the popular anti-free will literature, because Harris is a skilful writer and rhetorician with knowledge of both philosophy (first degree) and neuroscience (PhD). But even this least bad of the polemics has serious weaknesses, as we shall see.

Harris claims that free will is an illusion because our wills are "not of our own making", and then goes on to write that it is "actually more than an illusion (or less), in that it cannot be made conceptually coherent"[23] because of the *standard argument against free will* that we discussed above. But why should it be a problem that our wills are "not of our own making"? The answer to this comes in Harris's unconventional definition of free will, which he claims to be "the popular conception of free will". According to Harris, this popular conception "seems to rest on two assumptions: (1) that each of us could have behaved differently than we did in the past, and (2) that we are the conscious source of most of our thoughts and actions in the present".[24] He claims that both of these assumptions are wrong. Two questions immediately arise: is Harris right that the popular conception rests on these assumptions, and is he right in claiming that they are both wrong? To answer these questions, let us consider each of the assumptions individually.

Concerning the first assumption (that we could have behaved differently), Harris is probably right that most people make it, but can he justify his claim that it is wrong? Libertarians and compatibilists both have arguments that we could indeed have behaved differently. So what kind of counterarguments does Harris provide? His answer to the libertarians is breathtakingly dismissive. He writes: "Today, the only philosophically respectable way to endorse free will is to be a compatibilist – because we know that determinism, in every sense relevant to behavior, is true."[25] Several of the world's acknowledged leaders in the philosophy of free will (such as Robert Kane) are libertarians, and the question of behavioural determinism is currently a major subject of philosophical debate. But Harris, who is not even a specialist in this area, feels free to dismiss the whole of libertarian philosophy in a single sentence as "not respectable"! No attempt to consider the libertarian arguments, just a contemptuous dismissal!

Harris's treatment of compatibilism is more serious, but in my opinion he fails to give adequate attention to several of the main compatibilist arguments, including the point that the phrase "we could have behaved differently" in normal parlance implies "if we wanted to".

But it is Harris's second assumption (free will implies "that we are the conscious source of most of our thoughts and actions in the present") that is really bizarre. Harris spells out what he means by this: that to have free will we would need to be aware of all the factors that determine our thoughts and actions, and to have complete control over them. He claims that this is an important part of the popular conception of free will, and he vigorously attacks it, proving triumphantly that we do not have this kind of awareness or control. Therefore free will does not exist, QED. But I have never met anyone who held this conception. Reviewers of Harris's book such as Russell Blackford agree that this view is held neither by the general public nor by philosophers.[26] The views of the general public on free will have in fact been studied by various authors including Eddy Nahmias, but the second assumption has never been reported. We certainly don't have this kind of free will, but as Alvin Plantinga points out "not even God could have that kind of freedom" because God is *necessarily* all-knowing, all-powerful, and perfectly good and did not choose that character.[27] In short, Harris attacks an impossible conception of free will that nobody holds.

But even if some people did hold Harris's impossible conception of free will, would that justify his claim that free will is an illusion? Surely not! Let's take an example. Probably many people have incorrect concepts of what electrons are, since schools often teach that they are tiny spheres orbiting around atomic nuclei, which by the standards of modern quantum physics is wrong. So would that justify the claim that electrons don't exist? No! This would only disseminate confusion and error. That's what Harris does with free will!

The next question has to be what conclusions Harris draws from his attacks on free will. He has defined free will in a nonsensical way and proved triumphantly that it is nonsensical. In the second half of his book, we find that his conclusions are not particularly radical. He accepts the notion of personal responsibility (suitably defined). He accepts the need for a criminal justice system; and unlike many secularists he is even open to the idea that the principle of *retribution* (punishment on the basis of what one deserves) might play a role in deciding the sanction, providing that the decision is "scientifically informed" and that the punishment also serves as a deterrent and a means of rehabilitation (we shall examine this question in Chapter 9). In short, despite his rejection of the term *free will* (defined in his unconventional way), it turns out that Harris's beliefs about ethics, responsibility, and criminal justice are fairly close to the ones I defend in Chapter 9. It may seem strange that an atheist, who is outspoken against free will, draws practical conclusions rather similar to those of a Christian defender of free will such as myself. On the other hand, rejecting a nonsensical notion of free will that nobody holds would not be expected to have a major effect on one's worldview.

Conclusions

- It has become fashionable in recent years to claim that neuroscience refutes free will, although this is only a minority position among academic philosophers.
- Those who use neuroscience to attack free will mostly use two kinds of argument: a *general argument* based on the general principle that the brain's neural circuits obey the (almost) deterministic laws of physics and chemistry, and a *specific argument* based on the timing of conscious decisions with respect to the relevant neural events. The present chapter dealt only with the general argument, and the specific one will be the subject of the next two chapters.
- This chapter discussed the current debate between compatibilists, who believe that brain determinism is compatible with free will, and

incompatibilists, who deny this. This debate turns to a great extent on the definition of free will. I tend to favour compatibilism.

- Among incompatibilists, those who accept free will are called libertarians. They have to explain how indeterministic events in the brain could provide for free will without causing randomness detrimental to responsibility. The debate on this is ongoing and complex, involving difficult questions about the possible contributions of quantum theory, and the resistance of the brain to the effects of thermal noise. I draw attention to difficulties for libertarianism, but I think that some forms of it may still tenable.

- My main conclusion is that neuroscience does not refute free will, provided that it is defined in a moderate and realistic way.

- I end by discussing the regrettable strategy of anti-free will propagandists such as Sam Harris, who redefine free will in a nonsensical way so that they can then go on to show it is nonsensical.

- But the anti-free will propagandists have a second weapon. They deny not only the freedom of the will, but also the *efficacy* of conscious will, and this is the subject of the next two chapters.

6

Electrophysiology-Based Attempts to Refute the Efficacy of Conscious Will

Summary

Neuroscience and psychology are increasingly being invoked to cast doubt on the fundamental intuition that our intentions and decisions play a causal role in our behaviour. The initial attack was launched 30 years ago with the famous experiment of Benjamin Libet on the timing of decisions to perform simple movements. I here summarize the intense debate that has resulted and argue that the Libet experiment, and other related experiments, do not justify the iconoclastic claim of the anti-conscious-will lobby.

> **I went over to tea one day and announced… that the seat of the Will had been discovered! It was at or near the anterior cingulate.**
> **Francis Crick, *The Astonishing Hypothesis*, 1994**

Does the Conscious Will Do Anything?

The previous chapter was about whether our wills are *free*, despite the twin problems of determinism and indeterminism. The present chapter and the next are about whether our wills – our conscious wills – are *efficacious*. My use of the term "conscious" to qualify "will" may seem redundant, because for most of us the will is by definition conscious. I use it because those who deny the efficacy of our wills regularly refer to "conscious will", and the term "unconscious will" is sometimes used.

That people do some things on purpose, like switching on the television, but not others, like blinking, seems to most people obvious and undeniable. The efficacy of our conscious volition is surely our most direct and basic percept! But over the last 30 years there have been increasing attacks on this very notion, the efficacy of the will. Conscious will is dismissed as an ineffectual epiphenomenon (side effect) or even an illusion. It is claimed that our experiences of intending, willing, and deciding are merely delayed read-outs, informing us after the event of an unconscious "decision" made by the brain. Consciousness is not denied, but is claimed not to affect our behaviour. To argue thus is to threaten the very heart of our understanding of who we are: selfhood and human relationships, morality and responsibility, sin and repentance.

The anti-conscious-will attacks are based on two kinds of information: neurophysiological and psychological. The present chapter deals with the neurophysiology-based attacks, originating in some famous experiments by Benjamin Libet and his colleagues in the 1980s, and the next chapter deals with the psychology-based attacks. These two kinds of attack have received enormous attention from the media, which tend to give far more publicity to iconoclastic papers attacking our fundamental intuitions than to sober reports refuting the attacks. But the fact is that the overwhelming majority of recent papers contradicts the claims of the anti-conscious-will propagandists.[1]

The Libet Claim About the Initiation of Simple Movements

The modern assault on the efficacy of conscious will began with the neurophysiological experiments of Libet and his collaborators in the 1980s,[2] which have been interpreted by the authors and by many others as showing that our brains have already made the "decision" to make simple voluntary movements before we are consciously aware of the will to move, implying that our conscious will is not involved in the initiation of the movement. For brevity, I shall refer to this controversial claim as the *Libet claim*, and shall call this "decision" the *neural decision*. The Libet claim continues to be hotly debated.[3]

Before going into details about the Libet experiment, I must first provide some information about what happens in the brain when we decide to make a voluntary movement.

The Neurophysiology of Voluntary Movement

It is important to be clear about what is, and is not, being claimed when a movement is called voluntary. Even though these movements involve, by definition, an act of will, this is not to say that every aspect of a voluntary movement is conscious or willed. For example, a person engaged in conversation while walking home may be unconscious, or only marginally conscious, of his walking movements, but his walking is voluntary in the sense that he intended to walk home. Likewise, the movements of a tennis player as she serves are voluntary, but their control involves many automatic subroutines in the cerebellum and elsewhere. Furthermore, to claim that voluntary movements are caused by conscious acts of will is not to deny that the latter arise out of brain processes that are largely unconscious.

The neural circuits involved in voluntary motor control are exceedingly complicated, and I here give only some basic information that is necessary for understanding the Libet experiment. Voluntary movements are controlled mainly by the motor cortex (in the back part of the frontal lobe) but in cooperation with many other motor centres including the basal ganglia and the cerebellum. Motor commands are sent from the primary motor cortex (and to some extent from other areas) to motor neurons in the brainstem and spinal cord, which in turn control the muscles. The initiation and programming of movements depends on activity in many cortical areas including the supplementary motor area (SMA) and the preSMA, and several cortical areas in the parietal lobe (Figure 6.1). These areas feed directly or indirectly into the premotor cortex and motor cortex. Electrical stimulation of the motor areas elicits movements, but not usually the urge to move, although stimulation of SMA at intensities too weak to produce a movement has occasionally evoked an irrepressible desire to move going beyond the patient's will.[4] In contrast, electrical stimulation of areas BA-39 and BA-40 in the parietal lobe (Figure 6.1) never elicits movements but produces an urge to move, experienced as if it really was the subject's own desire.[5]

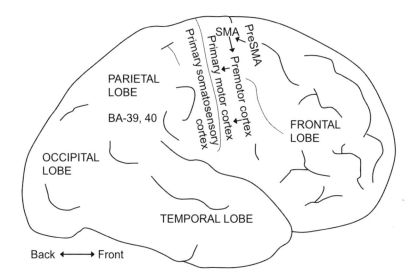

Fig. 6.1. *View of the human brain from the right side, showing cortical areas important for voluntary movement. SMA: supplementary motor area. BA-39, 40: Brodmann's areas 39 and 40.*

The Libet Experiment: a Challenge to the Role of Conscious Will

An important background to the Libet experiment was the discovery in the 1960s that before people make a voluntary movement, there is a slow build-up of electrical potential measured from the skull over the motor cortex, beginning as much as a second earlier for simple movements and even longer for complex series of movements.[6] This electrical change is called the readiness potential (RP).

Libet was interested in the relative timing of the RP compared with the movement and the conscious decision to move. He therefore asked his experimental subjects to perform simple movements, in most cases flexing the fingers or wrist, and to estimate the time (W) of conscious awareness of the urge (or will or decision) to move by reporting the position of a spot moving in a circle round an oscilloscope screen, about 25 times faster than the second hand of a normal clock. They were told to perform the movement whenever they felt like doing so, and to pay close attention to the time when they were first aware of the "urge to move". He also recorded the RP by electroencephalography, and the time of the movement itself was estimated from the electromyogram (electrical activity of the muscles). Libet found that time W came only about 200 milliseconds (msec) before the movement, whereas the RP began much earlier, usually about 550 msec before the movement and 300–400 msec before "W" (Figure 6.2). The fact that the change in brain potential occurred well before the conscious decision was interpreted by Libet and by many commentators to imply that the brain had already "decided" to move before the conscious decision to act, implying that the latter was not the true cause of the movement. They deduced that conscious will is too slow to make things happen, and that volitional acts must result solely from unconscious processes in the brain, not from conscious willing, implying that our intuitive notion of conscious will must be an illusion.

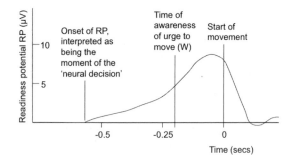

Fig. 6.2. *Schematized readiness potentials (RPs) in relation to the time of awareness of the "urge to move" (W) and the start of the movement (defined as time 0), as in the Libet experiment. Since these scalp-recorded potentials are very small, the experimenters had to average about 40 raw recordings to obtain reproducible results. Libet found that "W" occurred 300–400 msecs after the RP onset.*

There appeared to be a small loophole in that Libet's subjects still had the power to *veto* a movement in the 200 msec between time W and the movement. He therefore argued that even though the *initiation* of the movement was not the result of conscious will, its *vetoing* was. This argument was important to Libet himself, who did not wish to deny our fundamental intuitions about consciousness and free will, but its experimental basis has not been investigated in detail.

The Libet experiment provoked considerable interest and intense controversy, and stimulated further experimentation.

Single Neuron Recordings During the Libet Experiment

It is rarely possible to record from single neurons in the brains of humans, but this can occasionally be done in epilepsy patients using electrodes that have been implanted to localize the zones that cause seizures. Thus, remarkably, Itzhak Fried and his collaborators managed to record from more than 1,000 neurons in the medial frontal cortex of epilepsy patients (and especially in the supplementary motor area, which generates most of the early part of the RP) as they performed the Libet experiment. It was found that a few neurons changed their firing rate (by an increase or a decrease) almost 1.5 seconds before time W, and many more neurons did so subsequently, with about 25 per cent of the neurons firing several tenths of a second before W. The authors interpret their findings as indicating that the experience of will emerges as the *culmination* of premotor activity starting several hundreds of milliseconds before awareness.[7] In other words, they interpreted the early activity as leading up to the decision, but not as constituting the decision.

Criticisms of the Libet Claim

Despite the fame of the Libet experiment and its frequent acceptance in popular and semi-popular writings, it has been the subject of intense controversy. Most of the criticisms have focused on difficulties in judging the time of awareness, in interpreting the RP, or in the philosophical interpretation, as is discussed below.

Problems of Judging the Time of Awareness

It was central to Libet's claim that the RP began distinctly before time W. The published data of several groups do indeed support this claim, but critics have objected to the reliance on subjective recall after the event to determine time W, because there is evidence that this can be very unreliable. Furthermore, those such as Alfred Mele who have tried the experiment for themselves have found that W is difficult to define.[8] I have done this too, and you may wish to try it using a "clock" available on Bob Doyle's "information philosopher" website.[9] When I try this, I find it very hard to judge the precise time when I decided to move my finger/wrist. It would be useful to be able to quantify the reliability of our judgments, but this is hard to do for a purely subjective decision. Because of this difficulty, several research groups have instead measured how reliable people are at judging the time of *perceptual* events, which is easier to do. Several groups found serious biases, which depended, for example, on the modality of the stimulus (visual or auditory or tactile) and on the speed of the clock.[10] This raises doubts about whether one can trust the timing judgments in the Libet experiment. A different critique of the timing was made by Dennett and Kinsbourne,[11] who pointed out that Libet's experiment involves an attention shift from the participants' subjective intention to the clock, which may have introduced temporal mismatches between the felt experience of will and the perceived position of the clock hand. A further complication is that transcranial magnetic stimulation applied over the preSMA *after the movement* affects the subject's estimation of time W.[12] This shows that the estimation of W depends partly on neural activity occurring after the movement, emphasizing still further the difficulty of relying on subjective recall after the event.

To try to solve some of the above problems, Matsuhashi and Hallett devised a rather complicated alternative methodology for estimating time W. With this, they found that the RP (which they called BP1) occurred before W in only about two-thirds of the subjects; worse, the lateralized RP (LRP), which we shall discuss below, always occurred *after* W.[13]

In view of the controversy about the measurement of subjective timing, the media gave considerable attention to a paper published in *Nature Neuroscience* that used functional magnetic resonance imaging (fMRI) in a Libet-like experimental situation, and included in the summary a claim that a "decision can be encoded in brain activity of prefrontal and parietal cortex almost 10 sec before it enters awareness".[14] After all the subtle debate about a few hundreds of milliseconds, 10 sec was an enormous time, and the wording of the summary gave the impression that the temporal priority of the neural decision with respect to the subjective one was finally established. I assume that some journalists and bloggers only had access to the summary (available free on the web) and not to the full paper, because the main text made only the much weaker claim that the activity of prefrontal and parietal cortex was *correlated with the decision* (to use the left or right hand) with 60 per cent prediction accuracy, up to 10 sec before the conscious decision. That's very different! It is actually rather difficult to deduce the time of a decision from recordings of neural activity, but one would expect that the correlation would gradually rise during the prior deliberations, finally reaching close to 100 per cent, not 60 per cent (which is not very different from chance – 50 per cent), at the moment of decision. The paper provided interesting information about brain activity leading up to a decision from a surprisingly long time beforehand, but did nothing to rescue the Libet experiment from the criticisms about timing. Another serious problem is that subsequent research suggests that the early (-10 sec) slightly-better-than-chance prediction rate may have resulted from subtle experimental biases.[15]

The overall conclusion on timing has to be that the problems are serious and have not been resolved.

Doubts as to Whether the Readiness Potential Reflects a Decision to Move

The Libet claim assumes that the RP reflects a neural "decision" to move, and that the neural activity underlying the RP causes both the will to move and the movement. Even if these latter assumptions of causality could be demonstrated, this would not be sufficient to validate Libet's claim that the RP reflects a "decision", because this must presumably be caused by a chain of earlier neural events, and the RP might merely reflect some of these. But the Libet claim certainly assumes causality. This is part of the claim, and it has never been proved.

To be precise, we are really talking about the *earliest part* of the RP, because the timing argument focuses on the RP's onset. To attribute such a decisional and causal role to this *earliest part* of the RP seems surprising, because it originates mainly in the SMA (Figure 6.1), which has been known for more than 30 years to be strongly activated even when subjects merely imagine a complex movement *without actually performing it*.[16] This is not to deny that activity in SMA can cause movements in some cases, such as when it is stimulated electrically, but it cannot be assumed that the earliest part of the RP necessarily reflects neural processes underlying a decision to move. And, as I spell out below, there are at least five specific reasons to doubt this (there are in fact more, but five will do for now).

First, even though electrical stimulation of the SMA can cause movements, it only rarely causes an urge to move, which is evoked much more readily by stimulation of parietal areas, notably areas 39 and 40 (shown in Figure 6.1). Only when these areas are stimulated does the patient feel that the urge was her own, not alien. This suggests that the RP does not cause the will to move.

Second, if the RP truly caused the conscious will and the movement, as Libet's supporters claim, one would expect trial-to-trial variations in the onset of the RP to correlate with trial-to-trial variations in time W (i.e. trials with an early RP should also have an early time W). Haggard and Eimer tested this, using a variant of the Libet experiment, and found there was little correlation, ruling out the RP as a cause of the will or decision to move. They did, however, find that the "lateralized readiness potential" (LRP: i.e. the RP from the cortex on the side opposite the movement minus the RP from the same side) gave a positive correlation, suggesting that the brain processes underlying the LRP might cause the will to move.[17] Thus, at the time of publication, their results seemed compatible with a revised version of the Libet claim, because the LRP seemed to fulfil the role formerly attributed to the RP. However, the LRP occurs later than the RP, and subsequent experiments have sometimes found that the LRP occurs after time W as is discussed above, so the LRP seems a fragile candidate to replace the RP. Moreover, a 2013 paper has failed to repeat the findings of Haggard and Eimer and concludes that both the RP and the LRP reflect brain processes independent of will and consciousness, refuting the Libet interpretation.[18]

Third, experiments by Herrmann et al. cast further doubt on the interpretation of the RP as causally related to the decision and movement.[19] These researchers used a modified version of the Libet experimental paradigm, in which the participants were instructed to press one of two buttons, depending on a presented stimulus. An RP occurred well before the motor response, as in the Libet experiment. But, importantly, it occurred even before the stimulus presentation, so it clearly did not reflect a decision to press one or other button. The authors argue that the RP does not specifically determine the movement, but may reflect a general expectation (which is what the RP was initially thought to be by its discoverers, Kornhuber and Deecke, to reflect not a decision but a state of readiness, hence its name).

Fourth, Trevena and Miller devised a modified version of the Libet experiment in which participants made spontaneous decisions to move, or not, and found that the RP was no greater before a decision to move than before a decision not to move, which is not what one would expect if the RP reflected a neural decision to move.[20]

Fifth, computational analysis combined with some additional experimentation suggests that the neural decision to move occurs only very late during the time-course of the RP, not at its onset.[21]

There are thus very strong reasons to doubt that the earliest part of the RP reflects neural events underlying a decision to move. This further undermines the Libet claim.

Philosophical Implications of the Libet Claim

Even if the Libet claim, that our brains initiate movement before we are aware of the will to move, were to be accepted – which is by no means warranted, as we have seen – there is also debate about the philosophical implications.

I have systematically used the term "conscious will" rather than "free will" because the Libet experiment is more relevant to the efficacy of the will than to its freedom. Nevertheless, many supporters of the Libet claim, including Libet himself,[22] have used the term "free will" and have attempted to draw implications about human responsibility. This has aroused further controversy, because many critics have pointed out that Libet's experimental paradigm was irrelevant to the question of free will and responsibility. When we talk about free will, we are usually referring to choices between a variety of options, often with moral implications, and this may require careful deliberation over a period of minutes or hours or days. The Libet experiment is just the opposite. The subject was not making a moral decision, and was not even deciding *whether* to move, but only *when*. The *whether* decision was resolved by agreeing to take part in the experiment. Moreover, the subjects were specifically instructed not to deliberate but to act *spontaneously*, and in their original 1983 paper Libet et al. explicitly pointed out that their conclusions applied only to spontaneous, rapidly performed movements. Thus, even if we ignored the above arguments and accepted that the finger/wrist movements in the Libet experiment were not the result of conscious will, this conclusion could not automatically be extended to situations of human and ethical significance.

The Conceptual Framework of the Anti-Conscious-Will Lobbyists

As we have seen, debates about the Libet claim are situated at the intersection between neuroscience and philosophy. It is difficult to be expert in both areas, and I find it striking that prominent neurobiologists using Libet-style experiments to attack the efficacy of conscious will often seem to have rather obscure notions of the positions that they claim to refute. This is true of motor system specialist Patrick Haggard, a former collaborator of Libet and pre-eminent exponent of the Libet claim and its supposed implications against "free will", who appears to have in mind only rather marginal notions of the will. For example, in a major review published in 2008 on the neuroscience of volition, he mentions the idea that the brain's circuits might be influenced by "an unspecified and uncaused cause (the 'will')", rejects this, and concludes the article by stating that "modern neuroscience is shifting toward a view of voluntary action being based on specific brain processes…".[23] This gives the impression that "modern neuroscience" is gradually triumphing against the illusion of "uncaused cause (the 'will')", but this is confusing for at least two reasons. First, only a tiny minority of modern philosophers conceives of the will as an "uncaused cause", so why use such a marginal definition? Second, the wording about modern neuroscience "shifting towards a view of voluntary action being based on specific brain processes" is bizarre, because this has been the standard view in neuroscience for over half a century.

Finally, it is worth noticing that those who use the Libet claim to deny the efficacy of conscious will are committing themselves to a very awkward conceptual position that might be called *semi-epiphenomenalism*. The term *epiphenomenalism** refers to the view that our mental phenomena (our conscious thoughts, feelings, etc.) are in reality mere *epiphenomena* (side effects), being caused by physical events in the brain but having no influence on the brain or on anything. And yet, when it comes to estimating the time when the will to move occurs, these same advocates of the Libet claim have to assume that conscious will is efficacious after all, because they need it to influence the movements involved in reporting it. If the experimental subject says that her will to move occurred when the clock showed time 470 msec, this implies that the act of willing caused a chain of brain events that caused her speech apparatus to produce the words "470 msec". Otherwise it would be impossible to report the time of willing. Thus, the advocates of the Libet claim have to assume that conscious will is efficacious with respect to the movements involved in reporting its timing even though they claim it is inefficacious for the simple movements that were under study.

Conclusions

- The Libet experiment has frequently been claimed to show that conscious will is inefficacious, a mere epiphenomenon. However, many neuroscientists and most philosophers deny this.

- At the neurophysiological level, it has not been shown convincingly that a neural "decision" sufficient to cause a voluntary movement occurs before the time of awareness of the decision to move.
- Even if this could be shown, it would not undermine the conceptions of free will that are defended by most philosophers.
- However, the anti-conscious-will lobby has another string to its bow, and we address this in the next chapter.

7

Psychology-Based Attempts to Refute the Efficacy of Conscious Will

Summary

The previous chapter dealt with the challenge to the efficacy of conscious will raised by the Libet experiment, and I argued that this challenge fails philosophically and has been further undermined, especially over the last five years, by an accumulating weight of neurobiological evidence. But the anti-conscious-will lobby has a second string to its bow: a variety of psychological phenomena indicating the importance of unconscious brain processes in decision-making and voluntary behaviour. I here discuss current understanding of unconscious brain processes and criticize attempts by Daniel Wegner and others to elevate their importance to the point of denying the efficacy of conscious will.

Freedom stretches only as far as the limits of our consciousness.
Carl Jung, *Paracelsus the Physician*, 1942

Our sense of being a conscious agent who does things comes at a cost of being technically wrong all the time.
Daniel Wegner, *The Illusion of Conscious Will*, 2002

Wegner on the "Illusion of Conscious Will"

This chapter, like the previous one, deals with an attack against the efficacy of conscious will, but in this case the data on which the attack is based come not from electrophysiology, but from psychology. These data are tremendously diverse, but they were brought together in an influential book, *The Illusion of Conscious Will*, published in 2002 by social psychologist Daniel Wegner. Since this field has not advanced much since 2002, I shall focus on Wegner's book.

Wegner's book gathers together numerous reports of curious psychological phenomena and uses them to support his claim that the everyday feeling of conscious will is an illusion and that our so-called voluntary behaviour arises entirely from unconscious mental processes. In this chapter, I review briefly the intense debate that resulted from the publication of Wegner's book and draw attention to more recent experiments on the complementary roles of conscious and unconscious cognition. While not denying the role of unconscious processes, I shall argue that conscious ones are also very important and that the anti-conscious-will lobby has failed to make an adequate case to justify its extreme claims.[1]

Cognitive Psychology and Unconscious Mental Processes

Before addressing in detail these attacks against the efficacy of conscious will, it is worth considering some more sober evaluations from experimental psychology. The notion of unconscious mental processes was of course central to the conceptions of Sigmund Freud (1856–1939), but it was discussed well before his time. Partly as a reaction to Freudianism came a period dominated by behaviourism (early and middle twentieth century) when it was virtually taboo to discuss questions of consciousness or unconsciousness or mind. The behaviourist stranglehold was gradually broken during the cognitive revolution in the 1950s and 1960s, opening the way to new studies of consciousness and unconsciousness. Over the last 40 years or so, the nature of consciousness and the relationship between conscious and unconscious processes have become flourishing research fields.

I should at this point clarify my use of the words *mind* and *mental*. They are sometimes used to refer exclusively to *conscious* thought, but in modern psychology and philosophy of mind they generally refer to high-level cognitive processes that are *not necessarily conscious*, and I shall adopt this usage. As we shall see, consciousness is considered to arise out of mental processes, without being necessary for all of them.

It is worth bearing in mind, however, that it is difficult in some cases to determine whether someone else's mental processes are conscious or unconscious. A striking example of this occurred in research on "split-brain" patients (whose corpus callosum – the massive fibre tract linking the two cerebral hemispheres – has been sectioned). The question arose whether the subdominant (usually right) hemisphere of these patients was conscious. This hemisphere usually lacks language capacity, making it difficult to ask the right hemisphere whether it is conscious, because it cannot understand the question. Some very eminent authorities including Nobel Prize-winning neuroscientist Sir John Eccles and philosopher Sir Karl Popper concluded that the right hemisphere was *not* conscious.[2] In contrast, most specialists, including Roger Sperry, who won the Nobel Prize for his experiments on split-brain patients, disagreed with Eccles and Popper and argued that the right hemisphere *was* conscious.[3] I tend to side with Sperry, but the question remains unresolved, because nobody has been able to provide a decisive proof of the right hemisphere's consciousness, and there is still ongoing debate about this. Split-brain patients constitute of course a special case, but they illustrate well the point I am trying to make – namely, that research on conscious versus unconscious mental processing relies to a great extent on the subject's ability to communicate about her inner experience, which usually requires language.

The Combination of Conscious and Unconscious Mental Processes
Despite this problem, there is today something of a consensus that our behaviour results from a combination of conscious and unconscious mental processes. If all our mental processes were conscious, we would be swamped with details and our decision-making and behaviour would be too slow.

For example, learned motor tasks such as riding a bicycle rely to a great extent on automatic neural subroutines of which we are largely unconscious. These subroutines depend on neural activity in the cerebellum and elsewhere, and are developed as the person learns to ride the bicycle. At first, she needs to think about her movements, but as learning proceeds they progressively become automatic. A conscious component remains, however, even in an accomplished cyclist. She is conscious of the fact that she is riding a bicycle, and she can if she wishes pay attention to her pedalling or to the subtle body movements that maintain her balance, but most of the complex calculations needed for cycling are performed automatically and unconsciously. This is useful to the rider, because she can devote her conscious thought processes to other purposes. In patients who have a cerebellar lesion, however, the automaticity is lost and they need to pay great attention to motor tasks that would be automatic for other people.

Intuition is another example of automatic processing. Intuition is the ability to arrive at a conclusion, often correctly, without reasoning. We just know (or at least think we know) that this person is a liar or that that financial deal is worth accepting, without being able to say why. The conclusion is conscious, but the thought processes leading to it are unconscious. A book by social psychologist David Myers reviews numerous investigations of the strengths and weaknesses of intuition (considered automatic or "non-deliberate") as compared with "deliberate" (reasoned) thought.[4] Some individuals have developed remarkable intuitive skills in particular areas through intensive practice. For example, top-level chess players can often reproduce a complicated chessboard layout after a mere five-second glance. Intuition has the advantage of being fast and almost effortless, but it can sometimes lead us astray. In some cases, "gut feelings" can be disastrously wrong, as I mention below in the context of investment decisions.

Models of the Relation Between Conscious and Unconscious Processes

We looked briefly in Chapter 2 at the neuroscience of consciousness, and saw that some brain processes give rise to conscious thoughts whereas others do not, although the criteria determining which neural activity will give rise to consciousness are still not well understood. As a kind of shorthand I shall describe this brain activity as "conscious", although philosophers such as Peter Strawson and Paul Ricoeur have pointed out that it is not strictly the brain activity that is conscious, but the *person*. The *neuroscience* of how conscious processes interact with unconscious ones is currently unclear, but we here approach this subject at the level of *psychology*. The psychological literature on the conscious–unconscious relationship is considerable, and a great deal has become clear over the last 30 years. For simplicity, I shall focus on just two well-known models of how conscious and unconscious mental processes interact.

Selective attention is a key determinant of consciousness in Bernard Baars's famous *global workspace theory*.[5] The term *workspace* is computer jargon, and the term *global* here means not localized; thus, the phrase *global workspace* refers to a distributed network of neurons that may involve many parts of the brain. According to Baars, conscious mental processes (those rooted in the global workspace) are the ones that are in the spotlight of our brain's attentional mechanisms, whereas unconscious ones are those outside the spotlight. How this is worked out at the neural level is a major unanswered question that is under investigation.[6] The global workspace is considered to broadcast its output to many brain areas that are functioning at an unconscious level. Baars is not saying that attention is the *only* factor determining whether brain activity will give rise to consciousness; other factors are probably involved, but selective attention is the key factor that the theory emphasizes.

Speed of thought is the key factor in the other model that we discuss, as described in Daniel Kahneman's book, *Thinking, Fast and Slow*,[7] which focuses on the way fast and slow thought processes lead to our decisions. The model was developed by Daniel Kahneman, Amos Tversky, and others, and is backed up by a great deal of experimental data. This research led to Daniel Kahneman's Nobel Prize in Economic Sciences in 2002. He is a psychologist, not an economist, but he was awarded the economics prize because the research has important implications for the way people make economic decisions (as well as decisions in other fields). He conceives of our brains as functioning on two levels: "system 1" and "system 2". System 1 is automatic and unconscious, whereas system 2 is deliberate and conscious. System 1 analyses incoming information, makes judgments, and initiates responses, all this occurring quickly and automatically ("thinking fast"). Our intuitive judgments are made through the rapid functioning of system 1, as are our routine behaviours. In contrast, system 2 is slow, rational, and calculating ("thinking slow"). It is called into action for making decisions in complex or unusual situations. The book is packed full of data confirming this system 1–system 2 distinction. In one experiment, participants were divided into two groups, both of which had to solve the same problem. For group A, the instructions were set out in clear, easy-to-read type, whereas for group B they were in hard-to-read type. One might think that the group B participants would be at a disadvantage, but in fact they did better than those in group A! Kahneman argues that this was because those in Group B were obliged to bring system 2 into play in order to read the type, and that having been activated for reading the type, system 2 kept going and solved the problem. Kahneman's research is relevant to the debate about conscious will because it shows what an impressive part of our decision-making results from fast-unconscious thought processes. However, unlike Wegner (see below), Kahneman does not deny the importance of conscious thought. Quite to the contrary, he emphasizes the importance of the slow-conscious system, and shows how error-prone the fast-unconscious system can be, even when the person is convinced he is correct. This is one of the reasons why he won a Nobel Prize in economics, because, with his colleague Tversky, he revealed the "illusion of expertise and certainty" by experts making economic and investment decisions. Kahneman also considers that our intellectual productivity depends crucially on how willing we are to spend the time and effort required by the slow system.

Unconscious Motivation

The aspect of unconscious processing that is most relevant to this chapter is *unconscious motivation*, because motivation is what lies behind our *willing* and we need to address Daniel Wegner's controversial claim that conscious will is an illusion and that the motivation for all our acts is entirely unconscious. The modern era of experimental research on unconscious motivation is often considered to have been initiated in 1977 by a review by Nisbett and Wilson.[8] These authors argued that people lack insight into their own mental processes, because they are rather inaccurate in describing the influences that caused their behaviour. A more recent review in *Science* emphasizes the importance of what the authors called "unconscious will",[9] and mentions many examples including people's tendency to talk more softly when there is a picture of a library on the wall, or to keep their desk tidier when there is a scent of cleaning agent in the air. They may be vaguely conscious of the picture and the scent, but they are unconscious of the influence that these have on their behaviour. This use of the adjective "unconscious" to describe "will" is unconventional, and arguably self-contradictory, because in everyday language when we speak about the will we are referring to conscious wishes. I think it would be more appropriate to speak of unconscious *motivation*, and to reserve the word *will* for conscious willing as in everyday language, but to avoid possible misunderstanding I shall sometimes refer to conscious will to emphasize that I am using the word in its conventional sense.

For reasons such as those in the previous paragraph, most psychologists consider that motivations and decisions are influenced unconsciously. There is ongoing debate about the importance of the unconscious influences, and a review in 2014 criticizes several of the landmark studies on methodological grounds and goes so far as to state in the conclusion that "evidence for the existence of robust unconscious influences on decision making and related behaviors is weak and many of the key research findings… can be plausibly explained without recourse to unconscious influences".[10] This is, however, a minority view at present.

In short, there is debate about the extent to which our consciously willed decisions and actions may be biased by unconscious processes. Most accept that unconscious bias can be significant. But this is quite different from the extreme claims of the anti-conscious-will lobby that unconscious processes are all-important and that conscious will is totally inefficacious. We now consider their arguments.

Daniel Wegner's Multi-Pronged Attack on the Efficacy of Conscious Will

Daniel Wegner was a professor of psychology at Harvard and the 2011 winner of the American Psychological Association Award for Distinguished Scientific Contributions. His attack on the efficacy of conscious will is enshrined in his provocative and influential 2002 book, *The Illusion of Conscious Will*, which draws on a wide range of psychological literature to support his view that conscious will is an illusion. By this he means that conscious will is just a "feeling" without causal potency, a post-hoc interpretation. He claims that we do not really make consciously willed choices in any objective sense. He states: "Both the legal and the religious free will theories assume that the person's experience of conscious will is a direct sensation of the actual causal relation between the person's thought and action,"[11] and he makes clear that this assumption is the main object of his attack.

In support of his claims, apart from some pages devoted to the Libet experiment (see previous chapter), which Wegner finds totally convincing, Wegner's main focus is on numerous strange phenomena where notions of self and agency are distorted. These include cases of automatism (such as automatic writing, the movement of Ouija boards, and water dowsing), obedience to post-hypnotic suggestion, and delusions about who is the real agent in multiple personality disorder, spirit possession, and mediumship (interpreted as delusions explicable in naturalistic terms). He shows that our drive to consider ourselves as causal agents is so strong that it can lead us to take responsibility for actions that we did not intend, as in cases of patients with the corpus callosum sectioned who *confabulate* (make up stories) to explain behaviour controlled by their non-dominant (usually right) hemisphere. He also reports his own ingenious experiments where subjects are tricked. For example, a person whose arms are hidden under a robe and is watching himself in a mirror can be induced to believe that someone else's moving arms, extending through holes in the robe, are his own and are being moved according to his own volition.

Wegner's controversial claims have been debated in great detail by numerous authors including Alfred Mele,[12] and a wide variety of attitudes toward these claims is represented in a multi-author volume edited by Susan Pockett.[13] I here give only a superficial survey of the debate, beginning with some general criticisms followed by more specific ones, and then moving on to research performed since the publication of the book in 2002.

A major objection to Wegner's thesis is that his claims are too strong. Critics quite rightly argue that the demonstration of illusions or confabulations in contrived situations or in brain-damaged patients is insufficient to support Wegner's strong general claim that conscious will is always illusory even in ordinary situations and in people with undamaged brains. Other frequently expressed general criticisms include the following.

1. Wegner's assumption that the will is just a *feeling* confuses the *experience of will* with the *will* itself. Our experience of something is by definition a feeling, but that does not deny the reality of what is being experienced.

2. Even though Wegner explicitly rejects Cartesian interactionism (see Chapters 1 and 10), some philosophers consider that he does nevertheless make Cartesian interactionist assumptions.[14]

3. His use of the word "illusion" (as in the title of the book) does not even fit his own theory, because although he denies the conscious will's efficacy, he maintains that it is often accurate in its indication of cause and effect and is useful as a guide to understanding ourselves.[15]

4. Even if Wegner were correct in his claim that our explanations of our motivations are after-the-fact reconstructions based on incomplete information, this would not justify his use of the loaded word "confabulation" for normal situations,[16] because our explanations are often accurate.

5. A less common criticism is that of parapsychologist Edward Kelly, who objects that naturalistic interpretations (ones in terms of standard scientific assumptions) are too readily invoked for paranormal phenomena.[17]

As for the details, the book describes such a wide range of phenomena that it is necessary here to select. I shall focus on just two examples.

Automatisms – the subject of Wegner's Chapter 4 – are movements that appear to be consciously controlled but are not accompanied by a feeling of conscious will. He uses them to support his main thesis of the disconnection between actions and conscious will. As an example, let us consider Wegner's discussion of table turning in his Chapters 1 and 4. This curious phenomenon began in the context of the nineteenth-century spiritist movement. People sat around a table with their hands on it, believing (perhaps hoping) that a spirit might intervene, and after some time (which could be almost an hour) the table would begin to move. The cause of this was first studied scientifically by Michael Faraday, who placed force measurement devices between the participants' hands and the table, and found that the source of the movement was their hands. The gentle pressure from the hands of several participants was enough to move the table, even though they were not conscious of contributing to the movement.[18] It appears also that such movements only occurred when the participants were expecting a spirit to act, so the conscious expectation of movement apparently led to the movement via an unconscious mechanism. Wegner provides many such examples of unconsciously mediated movement and argues that this undermines our presuppositions about voluntary control. I find this to be grossly overstated. We all know that our thoughts can bias our movements and our posture without our being aware of it. The thought of a delicious meal awaiting me makes me walk faster without my being conscious of my increased speed. I slouch in my chair when disappointed, without meaning to do so. That unconsciously mediated biases exist is widely accepted and unproblematic, but this does not justify the much stronger claim that conscious will plays no role at all.

Protecting the illusion is the title of Wegner's Chapter 5, which claims that we think of ourselves as "ideal agents" who have goals and know consciously what the goals are before we pursue them. Wegner maintains that this is "all a fabrication, of course" and gives numerous examples of people who invent false stories about their motivations to justify their mistaken belief that they were acting as ideal agents. Wegner gives examples of this happening in ordinary situations and more strikingly in situations of brain damage or of hypnotic suggestion. As an example of the latter, he mentions a nineteenth-century hypnotist who said to a hypnotized woman: "After you wake up you will take a book from the table and put it on the bookshelf." She did just that and explained her motivation by saying, "I do not like to see things so untidy; the shelf is the place for the book…" This seems to me to fall far short of justifying Wegner's strong claim that conscious will is an illusion. The fact that we invent (or, more often, complete) retrospective explanations of our intentions when they are unknown (in this case) or forgotten (in some other cases) may tell us something about the difficulty of recalling our intentions in special cases such as the ones Wegner mentions. But to extrapolate from this to the claim that conscious will never affects our actions seems to me the height of temerity. To take an analogy, a naïve hypothesis might suggest that when we look at an object, say a grid of parallel lines, with only one eye open, we should see a gap in the lines where they go through the "blind spot", corresponding to the region of retina where there are no photoreceptors. We don't. Our brains interpret the gap as being due to the blind spot and therefore "fill it in", and we see the lines as continuous through the blind spot. This happens automatically, without our being aware of it. A Wegner-style visual scientist might be tempted to deduce that our vision is *illusory*, because the visual image that we see is *constructed*. Well, yes, the more we learn about vision the more we understand that it involves a great deal of construction – and our ability to interpret what we see depends on this. Constructed, yes; illusory, no! Visual illusions can occur, of course, but it would make no sense at all to say that *all our vision* was illusory. We know also that memory is an active, constructive process, and that we fill in gaps to produce a coherent account. I find it unsurprising that we fill in gaps in our memories of our motivations, but this does not refute conscious will.

Thus, I do not think the arguments of Wegner and his supporters are sufficient to justify his strong claim that conscious will is an illusion. In asserting this, I do not mean to dismiss Wegner's idea that the brain mechanisms for being aware of our willing may be separate to some extent from the mechanisms leading to the willed action. This seems to me an interesting open question, whose future elucidation will require some very detailed neuroscientific investigations. These have not yet been performed.

Conclusions

- Most, although not all, psychologists consider that "automatic", unconscious mental processes, inaccessible to introspection, play an important role in our decision-making. The unconscious processing has the advantage of speed, but it suffers the disadvantage of being open to blatant errors in certain situations, as the research of Daniel Kahneman and his colleagues emphasize.

- But it is one thing to accept the role of unconscious mental processes and quite another to deny the efficacy of conscious ones! In his book *The Illusion of Conscious Will*, Daniel Wegner goes to such an extreme. He reviews a wide range of situations where notions of self and agency are distorted, and attempts to deduce that the everyday feeling of conscious will is an illusion and that our so-called voluntary behaviour arises *entirely* from unconscious mental processes.

- I have argued in this chapter that Wegner's extreme conclusion is not justified by the data that he reviews.

8

Ethics and the Brain

Summary

This chapter shows that our moral understanding and decision-making, like all our psychological traits and behaviour, depends on the brain. Moreover, certain regions of the brain are particular involved in morality-related thinking. This raises subtle questions about the relationship between neuroscience and ethics, and about the responsibility of people with brain damage. It has even been claimed that neuroscience provides a basis for ethics, but I argue that this is not the case.

Morality is a weakness of the brain.
Arthur Rimbaud, *A Season in Hell: Ravings II*, 1873

The thief and the murderer follow nature just as much as the philanthropist. Cosmic evolution may teach us how the good and evil tendencies of man have come about but, in itself it is incompetent to furnish any... reason why what we call "good" is preferable to what we call "evil"...
Thomas H. Huxley, *Evolution and Ethics*, 1894

Genetics, Neuropsychology, and Ethics

We have already looked at three major challenges to free will and responsibility. Chapter 5 faced up to the challenges that come from considering the brain as a physical system obeying the laws of physics and chemistry, which are almost deterministic. Then, Chapters 6 and 7 considered recent claims to refute the *efficacy* of conscious will, based mainly on the neurophysiological experiments of Benjamin Libet and the psychology-based arguments of Daniel Wegner. I argued that the efficacy of conscious will can survive this double onslaught. But we have not exhausted the challenges to free will and moral responsibility. In this chapter and the next we turn to a new set of difficult questions coming from the areas of human neuropsychology and genetics. This chapter focuses on the relationship between ethics and neuroscience. The next extends the discussion to issues of genetics, determinism, and criminal responsibility.

The Brain and Morality

The Brain's "Moral Network"

Evidence from brain imaging and from studying the consequences of brain lesions indicates that many different regions of the brain are involved in *moral cognition* (i.e. our moral awareness and decision-making), and that these are connected together to form a so-called "moral network". The different parts of this network are involved in particular aspects of our moral cognition. For example, a complex group of brain structures called the limbic system plays a key role in the *emotional* aspects of morality – the feelings that inform our ethical values – whereas other regions are involved when we use *rational thought* to work out which of several options is most justified morally. It is generally accepted that this moral network exists, but that is not to say that it deals *solely* with moral questions, because many parts of it seem to be involved in other kinds of thinking as well that are unrelated to moral issues.[1]

The distinction between emotion-based morality and reason-based morality has ancient roots, and is inherent in some of the Greek words used in the New Testament. Thus, for example, the various New Testament Greek words relating to love imply emotion and reason to different extents. There are several of these words, but I here mention just two. On the one hand, there is *agape*, the New Testament word that is used for God's love, and for the love of those who love in the way that God loves. *Agape* is not about emotion. It refers to the unconditional intention to promote the well-being of others (even when our emotions are not at all positive). But there is another word, often translated *compassion* (Greek *splangchnizomai*), that has much stronger emotional content. This word comes from the Greek word for bowels, because the Greeks thought they were the seat of pity and compassion. The related verb can be translated as to be "moved with compassion", and this wording is often used about Jesus. He himself used it in his famous parable about the "prodigal son", whose loving father was "moved with compassion" when he saw his son coming home. Bearing in mind that the rational and the emotional aspects of morality are dealt with in different brain regions, it would seem that the neural events underlying these two kinds of love are separated in the brain.

The subject of how different brain regions are involved in our moral feelings and decisions is complicated, and in the present chapter I shall avoid going into too much detail about this. Our main concern is not the details, but the basic principle that certain brain regions underlie our morality and that these can be defective. This will lead us on to difficult questions about moral responsibility in the next chapter.

The Prefrontal Cortex and Moral Behaviour

Among the several brain regions involved in the moral network, I shall here focus on the prefrontal cortex, which plays a very important role in moral decision-making. It is the large expanse of cerebral cortex in the frontal lobes, lying in front of the motor areas (Figure 2.1). If you compare the sizes of different cortical regions in the brains of chimpanzees and humans, the prefrontal cortex is the region that is the most increased in relative terms in humans. This is not surprising, because it is involved in mental processes and behaviours that are much more developed in humans than in any other species, including the planning of complex behaviour, decision-making of different kinds, and the moderation of social behaviour, including our ethical beliefs and decisions. These are important aspects of our personalities, and damage to the prefrontal cortex can have devastating effects on personality, leading people to lose their moral inhibitions and/or their moral understanding and to become totally irresponsible.

An early and well-known case of this was the one (mentioned in Chapter 2) of Phineas Gage, the railway construction foreman whose personality was changed after an accident that caused severe damage to his prefrontal cortices. He became irresponsible, impulsive, and uninhibited. Since then, numerous other studies have confirmed that people who have suffered damage to the prefrontal cortex are, like Gage, uninhibited, impulsive, and unconcerned about the consequences of their behaviour.

Brain Function During Moral Cognition

A valuable way to investigate which brain regions are involved in moral cognition is to use functional brain imaging to find out which areas change their level of activity when people think about moral questions. I mentioned two reports on this subject in Chapter 2, but there have been many such studies, using a variety of different moral questions for the subjects to think about while their brains were being scanned. I here give just two more examples.

One study used functional magnetic resonance imaging (fMRI) to help clarify what it is that makes some people behave honestly when confronted with opportunities for dishonest gain. The researchers had in mind two main hypotheses: honesty might result from active *resistance* to temptation, or it might result from the *absence* of temptation. To distinguish between these hypotheses, researchers performed functional brain imaging in people confronted with opportunities for dishonest gain. The subjects were able to gain money by accurately predicting the outcomes of computerized coin-flips. In some trials, they had to state their predictions in advance, so there was no opportunity for cheating. But in other trials, they were rewarded on the basis of their own reports of their accuracy, allowing them to gain money dishonestly by lying about the accuracy of their predictions. The researchers knew when subjects behaved dishonestly, because their levels of accuracy were then much higher than could be expected on a chance basis. The results showed that people who regularly behaved honestly exhibited no additional activity in brain regions known to be involved in self-control (such as the lateral prefrontal cortex), whereas those who often behaved dishonestly did exhibit increased activity in control-related prefrontal regions, and this occurred independently of whether they were behaving honestly at the time of the brain scan.[2] It would seem, then, that in this task the people who regularly behaved honestly did so more or less automatically. This was just natural to them, and they didn't need to think about it. On the other hand, those who behaved dishonestly seem to have been involved in some kind of inner conflict. The brain regions involved in self-control were activated, but the desire to get more money was often too strong.

Another study compared brain activity in "easy" moral decisions (low-conflict ones such as whether you would assist a weeping child who had been assaulted) and in "difficult" moral decisions (high-conflict ones such as whether if you were hiding with the rest of your family during wartime and your baby started to cry, you would suffocate him to save the rest of the family). Brain imaging (fMRI) showed that different areas were activated (on both sides of the brain) in the two kinds of moral decision. During the easy ones, the activation was mainly in the ventromedial prefrontal cortex, but during the difficult decisions it was mainly at the junction between the temporal and parietal cortices.[3]

The Teacher Who Lost His Self-Control

A schoolteacher in Charlottesville, USA, had been a responsible and respectable man throughout his career until the change that turned his life upside down. To his own surprise, he began consulting child pornography websites and visiting prostitutes. These behaviours were new, although he had a pre-existing interest in pornography. Then he started to make sexual advances to his pre-teenage stepdaughter, which led his wife to call the police. He was found guilty of child abuse and was evicted from his home. He said he found his new behaviour totally unacceptable, but his desire was so strong that it overcame his self-control. He was treated with drugs for paedophilia and was enrolled in a behavioural rehabilitation programme, but he was soon expelled from the latter because he kept proposing sex to the women. Having "failed" rehabilitation, he was sentenced to prison, but on the evening before the scheduled date for going to prison, he showed up in a hospital complaining of headaches and saying he was afraid he would rape his landlady. A brain scan was performed, revealing a large brain tumour in the orbito-frontal region of the right prefrontal cortex. Removal of the tumour eliminated the licentious behaviour and the paedophilia disappeared. A year later the tumour began to grow back, and the strong desires returned, but removal of the new tumour once again solved the problem.[4]

It is not known exactly why the tumour had the effects it did, but many other reports confirm the role of the *orbito-frontal cortex** and other prefrontal regions in self-control. It therefore seems to me plausible that the pressure of the tumour may have deactivated these self-control regions thereby freeing pre-existing desires. Even though we do not understand the details, cases like this one highlight the fact that disruption of brain function affects not only perceptual and motor processes, but also morality.

This raises the difficult question of responsibility. If the teacher had raped his landlady, should the presence of the tumour be considered an argument for diminished responsibility? I think it should, because in this case it was very clear that the tumour seriously impaired the brain mechanisms of self-control, since its removal restored him to his normal state. Moreover, the teacher tried to avoid temptation and to resist his desires.

But this invites the question of how I can hold such a view when I previously accepted the arguments of compatibilists that physical determinism in a normal brain is compatible with responsibility and free will. Why should determinism have different consequences in the teacher's abnormal brain than in a normal brain? The crucial difference, in my opinion, is that the tumour was not integrated into the circuitry of the brain and can be considered an external disruption of brain function that went against the will of the teacher.

We will come back to the question of diminished responsibility in the next chapter, in the context of determinism by a combination of genes-plus-environment.

Does Neuroscience Provide a Basis for Ethics?

Having shown that our ethical decision-making and behaviour are rooted in the brain, we need to look at a controversial question that arises. Can neuroscience provide a *basis for ethics*? The standard answer is "no", but Sam Harris has recently contested the standard view.

It was the Scottish philosopher David Hume (1711–76) who first argued that facts, including scientific facts, cannot provide a basis for ethics because there is no valid way of arguing from *what is* to *what ought to be*. In more technical terms, *descriptive statements* (about what is) are fundamentally different from *prescriptive statements* (about what ought to be), and there is no way of getting from one to the other. This is known as the *is–ought problem*, or *Hume's Guillotine*. English philosopher G. E. Moore (1873–1958), one of the founders of analytical philosophy, made some more technical arguments for a similar position, and referred to attempts to cross the is–ought divide as the *naturalistic fallacy*. The arguments of Hume and Moore are widely accepted.

How, then, can we decide what actions are right or wrong? The traditional approach in most societies has been to base ethics on divinely sanctioned laws. It is wrong to steal, murder, or commit adultery because God says so. This does indeed provide a basis for ethics providing one is convinced that God exists and is good, but many philosophers do not accept this and therefore reject the traditional approach. Atheists reject it because they deny that God exists, and philosophers who believe in God, including Immanuel Kant, have raised the difficulty of how we can be sure that God is good.

But on what, then, do those who reject the traditional approach base their ethics? What approaches do they propose for deciding between right or wrong? Many different solutions have been proposed, including *utilitarianism** (considered in the next chapter) and *moral relativism*, but there are difficulties with all these approaches. I cannot here explore systematically the various possibilities, because the subject is vast and complicated and it would take us too far away from our theme of neuroscience. Instead, I shall focus on one much popularized claim by Sam Harris, in *The Moral Landscape*,[5] that we can sweep aside all these philosophical positions because the is–ought divide can be crossed after all. Central to his claim is the idea that neuroscience can provide an adequate basis for ethics.

The Moral Landscape

Prior to publication the book received unconditional praise from some members of the advisory board of Harris's *Project Reason*, including Richard Dawkins, whose words were reproduced on the dust jacket: "I was one of those who had unthinkingly bought into the hectoring myth that science can say nothing about morals. To my surprise, *The Moral Landscape* has changed all that for me. It should change it for philosophers too." But the philosophers did not agree. Their reviews of the book were almost uniformly negative. For example, fellow atheist Simon Blackburn wrote that Harris "joins the prodigious ranks of those whose claim to have transcended philosophy is just an instance of their doing it very badly".

What then was the problem? It was that Harris smuggled in a crucial assumption. He wrote that "questions about values – about meaning, morality, and life's larger purpose – are really questions about the well-being of conscious creatures. Values, therefore, translate into facts that can be scientifically understood".[6] He then went on to argue that with the help of neuroscience we should in principle be able to evaluate people's well-being and hence be able to maximize it, enabling us to make moral decisions without any need for religion (which Harris attacks repeatedly) or for moral philosophy.

The problem with this is that Harris doesn't cross the is–ought divide at all. Instead, *he assumes right from the start* that the well-being of conscious creatures should be maximized. I am not saying that this is a bad assumption to make. It is essentially the one made by Bentham and Mill, the founders of utilitarianism, a position that we shall discuss in Chapter 9. As Mill himself pointed out, it is close to the injunction of Jesus to love one's neighbour as oneself. Why then was Harris's book so widely condemned? It is that he claimed to have found a way of crossing what he calls the "firewall between facts and values", but served up something very close to traditional utilitarianism.

I am not trying to say that Harris's book is all bad. It is very readable and contains a great deal of interesting information. But it does not solve the is–ought problem. Neuroscience does not provide a basis for morality.

Conclusions

- Moral decision-making depends on the brain just as do all our other psychological and behavioural functions. Moreover, brain damage can profoundly undermine our ability to behave ethically.
- This raises difficult questions about human responsibility and criminal justice that will be discussed in the next chapter.
- Despite the centrality of brain activity in moral decision-making, neuroscience does not provide a basis for morality.

9

Bio-Environmental Determinism and Criminal Liability

Summary

This chapter focuses on the question of determinism by the combination of genes-plus-environment. If our brains are thus determined, how can we be free and responsible? And what about criminals? Many of them have abnormal brains. Is this because of bio-environmental determinism? Are they responsible for their crimes?

Liberty means responsibility. That is why most men dread it.
George Bernard Shaw, *Man and Superman*, 1903

I became acquainted with the last stage of that corruption in my second concentration camp, Auschwitz. The gas chambers of Auschwitz were the ultimate consequence of the theory that man is nothing but the product of heredity and environment; or as the Nazi liked to say, "of Blood and Soil."
Viktor E. Frankl, *The Doctor and the Soul: From Psychotherapy to Logotherapy*, 1982

Why Do People Commit Crimes?

The previous chapter showed that our moral understanding and decision-making, like all our behaviour, is rooted in our brains, and that damage to certain brain regions can profoundly undermine our ability to behave morally. This leads on to major issues that are dealt with in the present chapter.

- Are the brains of criminals different from those of other people?
- If these differences exist, is this because of genetic and/or environmental influences?
- Is criminal behaviour *predetermined* by genes and environment?
- In the light of neuroscientific and genetic understanding, should the legal system be changed?

Neurocriminology

Several studies have shown that there are differences between the brains of psychopaths (people who lack empathy and remorse) and criminals, as compared with the brains of "normal" people. This has direct implications for the debate about whether criminality is the result of social conditions or of biology or both. After the Second World War the general tendency was to attribute crime to social factors or to psychological disturbances, and not to biology, but the pendulum has swung back in the direction of biology, as is recounted in a controversial recent book by Adrian Raine,[1] who describes himself as a "neurocriminologist".

Most modern studies of the brains of criminals have used some form of brain imaging. Some of them have focused just on the structure of the brain (e.g. the sizes of different regions), and this is called *structural brain imaging*. Others compare the functional activity of different regions (*functional brain imaging*).

Structural brain imaging has been used to compare the sizes of various brain regions in psychopaths or in people with particularly violent or antisocial behaviour, as compared with "normal" people. Many such studies have been performed, and these have regularly shown significant differences, especially in the prefrontal cortex.[2] For example, one study assessed whether different parts of the brains of psychopaths were larger or smaller than the corresponding regions in the general population. It was found that some regions were significantly smaller in psychopaths, notably parts of the orbito-frontal and fronto-polar cortices, both known to be involved in moral behaviour.[3]

Many other studies have compared the *functions* of different brain regions. One method of doing this is to use positron emission tomography to measure the levels of glucose metabolism in different brain regions, providing an indication of their amounts of electrical activity. One such study showed that people with a life history of aggressive and impulsive behaviour had on average a lower than normal metabolic rate (implying reduced electrical activity) in several regions of prefrontal cortex (orbito-frontal, anterior medial frontal, and anterior frontal).[4] Another study distinguished between two different kinds of murderer, showing that glucose metabolism in the prefrontal cortex was reduced in those with strongly emotional and impulsive personalities, but was virtually normal in murderers of the calculating, predatory kind. These latter were characterized by excessive metabolism (and presumably electrical activity) in various subcortical brain regions, and it was apparently this that predisposed them to aggressive behaviour.[5]

Moral and Criminal Responsibility in Cases of Brain Pathology

A natural interpretation of the above studies is that the differences between the brains of "normal" people versus those of psychopaths or violent criminals are a major factor in causing the aberrant behaviour of the latter. This is not certain, however, because correlation does not imply causation, so the finding of differences in the brains of criminals does not prove that the differences caused the criminal behaviour. Moreover, the brains of many criminals cannot currently be distinguished from those of ordinary people. In particularly striking cases, such as the teacher who lost his self-control (previous chapter), the causal relation between the brain abnormality and a behavioural problem can be clear, but such cases are exceptional. In most cases it is very difficult to know what caused the aberrant behaviour.

The Brain and Criminal Lawsuits

Nevertheless, lawyers are increasingly using neuroscientific arguments in their attempts to establish diminished responsibility for their clients.

The first major instance of this was in 1991 in New York. Herbert Weinstein, a retired advertising executive aged 65, strangled his wife and then threw the body out of the window of their twelfth-floor apartment to simulate a suicide. During the trial, Weinstein admitted everything, but argued that he was not responsible for murdering his wife, because brain imagery showed a cyst in the protective layers covering the upper part of the right frontal lobe associated with a decreased volume of this part of the brain. The defence lawyers argued that this explained the aggressive behaviour. The prosecutor replied by arguing that it was invalid to use the new imaging techniques as these had not yet been sufficiently validated, and therefore maintained that the photographs based on these techniques should not even be shown to the jury. As a compromise, the judge ruled that the photographs could be admitted, but that the jury should not be told that the cyst was associated with the violence. The lawyers for the prosecution were so intimidated by the neuroscientific arguments of the defence that they accepted an agreement that the charge should be reduced from murder to manslaughter if Weinstein accepted to plead guilty, which he did.

As brain imaging continued to be developed in the 1990s, other cases soon followed. In one famous case, imaging was used to demonstrate not a brain disease, but a brain *immaturity*. In 1993, Christopher Simmons, aged 17, coldly concocted a plan of burglary with murder, in the state of Missouri, USA. He communicated his plan to several friends and managed to recruit two younger teenagers to help. Simmons convinced them to help him by saying that being minors would ensure that they would not get a heavy penalty. One of them dropped out, but Simmons and the other captured and bound the victim and threw her alive into a river where she drowned. Simmons was sentenced to death, but after several appeals (including one brought by the American Medical Association – AMA), the case was brought before the Supreme Court of (the State of) Missouri and then before that of the United States, who ruled that the death penalty was unconstitutional when the defendant was a minor. Advocacy for this conclusion relied heavily on neuroimaging data. According to the AMA:

> First, adolescents rely for certain tasks, more than adults, on the amygdala, the area of the brain associated with primitive impulses of aggression, anger, and fear. Adults, on the other hand, tend to process similar information through the prefrontal cortex, a cerebral area associated with impulse control and good judgment. Second, the regions of the brain associated with impulse control, risk assessment, and moral reasoning develop last, after late adolescence.[6]

The Supreme Court of the United States was convinced, and Simmons's penalty was commuted to life imprisonment.

Genes, Environment, and Diminished Responsibility

Genes and environment come into our present discussion, because they affect behaviour, mainly through their effects on brain development. By "environment" I mean all influences on an organism that act from outside it, from the effects on a foetus of its mother's hormones to housing and education.

Theories about the hereditary origins of delinquency took off in the early nineteenth century and reached their culmination in the second half of it with the publication of books proposing an almost total genetic determinism, such as *L'uomo delinquente* (*The Criminal Man*), published in 1876 by the Italian criminologist and physician Cesare Lombroso.[7] Influenced by phrenological and physiognomic studies, Lombroso believed that one could distinguish a "born criminal" by his physical appearance. He considered that about one-third of criminals can be recognized by their "primitive" or "atavistic" physical traits (jutting jaw, jug ears, etc.) to be "born criminals" but that the other two-thirds have only some of the inherited traits of criminality and are driven to criminality by environmental factors. Lombroso's notion of "born criminal" has been refuted by many authors, and nowadays nobody accepts full genetic determinism. But the more moderate notion of a *partial influence* of genetic factors (i.e. genetic *susceptibility*) has been quite widely accepted and is gaining ground.

In 2007, Abdelmalek Bayout, an Algerian, confessed before an Italian court to the murder of a Colombian, Walter Perez. His original sentence of 12 years in prison was reduced to 9 years and 2 months, because Bayout was suffering from schizophrenia. Then in May 2009, the sentence was reduced again by a year, on appeal, because of genetic anomalies, including but not limited to a particular variant of the monoamine oxidase A (MAOA) gene, as there were indications that the anomalies would tend to make a person more aggressive in stressful situations. The MAOA gene encodes an enzyme that degrades certain neurotransmitters (including dopamine, noradrenaline, and serotonin) that are involved in mood and emotionality. Bayout's variant of MAOA is less active than other variants, leading to higher levels of these transmitters and hence greater aggressiveness.[8]

Similar arguments have been used in other cases. For example, in the trial of Davis Bradley Waldroup a US jury reduced the charge from first-degree murder to voluntary manslaughter because he had the less active variant of MAOA and had also been abused in childhood, and these two factors have been shown to interact synergistically, by which I mean that the combined effect of the less active MAOA and the abuse is much greater than either effect alone.[9]

These are just two cases among many where genetic data were used in a trial to argue a reduction of liability. In most cases, however, the courts have rejected the genetic argument, for a variety of reasons. Nobody disputes that changes in genes such as MAOA affect emotions and impulsivity, and are therefore statistically associated with violent behaviour, but this does not in itself prove that responsibility was diminished, for several reasons. First, a statistical correlation does not prove causation; most people die in bed, but lying in bed is not the cause of death. Second, even when the statistics suggest a causal influence, if this is just one genetic factor among many (as is probably the case with MAOA, since hundreds of other genes probably also influence violent behaviour), we currently know far too little about the genome as a whole to be able to say if one murderer's genes were "worse" than those of another. Even apart from these objections, the implications of a strong correlation for responsibility can be debated. For example, nine out of ten murders are committed by people with the genetic peculiarity that they carry the Y-chromosome (i.e. they are males). Nobody disputes this, but should male murderers therefore be considered to have diminished responsibility? Should female murderers be punished more severely?

Environmental Influences on Criminality

A further complication is that heredity does not work alone, and that our environment contributes to the development of our personalities and our behaviour. Environmental factors that correlate with criminality include the effects on a foetus of its mother smoking or drinking strong coffee, abuse during childhood, a broken home, poor education, and poverty. Presumably the adverse consequences of all these factors for behaviour result from their effects on brain development. Some of them, especially childhood abuse, are occasionally accepted by a court as an indication of diminished responsibility, although such a decision can be criticized for reasons parallel to those above: a statistical trend showing that adults who had been abused in childhood commit more crimes does not strictly prove that responsibility is diminished.

Bio-Environmental Determinism and Moral Responsibility

But the situation becomes more complicated when one considers the *combination* of our heredity and our environment taken together, because it is widely believed that the two together almost completely determine who we are. Advocates of such *bio-environmental determinism* (determinism by genes-plus-environment) sometimes argue for a very broad application of the concept of diminished responsibility. Their idea is that anybody who commits a crime presumably does so as a result of his brain function. In some cases, we may be able to identify the abnormalities responsible (brain lesions, MAOA mutations, abuse in childhood, etc.), and we therefore ascribe diminished responsibility to the criminal. But, the argument continues, the causal link between brain function and behaviour is presumably present in all criminals, even when we cannot identify genetic or environmental or other factors favouring brain abnormalities. If they didn't have a crime-prone brain, they presumably would not have committed the crime. Therefore none of us is responsible! The argument for diminished responsibility becomes so broadly applicable that it is emptied of its substance. Responsibility cannot be diminished if it does not even exist.

We thus have two conflicting claims:

- The *diminished responsibility claim* applies in special situations of brain abnormalities (due to genetics and/or environment, or brain damage, etc.). It implies that particular individuals have diminished responsibility compared with the rest of us. Most legal systems accept this.
- The *no-responsibility claim* denies that responsibility can be diminished because it rejects the very notion of responsibility on the grounds of total determinism. Advocates of the no-responsibility claim invoke various kinds of determinism (and sometimes fail to distinguish between them) including physical determinism, which we dealt with in Chapter 5. But our focus here is on bio-environmental determinism and we now consider whether this undermines human responsibility – including criminal responsibility.

The Helplessness of Mr Puppet

There is an extensive literature on determinism and its implications for criminal law, but I shall focus on a single very influential paper by Joshua Greene and Jonathan Cohen.[10] They are highly respected cognitive neuroscientists and make a serious effort to bridge the gap between neuroscience and modern philosophy, but they make some outlandish claims.

They propose a particularly strong version of bio-environmental determinism. Its most common version is the claim that the genes-plus-environment combination determines our personality traits, but Greene and Cohen go further and claim that it determines even our *individual actions*.

They invent a "thought experiment", according to which a group of malevolent scientists design an individual ("Mr Puppet"), selecting every gene and controlling all his environment, to make it highly probable that he will perform some pre-specified criminal act. They argue that Mr Puppet is the victim of forces beyond his control and then jump to the conclusion that we are all just like him.

> *Thus, it seems that, in a very real sense, we are all puppets. The combined effects of genes and environment determine all our actions. Mr Puppet is exceptional only in that the intentions of other humans lie behind his genes and environment. But… this does not really matter. We are no more free than he is.*[11]

This is a very strong form of bio-environmental determinism, because it claims that genes-plus-environment determine not only our traits and tendencies, but even our individual actions – including, presumably, the writings of Greene and Cohen, although they do not mention this. In my opinion, this is simply wrong. Admittedly, a weaker form of bio-environmental determinism was widely assumed throughout much of the twentieth century, and many psychological investigations into the relative contributions of genes and environment to personality traits, intelligence, disease susceptibility, etc. still implicitly assume that the two together are entirely responsible for the trait being studied. But over the last two decades or so a wealth of new cell biological results has undermined this view. It has in fact long been understood that many events in our cells – and notably the *thermal motion* of molecules – are controlled neither by our genes nor by our environment, but only during the last decade has the importance of this for debates about bio-environmental determinism come to be understood.

At temperatures above absolute zero, all molecules and atoms and even subatomic particles are constantly in motion. This is called *thermal motion* or *thermal noise*. Temperature is in fact a measure of the amount of thermal motion in a system. Thermal motion is essential to cellular function – otherwise molecules would not diffuse, for example. But it has now become clear that thermal noise has major effects on fundamental events involved in the control of cellular function, including the synthesis of proteins and the functioning of ion channels. This introduces an important uncontrolled element into cellular function. The implications for behaviour are still only partly understood, but in 2012 I reviewed the available evidence in considerable detail, showing the importance of the uncontrolled events for brain development and brain function.[12]

Thus, even if the malevolent scientists were able to specify Mr Puppet's genes and environment with perfect precision, this would not enable them to pre-specify his behaviour. This is not, of course, to deny that our genes and our environment make important contributions to the development of our personalities and our behaviour, but Greene and Cohen's extreme claim that genes and environment determine all our actions is simply wrong, and even the weaker claim that these determine our personalities is exaggerated.

Principles of Criminal Justice

The point where these considerations become frighteningly practical and urgent is their application to criminal justice. I have mentioned two different questions, about the *theory of punishment* and about *diminished responsibility*. Our aim now is to come back to these themes and to reconsider them in relation to the notion of criminal justice. As I mentioned briefly above, neuroscientific determinists such as Greene and Cohen argue that the purpose of punishments should not be to establish justice, but to improve society. This view is called *utilitarianism* (or sometimes *consequentialism* – a term with a similar but slightly broader meaning). We need to look at this more closely.

Utilitarian and Retributivist Theories of Punishment

Our evaluation of the question of bio-environmental (and other) determinism will affect our attitude to the role of punishment in society. There are two main approaches: *utilitarianism*, which is justified on the basis of the future effects of the punishment, and *retributivism*, which is justified on the basis of the crime that has been committed and the need to atone for the damage already done.

Utilitarianism

Since the eighteenth century, the term *utilitarianism* has been used to describe both an ethical principle, and, more narrowly, a theory of punishment. At the core of utilitarianism is the idea that the moral worth of an action is determined by its outcome, and notably its tendency to promote happiness. Modern utilitarianism has its roots in the writings of Jeremy Bentham (1748–1832) and John Stuart Mill (1806–73), and was launched in 1776 when Bentham wrote in his *A Fragment on Government:* "It is the greatest happiness of the greatest number that is the measure of right and wrong."[13] A striking aspect of this utilitarianism is that it endeavoured to found ethics on an abstract principle rather than on divine fiat, which was not an option for Bentham and Mill since they were both atheists. However, Bentham claimed to have derived this principle from the writings of Joseph Priestley, a Unitarian clergyman, and Mill argued that it was inherent in the teaching of Jesus:

> *In the golden rule of Jesus of Nazareth, we read the complete spirit of the ethics of utility. To do as one would be done by, and to love one's neighbour as oneself, constitute the ideal perfection of utilitarian morality.*[14]

In the modern world, the importance of loving one's neighbour as oneself is of course widely accepted by adherents to many different religions as well as by atheists and agnostics, but thoroughgoing utilitarians who found their ethics and theory of punishment *solely* on utilitarian principles tend to be atheists or determinists denying free will and responsibility, or both. But it seems to me that Christians who accept divine fiat can still adopt a form of utilitarian ethics without denying the force of divine fiat, because to Christians, who believe that "God is Love" (1 John 4:8), the supreme divine command, stemming from God's very nature, is to practise *agape-love*, the resolute and unconditional intention to promote the well-being of others. A "Christian utilitarian" (the term has been used by several Christian ethicists including Joseph Fletcher) would thus be a Christian who systematically tries to promote the well-being of others.

Conversely, someone who accepts utilitarian *ethics* is not, as far as I can see, logically committed to adopting a *purely* utilitarian theory of *punishment*. Whether atheist or theist, she could consistently accept a role for retribution in her theory of punishment. However, hard determinism does seem to me incompatible with retributivism, because it denies that anyone deserves punishment, which is an essential part of the retributivist approach.

Thus, it is entirely logical that utilitarianism (or *consequentialism*) should be the approach of hard determinists Greene and Cohen (and many other deterministically oriented neuroscientists). For these authors, the sole criteria for deciding on the punishments of criminals should be the ability to achieve future social benefits, such as crime reduction.

Most modern legal systems are not exclusively utilitarian but do include utilitarian components, including:

- *Deterrence.* The fear of punishment should deter potential criminals.
- *Preventive incarceration.* Fear that a murderer or rapist may commit another crime would motivate the judge to impose a long stay in prison as a preventive measure to protect the public.
- *Rehabilitation.* In most Western countries, great efforts are currently being made to develop effective rehabilitation programmes, especially for young people. These attempt to reform criminals by various therapies, by education, and by allowing progressively more parole from prison so that the person can adapt to life in the outside world. Unfortunately, most rehabilitation programmes are still only moderately effective.

But modern legal systems usually also include some retributivist criteria, as we now discuss.

Retributivism

This is the view that a criminal should be punished because he *deserves* it. At its heart is the *principle of proportionality*: a serious crime should be punished severely, and a minor crime leniently, because that is only fair and just. There is also a psychological aspect, the feeling that a deserved punishment (called *retribution*) somehow "puts things right". The criminal is said to be "paying his debt to society". The concept has been accepted in most cultures throughout history. It is present in the law of Moses in the Old Testament, in several passages that prescribe the *lex talionis*, that punishments for injuring someone seriously should be on the basis "life for life, eye for eye, tooth for tooth, hand for hand, foot for foot" (Exodus 21:23–24; Deuteronomy 19:21), and similar ideas were formulated in the earlier Babylonian Code of Hammurabi (1772 BC). The underlying motivation for these laws seems to have been less brutal than might at first appear, because part of the purpose was to limit vengeance in primitive situations where relatives of the injured person were likely to take the law into their own hands. Moreover, once the ancient Israelites had settled into the "promised land", many Jewish rabbis interpreted the *lex talionis* metaphorically to mean that the punishment should include compensation but not physical injury. Famously, Jesus went much further, exhorting his disciples to "turn the other cheek" (Matthew 5:39).

In the Western world, in both medieval and modern law, the *lex talionis* has not been interpreted literally (except when the death penalty is imposed for murder, as still happens in some American states), but as an affirmation of the principle of proportionality. Modern retributivist theories have been greatly influenced by the eighteenth-century philosopher Immanuel Kant, who argued in favour of the retributive principle as the sole just basis for criminal punishment, writing: "Judicial punishment can never be used merely as a means to promote some other good for the criminal himself or for civil society, but instead it must in all cases be imposed on him only on the ground that he has committed a crime."[15] Thus Kant rejected utilitarianism categorically, but most modern legal systems, at least in the West, function on the basis of a pragmatic compromise between utilitarianism and retributivism.

Utilitarianism Versus Retributivism

As was discussed above, some hard determinists such as Greene and Cohen argue from neuroscience for a punishment system based exclusively on utilitarian principles. Even though I reject some of the extreme deterministic claims that motivate their position, I agree that utilitarian considerations – deterrence, preventive incarceration, and rehabilitation – should play an important role. But I would be reluctant to exclude retributive considerations completely, for several reasons.

First and foremost, to deny them completely would render all punishment unjust. In the words of C. S. Lewis:

Some enlightened people would like to banish all conceptions of retribution or desert from their theory of punishment and place its value wholly in the deterrence of others or the reform of the criminal himself. They do not see that by so doing they render all punishment unjust. What can be more immoral than to inflict suffering on me for the sake of deterring others if I do not deserve it? And if I do deserve it, you are admitting the claims of "retribution." And what can be more outrageous than to catch me and submit me to a disagreeable process of moral improvement without my consent, unless (once more) I deserve it? On yet a third level we get vindictive passion – the thirst for revenge... The good thing of which vindictive passion is the perversion comes out with startling clarity in Hobbes's definition of Revengefulness, "desire by doing hurt to another to make him condemn some fact of his own." Revenge loses sight of the end in the means, but its end is not wholly bad – it wants the evil of the bad man to be to him what it is to everyone else.[16]

Thus, C. S. Lewis makes a strong point that even though revenge is against the teaching of Jesus, it is rooted psychologically in a right idea, that the person who does wrong to others should have the truth revealed to him, that his evil should be to him as it is to others. There is something psychologically very right about the notion of retribution.

This psychological aspect has been acknowledged even by secularist Sam Harris,[17] who refers to an article by science writer Jared Diamond, contrasting the experiences of two people who both lost relatives through murder. One of these was a New Guinea highlander who supposedly avenged the death of a paternal uncle and felt content afterwards – although the highlander has since contested this. The other was Diamond's late father-in-law, who had the opportunity to kill the man who murdered his family during the Holocaust, but instead handed him over to the police. The murderer was released after only one year in jail, and the father-in-law was tormented by feelings of regret for the rest of his life. Diamond refers to the *psychological need for vengeance*. As a Christian, I cannot support the exercise of vengeance as such, but the idea that retributive justice administered by the state can bring psychological relief to those who have been wronged seems to me valid, a factor to be considered in seeking a correct balance between utilitarian and retributivist considerations.

Another value of retributivism lies in its *principle of proportionality*, which is needed to limit excessive punishment. Pure utilitarianism could justify acts that are fundamentally unjust, such as condemning an innocent person to satisfy an angry mob that considered him guilty.

A related question is that of *pre-emptive imprisonment*. It is already generally accepted in the Western world that the release of a prisoner on parole should be subject to an evaluation of how dangerous he is. Unfortunately, the psychologists' evaluations are not entirely reliable, with the result that murders and rapes are sometimes committed by prisoners on parole. But supposing the evaluation techniques improved greatly, permitting very accurate predictions of which prisoners were likely to commit violent offences. Obviously, parole would not be granted to the most dangerous prisoners. But what about those who had finished their sentence? Would they still be released, even if the probability of their committing another violent crime was high? On purely utilitarian principles, they would be kept in prison – perhaps in a comfortable five-star prison, but they would not be released. On purely retributivist principles, they would be released, despite the enormous danger to society. I think the best solution has to be a balance between utilitarian and retributivist principles, but I admit that finding the right balance is going to be very difficult.

A Christian View of the Balance Between Utilitarianism and Retributivism

Most legal theorists agree that the penal system should take account of both utilitarian and retributivist principles, although several secularists reject outright the notion of retribution. At the other extreme, some Christians give particular importance to retribution because of its importance in theology. Indeed, the very heart of Christianity, the conviction that Jesus died on the cross to obtain the forgiveness of sinners is founded on the notion of retributive justice. Jesus was paying retribution for humanity. But despite my acceptance of this theology, and despite my insistence on the relevance of retribution for penal policy, I think it is important to give at least equal weight to utilitarian considerations: deterrence, preventive detention, and rehabilitation. This is a vast subject, which I can only touch on here, but I would draw attention to the increasing emphasis by Christians (especially Mennonites) on the notion of *restorative justice*. This is a biblically based utilitarian notion. It includes rehabilitation, but is broader. It is a process where the different people affected by an injustice are brought together to discuss and to decide what should be done to repair the harm. Its fundamental idea is that because crime hurts, justice should *heal*. A useful summary is available in an article by two Mennonite authors, Ted Grimsrud and Howard Zehr, who has been called the "grandfather of restorative justice".[18] They argue that the Bible emphasizes "restorative justice" and go on to give a very positive evaluation of recent developments that emphasize restoration rather than retribution. These include victim–offender reconciliation programmes (in North America), "Family Group Conferences" for juvenile offenders (initially in New Zealand but now also in Australia), and "Sentencing Circles" (initially among native Canadians, but now in other contexts as well).

Finally, I think it is illusory to imagine that the state could establish retributive justice at the deepest level, which would need to take account of all our motivations and all our strengths and weaknesses. The law courts could never fully evaluate these. The ultimate judge is God, and he alone knows our hearts.

Diminished Responsibility Before the Law Courts

We now come back to the other difficult question mentioned above, that of *diminished responsibility*. I argued in Chapter 8 that if the teacher with a brain tumour had raped his landlady, his tumour should be considered grounds for diminished responsibility.

In contrast, I would be reluctant to accept the arguments for diminished responsibility of patients with a genetic variation tending to make them more impulsive or aggressive. A first problem is that the available genetic information is still very incomplete. While it is true that a change in a gene for MAOA can promote impulsivity and aggression, this is just one factor among many genetic and environmental influences on personality, most of which are unknown. It seems very artificial to modify a criminal sentence based on a single piece of genetic information, in such a context of global ignorance. Moreover, most of these impulsive/aggressive people can learn to exercise emotional self-control. They have this ability, which distinguishes them from the teacher with a tumour whose brain mechanisms of self-control seem to have been disabled.

Conclusions

- Some cases of criminal behaviour appear to be due, at least in part, to changes in the brain caused by genetics and/or or environmental influences during development, or to brain damage, but the causality is often difficult to evaluate.

- This raises questions about human responsibility and about criminal justice. We are not responsible for our genetic make-up, and have only a limited control over our environment, so to what extent are we responsible for our moral (or immoral) behaviour? If our responsibility is limited, why should anybody be punished?
- Issues such as these have major implications for the ongoing debate about whether criminal punishment should be based on utilitarian or retributivist principles. I here attempt to contribute to this debate by pointing out that the supposed determinism due to a combination of genes-plus-environment is very far from being total.
- I also argue, from a Christian point of view, that the debate between utilitarians and retributivists need not be an either–or dichotomy. A middle ground between the two views can be defended.

IV

The Soul and Religion

10

Does Neuroscience Debunk the Soul?

Summary

Neuroscience raises major problems for the Cartesian notion of a separate soul interacting with the brain, but is perfectly compatible with an embodied soul, which is in fact the biblical conception according to most scholars.

We must no more ask whether the soul and body are one than ask whether the wax and the figure impressed on it are one.
Aristotle, *De Anima*

To give up the illusion that sees in it an immaterial "substance" is not to deny the existence of the soul...
Jacques Monod, *Chance and Necessity*, 1970

When people discover that I am both a neuroscientist and a Christian, they quite often express surprise. They then frequently raise the question of the soul. They want to know how I can believe in one, when neuroscience explains thought and behaviour in terms of neural processes. It usually turns out that their concept of soul is close to that of Descartes: a separate thing outside the body that somehow modifies the functioning of the brain. They assume that all Christians must believe in this dualistic notion of a Cartesian, disembodied soul, and books criticizing the supposedly Christian view of the soul often make the same false assumption.[1] I don't believe in *that* kind of soul. But I shall argue that the teaching of the Bible is more readily compatible with a very different concept of soul, an *embodied soul*. This latter concept is perfectly compatible with the findings of neuroscience.

Various Concepts of Soul in Western Thought

Different Concepts of Soul

Throughout history most people have believed in some kind of soul, or life principle. Anthropologist Sir Edward Burnett Tylor (1832–1917) concluded that the concept of soul is present in all primitive societies. It is also widespread in most advanced and historic cultures and religions, although there are many disagreements about the details. For example, Hindus and a minority of Jews and Christians maintain that we have *intrinsically eternal* souls, but others deny this (Buddhists, most Jews and Christians, Western atheists).

To understand current discussions about the soul it is important to bear in mind the multiple ways in which the word has been used throughout history. I shall focus on Greek thought and its influence on Christian thinking.

Greek Concepts of Soul

The ancient Greeks used the word soul (*psyche*) in three very different ways. (1) The Epicureans thought the soul was a physical thing made of atoms. (2) For Plato and his followers, the soul was an eternal, immaterial, and incorporeal *substance** that temporarily inhabited the body but could exist and thrive without it. (3) To Aristotle and his followers, the soul was the "form" (i.e. *organizing principle*) of the body and inseparable from it.

In the Western world, most philosophical debate about the soul is related to the two great philosophical traditions descended from Plato and Aristotle (Figure 10.1) and their two different concepts of soul, so I emphasize below the differences between these traditions.

The Soul in the Platonist Tradition

The idea of the soul as a separate entity came into mainstream Western thought through the ideas of Socrates (c. 470–399 BC) as recounted in the writings of Plato (c. 424–348 BC). To the Platonists, the soul is an eternal "substance" that imparts life to the body but can exist apart from the body. For them, the soul is the "real me". In the *Phaedo*, the dialogue that Plato wrote about Socrates' last day of life, Socrates compares the body to a prison from which the soul escapes at death. When a friend asks Socrates how he would like to be buried, he replies:

Any way you like... that is, if you can catch me and I don't slip through your fingers.... I shall remain with you no longer, but depart to a state of heavenly happiness. (Plato, Phaedo, *115C)*

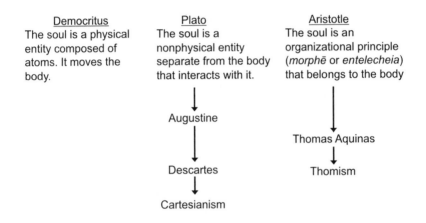

Democritus	Plato	Aristotle
The soul is a physical entity composed of atoms. It moves the body.	The soul is a nonphysical entity separate from the body that interacts with it.	The soul is an organizational principle (*morphē* or *entelecheia*) that belongs to the body

Augustine

Descartes

Cartesianism

Thomas Aquinas

Thomism

Fig. 10.1. *The soul in Western thought; three founding Greek fathers, three distinct concepts and two major Western traditions.*

Earlier in the *Phaedo*, Socrates writes:

*Does not death mean that the body comes to exist by itself, separated from the soul, and that the soul exists by herself, separated from the body? (*Phaedo, *64C)*

This Platonic concept of soul was introduced into Christian philosophy through philosophers such as St Augustine of Hippo (AD 354–430), but the enormous importance of this concept for more recent Western philosophy arises mainly from its central place in the writings of Descartes, as was mentioned in Chapter 1. Even today the average person often thinks of the soul as a Cartesian soul (or mind) existing independently of the brain and acting upon it. Philosophers often call this view *substance dualism*, but I shall avoid this terminology and refer instead to *interactionist dualism* (or *interactionism**) to make it absolutely clear that an *interaction* between the brain and a separate soul (or mind) is being envisaged. The problems raised by neuroscience for *interactionist dualism* do not apply to non-interactionist forms of dualism.

The Soul in the Aristotelian Tradition

Aristotle was a disciple of Plato, and agreed with his master that the soul gave life to the body, but he disagreed on many other points including the nature of the soul. Importantly, Aristotle rejected Plato's conception of the soul as separate from the body. He wrote:

> ... *those have the right conception who believe that the soul does not exist without a body and yet is not itself a kind of body. For it is not a body, but something which belongs to a body, and for this reason exists in a body*... (De Anima II, *2, 414a*)

For Aristotle, the soul is a *principle* inherent in the body. He described it as the body's form (*morphē*) or first actuality (*entelecheia*), meaning that it was an *organizing principle* that caused the body to acquire its structural identity. He also maintained that there was a hierarchy of three different soul functions:

- A *vegetative* or *nutritive* soul function, possessed by all living creatures (plants, animals, humans – monocellular organisms were unknown) and responsible for nourishment, growth and reproduction.
- An *animal* or *sensitive* soul function, possessed by animals and humans and responsible for sensation and movement.
- A *rational* soul function, responsible for conscious thought, reason, and speech.

This conception of there being three soul functions (or three souls in some writings) became generally accepted in antiquity and throughout the Middle Ages (Figure 10.2A), even by Platonists. In claiming that plants and animals were machines (Chapter 1), Descartes implicitly denied the existence of the vegetative and animal soul functions, which left only the rational soul (Figure 10.2B).

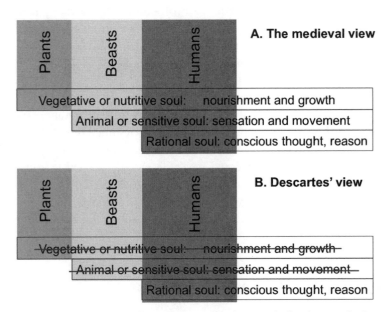

Fig. 10.2. *A. Diagram showing the medieval view of the three souls (or soul functions). B. Descartes abolished the vegetative and animal souls of medieval thought and declared plants and animals to be machines, but humans to be rational souls in machines.*

Differences between Platonists and Aristotelians

As we have seen, the most important difference is that Platonists were *dualists*, believing the soul to be a separate entity from the body, whereas the Aristotelians were closer to *monism**, the view that man is a psychosomatic unity. Their view is sometimes referred to as *hylomorphism** – from *hylē* (matter) and *morphē*(form), because they described the soul as the *form* of the body.

Another important difference concerns the brain. The idea that brain function underlies conscious thought goes back to Alcmaeon and the Hippocratic School, and Plato seems to have accepted this view. In contrast, Aristotle attributed sensation and movement to the heart, and psychological faculties such as imagination, reasoning, and memory to the whole organism,[2] but thought the brain was a cooling device for the blood.

Aristotle's views were adopted by many subsequent thinkers, but his powerful influence on Christian philosophy came mainly through St

Thomas Aquinas (1225–74), who was profoundly influenced by Aristotle and shared (approximately[3]) the latter's view of the soul as being a principle inherent in the body. Aquinas was enormously influential, and indeed he still is, especially among Roman Catholics.

Implications of the Two Concepts of Soul

The differences between the Platonic and Aristotelian traditions with respect to the soul are important in a neuroscientific context because Platonic (or Cartesian) dualism implies that a physical (and chemical etc.) account of the brain could never be entirely correct, because it would fail to deal with the influences coming from the soul. In contrast, Aristotelian monism has no such implication. This means that the challenge of neuroscience to the notion of a soul is far greater in the case of Cartesian dualism, so we need to look at this in some detail.

Cartesian Dualism

As is mentioned in Chapter 1, Descartes considered animals (and plants) as hydraulic (or pneumatic) machines, powered by the flow of the animal spirits in nerves considered (wrongly) to be hollow pipes. But he held that *man*, unlike animals, was more than a machine. When he wrote that animals were machines, he appears to have meant that they were *mere* machines, unthinking and unconscious, or at least not conscious in the way we are.[4] This was obviously not true of humans, so he invoked what he called the *rational soul* (or just *soul*) to explain human consciousness and thought. He thought of the soul (or *mind* – for him, *rational soul* had roughly the meaning of mind) as a separate entity that interacted with the brain. He thought the soul was non-physical and indivisible, existing in time but not in space – it had no size or position. Thus, man was a *soul in a machine*. He explained human reflex movements on the same hydraulic/pneumatic basis as in animals, but maintained that human thought and voluntary behaviour required an interaction with the soul.

Notoriously, Descartes maintained that the body–soul (or brain–soul) interaction occurred in the pineal gland, where the soul supposedly redirected small tissue movements so as to regulate the flow of the animal spirits, and where these could affect the soul. He chose the pineal gland as the interaction site because it is a single, unpaired structure appropriate for interaction with a unique soul, and because he believed (incorrectly) that it protruded into the middle (third) ventricle, a liquid-filled space in the middle of the brain, which he believed to be full of animal spirits.

Early Critiques of Cartesian Dualism

Descartes' proposal of the pineal gland as the site of body–soul interaction makes no sense at all in the light of modern understanding of the pineal's location outside the ventricle and of its role in secreting the hormone melatonin. Even in the seventeenth and eighteenth centuries, it was controversial for reasons that need not concern us, and other structures were proposed, including the corpus callosum, which is now known to be a very large tract of nerve fibres linking the two cerebral hemispheres. Advocates of soul–brain interaction have long since rejected the structures proposed for it in the seventeenth and eighteenth centuries, and its few remaining supporters now propose that it occurs in the cerebral cortex.

Quite apart from arguments about where the brain–soul interaction occurred, the very notion that a non-physical soul could interact with a physical brain has seemed incoherent to many people. One of the earliest objectors was the Princess Elisabeth of Bohemia (granddaughter of King James VI and I of Scotland and England), who maintained a long correspondence with Descartes. In 1643 Elizabeth, a devout Protestant, wrote:

> ... *it would be easier for me to concede matter and extension to the soul than to concede the capacity to move a body and to be moved by it to an immaterial thing.*[5]

Explaining how a non-physical soul or mind could interact with a physical brain continues to be problematic today, and there are additional problems with Cartesian dualism that were discussed in Chapter 5.

Neuroscience and the Cartesian Soul

Despite ongoing controversy, the Cartesian concept of an immaterial (non-physical) soul acting on a material brain was quite widely accepted by Westerners from the late seventeenth century until the mid twentieth century. Its dominance in the late nineteenth century, among both theists and sceptics, is implied by the following quotation from Bertrand Russell (1872–1970):

When I was young we all knew, or thought we knew, that a man consists of a soul and a body; that the body is in time and space, but the soul is in time only. Whether the soul survives death was a matter as to which opinions might differ, but that there is a soul was thought to be indubitable.[6]

As late as 1949, when Gilbert Ryle published his famous book *The Concept of Mind*, he referred to interactionist dualism as the "official doctrine". Since then, this view has declined and has become a minority position among academics, although it still has support from a few philosophers such as Goetz, Swinburne, and Taliaferro. The decline occurred for a variety of reasons, including the arguments of philosophers such as Ryle, Place, Smart, and Feigl in the mid twentieth century, but I shall here focus on two major problems raised by *neuroscience*.

The Interaction Problem

Even when Descartes was still alive, his dualism was criticized by correspondents such as Elisabeth of Bohemia who questioned whether a non-physical mind/soul could affect the brain. In modern terms, the problem is that a non-physical soul would have to exert effects on physical entities, whereas standard physics assumes that the behaviour of every physical entity is determined by the physical forces acting on it. Thus, the soul's influence would have to modify the entity's physically determined behaviour, thereby violating the laws of physics. Only two ways have been proposed for answering this objection.

One way is to suggest that the mind/soul might have physical powers. The idea that it might be physical, with a measurable mass, was debated early in the twentieth century following a report that the bodies of humans, but not those of dogs, lost weight at the moment of death,[7] but the evidence was poor and has never been confirmed. Since then, the only published reports on weight changes at death have involved animals. For example, tests performed on sheep showed an unexplained transient *increase* in weight shortly after death,[8] but there was no evidence for the departure of a physical soul with measurable mass. This does not rule out the possibility that the soul might be some kind of physical entity, perhaps with zero or immeasurably small mass. I know of no serious evidence for such a view, and it has no academic support, but it remains a remote possibility.

If we set aside the idea of a mind/soul with physical powers, the only other solution is to find a way for the laws of physics to be circumvented.

Modern proponents of this approach always invoke the indeterminacy (fuzziness) of quantum physics. I shall refer to this idea that soul–brain (or mind–brain) interaction might occur through the subtle mysteries of quantum physics as *quantum dualism*. It has spawned a vast literature of variable quality (if I type *quantum* and *soul* into Google, I get 12 million answers), but it is a minority view among academics. The idea is that owing to the indeterminacy of quantum physics, the workings of the brain-machine are only approximately determined by the laws of physics, allowing small soulish influences to sneak in. It would be beyond our present scope to grapple in detail with this difficult and controversial question, but Appendix 1 discusses briefly one of the main objections to quantum dualism – the problem that quantum indeterminacy is very small indeed, and probably much too small to affect the behaviour of neurons.

Thus, the interaction problem is a major difficulty for Cartesian dualism (even for modern versions). This does not in my opinion refute interactionism conclusively, but it weighs heavily against it. And neuroscience raises another major problem for interactionism, as I now briefly discuss.

What Tasks Remain for a Cartesian Soul?

We saw in Chapters 2 and 3 that a wealth of data from many branches of neuroscience indicates that the brain works mechanistically, and that the intimate relationship between mind and brain function is strongly supported. Particular tasks are performed in particular parts of the brain, and in some cases (such as visual recognition and the storage and retrieval of memories – Chapter 3) we understand in considerable detail how the neuronal operations are performed and can even simulate them with success. The simulations work, without any need to postulate help from a Cartesian soul.

In the light of this, modern interactionist dualists can no longer defend a full-blooded Cartesian approach in which all cognitive activity was ascribed to the non-physical soul. The only option left is to argue for a weaker form of interactionism, in which the brain performs part of the job and the soul does the rest. Physicist John Turl embraces this reality explicitly, arguing that the soul plays an overall supervisory role:

It may seem to the sceptical monist as if the dualist's soul is being squeezed into the last available gap of knowledge, possibly even where the experimentalist cannot reach. Prof. P. Clarke believes that "the only kind of substance dualism that is still even remotely defendable in the light of modern neuroscience is a limited one, invoking a separate soul acting on the brain only for very particular aspects of our humanity such as free will". But the reality is that the soul has been put back where it belongs – from filing clerk to chief inspector.[9]

Fair enough. If somebody is sufficiently convinced, for philosophical or theological reasons, in the existence of a non-physical soul of the limited "chief inspector" variety that John Turl proposes, this may still be defensible. Such a soul might exist and interact with the brain by means that are currently unknown. This remains theoretically possible, even though there is no experimental evidence to support it.

But, as a Christian (like John Turl), this is not where I would place my bets. With all due respect to the rich Platonist/dualist tradition in Christianity, I think a moderate form of monism is more defensible scientifically and also more true to the biblical conception of man.

The Biblical Conception of Man and the Soul

The biblical authors are very clear that humans are more than just matter. We transcend matter by our psychology and by our spirituality. There is also what some scholars call a body–soul *duality** (not dualism) in some biblical verses, as when Jesus exhorts his disciples not to be afraid of those who kill the body but cannot kill the soul (Matthew 10:28). But *duality* does not imply *interactionist dualism*, and over the last 60 years or so the latter has lost popularity among biblical scholars. This is mainly because advances in the analysis of biblical texts have tended to emphasize the unity of human nature, and to contradict any temptation to read Platonism into these texts. To illustrate the anti-Platonist arguments, we shall focus on current understanding of the words translated *soul* or *spirit* in the Bible.

Soul and Spirit in the Bible

In the Old Testament, the Hebrew word most often translated as "soul" is *nephesh,* which carries the basic idea of *life* or *vitality,* but which can take on many different meanings ranging from *personality* to *blood.* In Genesis 2, when God breathes into the nostrils of man the breath of life, man becomes a *nephesh,* which is translated "living being" in most modern

English versions but "living soul" in the Authorized (i.e. King James) Version. The meaning of man's becoming a *nephesh* is that he starts to live and move.

Other Hebrew words in the Old Testament can overlap in meaning with *nephesh*, particularly *ruah*, the word for "spirit", but whose primary meaning is air in motion. In many cases it means "wind", but it can also refer to the "breath of life" that the whole animal creation shares with man (e.g. Genesis 6:17). When translated spirit, it usually refers to the mind as expressive of the whole personality (e.g. Psalm 32:2), or it may refer to human inclinations and desires (e.g. Hosea 4:12) or to God's Holy Spirit.

Thus, neither *nephesh* nor *ruah* implies dualism. Neither is ever described as existing separately from the body. The Old Testament sees man as a unity.[10]

In the New Testament, interpretation is complicated by the fact that the original manuscripts were written in Greek, and so the available words carry the dualistic overtones of Platonic philosophy. However, the New Testament writers emphasize the unity of the human person and do not teach the idea of a disembodied soul. Thus, *psyche*, the Greek word for soul, carries meanings ranging from life and desire (in St Paul's letters) to the whole personality. And *pneuma*, the New Testament equivalent of *ruah*, is the word most commonly translated spirit (of man or of God) but has the primary meaning of wind or breath.

The point where the New Testament distances itself most clearly from Platonism is in the doctrine of the resurrection of the body, which is poles apart from the Platonic concept of an eternal, non-physical soul existing in isolation from the body. This is particularly clear in 1 Corinthians 15, where St Paul first affirms the resurrection of Jesus, and goes on to explain that after the dead are raised their body will be a "spiritual body", very different from the previous "natural body", but a body nonetheless. Nowhere does the Bible clearly affirm the notion of a disembodied soul or an intrinsically eternal soul.

The appreciation of this by twentieth century scholars was not entirely revolutionary, because there had always been a strong monistic strand in Christian thought due to the influence of Thomas Aquinas as we discussed above. Thus, Austin Farrer, an eminent Anglican theologian with *Thomistic** inclinations, criticized the dualistic views of neurobiologist (and future Nobel Prize-winner) John Eccles, writing:

We will have nothing to do with the fantastic suggestion, that what the supersensitive "reactors" in the cortex react to, is the initiative of a virtually disembodied soul. To what, then, are we to say that they do react? What else, than to the motions of the embodied soul, that is to say, other motions in the same nervous system?[11]

Current Debate Among Biblical Scholars

There is still, however, a degree of debate among biblical scholars. All agree that the Bible emphasizes the unity of human nature and teaches the resurrection of the body, not a Platonic concept of an eternal soul temporarily imprisoned in the body. Most, including Joel Green, maintain that the dominant biblical view of man is monism with no place for a *separate* soul. But others, including John Cooper, draw attention to New Testament passages that seem to teach an *intermediate state* after death during which we will temporarily be disembodied souls while waiting for the resurrection of the body. To emphasize both the unity of human nature and the soul's possibility of being separate from the body in the intermediate state, Cooper uses the terms *holistic dualism* and *dualistic holism*.[12]

How this theology links in to philosophy is not simple. Green and others at the monistic end of the theological spectrum clearly reject interactionist dualism. At the other end of this spectrum, holistic dualism tends to go hand in hand with a dualistic philosophy, but does not necessarily require interactionist dualism. For example, Thomas Aquinas believed in the intermediate state, but for humans and other organisms on this earth his concept of soul was embodied, not interactionist.

In fact, Christian philosophers and neuroscientists adopt a range of positions. All Christian neuroscientists (I know of no exception) and many (probably most) Christian philosophers reject interactionist dualism, but they also distance themselves at the other extreme from forms of materialism that reject conscious states as illusory. Instead, they mostly adopt an intermediate position, either a non-interactionist form of dualism such as emergent dualism,[13] or a moderate monist position such as *two-aspect monism** (also called *dual-perspective theory*), according to which our own subjective, first-person, account of our inner life and neuroscience's objective, third-person account of our brain's activity refer to complementary aspects of a single entity.[14] It is hard to choose between these moderate positions, but I personally favour two-aspect monism.

On the other hand, a significant minority of Christian philosophers (and physicists, but not neurobiologists in the post-Eccles era – see Appendix 1) rejects even moderate forms of mind–brain monism and continues to advocate interactionist dualism.[15] These authors are rarely explicit about the neuroscientific implications of their positions, but they seem to consider that a non-physical soul, separate from the brain, exerts a direct influence on brain activity.

Personal Identity After Death

A question arises if we think of the soul in Aristotelian/Thomistic terms as a kind of organizing principle inherent in the body. Won't this be destroyed at death? How then can we survive death? As I have discussed above, the Christian answer lies in the doctrine of the resurrection of the body.

But a further question then arises. If I am going to have a new, spiritual, body in heaven (as St Paul claims) but without a Cartesian soul, by what criterion will it be *me*? It may be helpful to take the analogy of a computer program. If you destroy the computer, you destroy the program. But the program can be reinstalled in a new computer and can then "live again". The important thing is that even though the information in the program was destroyed when the computer was destroyed, it was not really lost, because a copy was available. This is only an imperfect analogy, but I find it helpful for thinking about the resurrection of the dead. Our bodies will be different (and better, without weakness or disease!), but they will contain essential information about who we are. Our identity will be maintained.

Of course, this leaves many questions unanswered. How does this information get into the new body? Is the information perhaps stored in some hidden dimension? Or in the mind of God himself? We don't know! This is God's problem, not ours, but I see no reason to doubt that he can solve it.

Conclusions

- Neuroscience raises major problems for the Cartesian notion of a separate soul interacting with the brain, and virtually all modern neuroscientists reject the Cartesian soul, as do most philosophers.

- But the dualistic Cartesian conception, stemming from Plato and Augustine, is not the only Christian conception of soul. There is a strong monistic (in the sense of non-interactionist) tradition in Christian thought, stemming from St Thomas Aquinas and conceiving of the soul as an embodied principle.
- Recent advances in biblical research indicate that the monistic tradition is closer to the biblical concept of man. Such a notion is fully compatible with neuroscience.

11

Near-Death Experiences and Deathbed Visions

Summary

Powerful mystical experiences associated with death or the danger of dying are often cited as evidence supporting a dualist conception of the soul and belief in life after death. But are these experiences real or illusory? The debate is very polarized. A non-illusory status of the experiences is supported by their powerful subjective sense of reality, by their occurrence in virtually all cultures, and by claims that the experiences sometimes provide information not available by natural means. But critics reply that despite the universality of the experiences, their details are strongly influenced culturally, and they point out that many aspects of them can be evoked by drugs or by electrical stimulation of the brain. More rigorous testing will be needed before this debate can be resolved, but for the moment they do not refute the monistic concept of the mind–brain (or soul–brain) relation proposed in the previous chapter.

My experience showed me that the death of the body and the brain are not the end of consciousness, that human experience continues beyond the grave.
Eben Alexander III, *Proof of Heaven*, 2012

Taken together, the scientific evidence suggests
that all aspects of the near death experience have a
neurophysiological or psychological basis.
Dean Mobbs and Caroline Watt, 2011[1]

Paranormal Phenomena and the Soul

In the previous chapter I argued against the notion of a disembodied soul, but in doing so I ignored a whole range of *paranormal* phenomena that many modern dualists consider important evidence in favour of their claims. In this case, however, the notion of soul is not the dimensionless, unlocalized soul that Descartes postulated, but one that can be ascribed to a particular location. Rather than list all these phenomena, which are multifarious, I shall here focus on various striking experiences associated with the proximity (or apparent proximity) of death. The most famous of these are *near-death experiences* (NDEs), which often begin with *out-of-body experiences* (OBEs). Several books relating NDEs have been bestsellers among the general public, including a recent one by Harvard neurosurgeon Eben Alexander.[2] Other less well-known death-related experiences include *terminal lucidity*, the sudden return of mental clarity shortly before death,[3] and *deathbed visions*. Opinions on these have been very polarized. Many enthusiasts, including most of the experiencers themselves, maintain that these reports provide proof of soul–body dualism and of life after death. Others, including several neuroscientists, have taken a radically opposite position, dismissing them as mere illusions due to brain malfunction. The present chapter deals mainly with NDEs (including OBEs) and more briefly with deathbed visions, attempting to assess their validity.

Near-Death Experiences (NDEs)

The term *near-death experience* (NDE) refers to a set of experiences generally associated with the danger or proximity of death. NDEs often occur in situations of severe cerebral *ischaemia** (lack of blood flow to the brain) or *anoxia* (lack of oxygen), and in many cases the patient had been considered clinically dead before resuscitation, but NDEs quite often occur without cerebral ischaemia or anoxia. They may be triggered by stress, depression, or an emotional crisis, or by meditation, and sometimes occur spontaneously. The features of NDEs are similar in people who are near to death and in those who are not. About 4 per cent of the people in the Western world appear to have had NDEs, although the percentage has been claimed to be almost 40 per cent when the widest possible definition is used, including NDE-like phenomena during dreams.[4]

Individuals who experience NDEs usually report several of the following, and usually in the following order.[5]

1. A feeling of deep peace, well-being, and painlessness.

2. An experience of being outside their own body and of looking down on it as a spectator, thus observing the attempts at reanimation and hearing the remarks of the medical staff including sometimes their verification of death.

3. An inability to communicate with these people that they can see and hear.

4. An impression that their vision is better than normal.

5. Then, the feeling of being propelled through dark space, often through a long tunnel (although this is rare in several non-Western cultures) but sometimes across some other sort of symbolic barrier such as a doorway, a bridge or a river.

6. Arrival in a kingdom of light where they often have a "life review" in which they see all the events of their lives pass before their eyes.

7. An encounter with a supreme, and supremely loving, being of light, whom they identify as God or Jesus or Krishna etc. The light differs from mere earthly light in being vibrant and alive. They also meet other spiritual beings, whom they identify as deceased relatives or friends, or as angels. The spiritual beings are often described as being made of light, and sometimes the experiencers apply this description to themselves as well. Communication with these beings occurs through thoughts rather than words.

8. Finally, they return to their original location, sometimes via the same tunnel (etc.) and often after a spiritual being has explained that this is not their moment to die, because they are needed by their family or friends. They re-enter their body, and this moment usually seems to occur at the moment when the person recovers consciousness, suggesting that the soul that departed for the NDE was needed for consciousness.

Most experiencers are convinced that their NDEs were real, not illusory, and they are often profoundly affected by them. They may initially have been very disturbed by the NDE, associated as it often was with a severe medical emergency, but they usually report that its overall effects were positive because it led to a greater appreciation of the value of life and an enhanced feeling of empathy and tolerance toward others. Usually they lose all fear of death because they are convinced of the reality of life after death, even if they had no such conviction before the NDE. Often they devote the remainder of their life to the service of others.

While most NDEs are predominantly positive (at least in the Western world), as is described above, there are occasionally negative, frightening NDEs. These can be variants of the NDEs above, involving a tunnel experience and the realm of light, but are experienced as unpleasant because of feelings of anxiety, loss of control, and isolation. More rarely, the NDE can involve hellish imagery with the presence of demonic beings, frightening animals, or suffering fellow humans.[6]

NDEs Throughout History and in Various Cultures

Even though the current intense interest in NDEs is fairly recent, they have been reported throughout history in many different cultures. An NDE was mentioned even by Plato. Near the end of Plato's *Republic,* Socrates tells about a Greek soldier, Er, who was injured and considered killed in combat. But when the dead were taken up for burial ten days after the battle, Er's body was undecayed although he showed no signs of life. Before his comrades could bury him, Er came back to life and told them what he had seen in the afterworld, on the other side of bodily death. According to Er's account, when his soul left his body he found himself with many other souls on a journey to a marvellous place where he saw many marvellous things including judges who determined the fate of the just and the unjust. The judges told Er to observe and learn and then go back to earthly life and tell what he had seen. It seems plausible that NDEs may have contributed to the ancient and widespread belief in disembodied souls.

In recent years, NDEs have been studied in many different cultures in addition to the Western world (China, India, Thailand, Tibet, Guam, Hawaii, Maoris in New Zealand, etc.).[7] They occur in all these cultures, with striking similarities but also substantial differences. In all these cultures the NDEs often include feelings of euphoria or sometimes of horror, an OBE, the crossing of some sort of barrier or a void (only rarely a tunnel in non-Western cultures), a visit to a supernatural world, and seeing the dead and/or religious figures. The life review experience is also common in major Asian societies (China, India, Thailand, Tibet), but the small number of cases examined up to 2005 in hunter-gatherer societies (30 cases) and the Pacific area (9 cases) revealed only one case of a life review. But even though the occurrence of many of the features is universal, their detailed characteristics are strongly influenced by expectations. For example, even though the visit to a supernatural world occurs in all cultures (and is often experienced even by secular Western atheists), the details of this world are strongly dependent on the culture or expectations.

A study of Thai NDEs illustrates this culture-dependence well. Thai culture is more than 95 per cent Theravadin Buddhist, and is strongly influenced by the *Phra Malaya*, an ancient book that recounts the experiences of a medieval monk (Phra Malaya) during meditation. It describes his descent into the underworld where Yama, the Lord of the Dead, assigns those who have recently died to their appropriate rebirths as a human or an animal or into any of 14 hells or 9 heavens. The monk visits the different hells and witnesses numerous tortures being inflicted on people because of their sins. The influence of the *Phra Malaya* on Thai NDEs is very clear. They almost always involve being taken by Yamatoots (Yama's messengers) to be judged by Yama. In five of the ten cases referred to in an article by Todd Murphy about NDEs in Thailand, the NDEer made a tour of the different hells, witnessing terrible tortures, but none of them actually suffered the tortures. The prevalence of light and of a positive effect in Western cultures was absent, and Yama was very different from the loving being of light in Western NDEs. The distinct cultural flavour of these judgments is illustrated by the following:

I climbed these stairs and found myself in the judgment hall of Yama's palace. I knew that they were ready to judge me for my sins. A giant rooster appeared who told Yama that I had killed him. He emphasized that I had tried to kill him again and again. The rooster said that he remembered me exactly. An entire flock of roosters also appeared and testified that I had killed them, as well. I remembered my actions, and I had to admit that the roosters had told the truth. Yama said that I had committed many sins, and sentenced me to many rebirths both as a chicken, and many other kinds of birds as well... But, quite suddenly, an enormous turtle appeared. It screamed at Yama, saying "don't take him; he is a good human, and he should be allowed to live." Yama asked the turtle "What did he do to help you?" The turtle answered. "Long ago, I almost died because another of these humans wanted to eat me. This man prevented him, and so I was able to live out my life."[8]

The important cultural differences between NDEs make it difficult to accept them as objective, undistorted experiences of a spiritual world, but do not prove them to be totally illusory.

Neurobiological Critiques of NDEs

Those who seek a biological explanation for NDEs underline the fact that several aspects of them, and especially OBEs, can be produced artificially, by brain stimulation or by drugs. Recent reviews of the neurobiology of NDEs offer a variety of perspectives, ranging from a polemical insistence that they are illusory[9] through cautious scepticism[10] to a philosophically argued opposition to materialistic "dogma".[11] There are far more neurobiological data on OBEs than on the other aspects of NDEs.

Neurobiology of Out-of-Body Experiences (OBEs)

OBEs are not always associated with NDEs. A dream-like illusion of floating above one's own body can occur in association with the wake–sleep cycle,[12] and OBEs can be induced by extreme physical effort, by drugs, by meditation, or in other ways without the occurrence of other NDE phenomena. They can also be induced by electrical stimulation of the brain.

Electrical brain stimulation is sometimes performed in patients prior to surgery. In such cases, the patients are conscious, being anaesthetized only locally, as was the case in the famous experiments of Canadian brain surgeon Wilder Penfield in the 1950s. During stimulation of the right temporal lobe (at the side of the brain), one of his patients exclaimed, "Oh God, I am leaving my body." A similar case was observed more recently and described in detail.[13] Moderately weak electrical stimulation of the right angular gyrus (near the boundary between the parietal and temporal lobes) evoked the sensation of falling from a height. Slightly stronger stimulation evoked an experience that resembled an OBE. The patient said, "I see myself lying in bed, from above, but I only see my legs and lower trunk." In fact, the patient was lying in bed with her upper body supported at 45°, and so despite the illusory shift in the patient's vantage point, her description that she could only see her legs and lower trunk was correct. Subsequent stimulation led to illusions of lightness and floating close to the ceiling. When the patient was instructed to watch her legs, stimulation of the same site provoked the impression that her legs had become shorter or that they were moving toward her face. The region stimulated is known to be involved in the awareness of body position, so the authors interpreted the patient's sensations as resulting from a distortion of this awareness. These and other data (involving lesions, epileptic phenomena, etc.) establish a clear link between OBEs of neurological origin and aberrant activity near the right temporo-parietal junction, which is known to be involved in the integration of multisensory body information (tactile, proprioceptive, vestibular, visual, etc.) and hence in body self-consciousness, the feeling of being an entity localized at a position in space.

OBEs share some features in common with two neuropsychiatric conditions: *autoscopy* and *heautoscopy*. In autoscopy, an individual has the impression of seeing a second version of his own body, but unlike in an OBE, he feels that his "self" is located in his real body, not in the illusory one. Heautoscopy is intermediate between autoscopy and an OBE, in that the patient feels uncertain whether his "self" is in the real body or in the illusory one. There is evidence that autoscopy and heautoscopy, like OBEs, can be due to disturbances near the right temporo-parietal junction. An illusion of being outside one's physical body can be induced even in healthy individuals by experimentally inducing a mismatch between visual and tactile information, and in such cases the subjects no longer perceive their body to be part of themselves.[14] Data such as these support the view that OBEs may be illusory experiences resembling autoscopy and heautoscopy, although there is debate about the extent to which these neuropsychiatric or induced experiences resemble true OBEs.

Taken together, the above evidence indicates that OBEs can be illusory. Whether this applies to the OBEs associated with NDEs is an open question, but the fact that OBEs can be illusory puts the burden of proof on those who claim that they are sometimes a genuine, non-illusory phenomenon.

Neurobiology of Otherworldly Aspects of NDEs

An OBE is only the initial part of an NDE, and the other components, involving entry into another world, have never been produced by brain stimulation. Attempts have been made to explain them in neurobiological terms, although several of these seem to me little more than guesswork.

The most plausible (or least implausible) of these attempts have focused on the fact that the modification of brain activity by drugs can lead to several features of an NDE. Several substances can occasionally have such an effect, including various psychedelic drugs including *N,N*-dimethyltryptamine (DMT), ayahuasca (which contains DMT),[15] and LSD, but also ketamine, an anaesthetic that is also used as an antidepressant and as a recreational drug. The most striking example known to me is the experience of an LSD user cited by Oliver Sacks in his book *Hallucinations*:

> *Then I left my body and hovered in the room above the whole scene, then found myself traveling through a tunnel of beautiful light into space and was filled with a feeling of total love and acceptance. The light was the most beautiful, warm and inviting light I ever felt. I heard a voice ask me if I wanted to go back to Earth and finish my life or… to go in to the beautiful love and light in the sky. In the love and light was every person that ever lived. Then my whole life flashed in my mind from birth to the present, with every detail that ever happened, every feeling and thought, visual and emotional was there in an instant. The voice told me that humans are "Love and Light."*[16]

Various explanations have been proposed for individual components of NDEs, but these seem to me ad hoc at best. Thus, differences in ischaemia between the central and peripheral parts of the retina, or in their representations in the primary visual cortex, have been proposed to explain the tunnel experience, but such differential sensitivities cannot explain how the tunnel experience can occur in people who are clearly not ischaemic/anoxic, nor why the symbolic barrier that is traversed is only sometimes a tunnel and can be a bridge or a river or a fence, and they do not readily account for the absence or rarity of the tunnel experience in most non-Western societies.

Also, the fact that Alzheimer's or Parkinson's disease patients sometimes have hallucinations of ghosts or monsters, and the claim that electrical stimulation near the angular gyrus can cause a "sense of presence" have been invoked to explain the meeting with friends and relatives and angels during NDEs, but the vague crudeness of these hallucinations is in striking contrast to the NDEers' conviction that they clearly identified particular friends and relatives. Finally, various psychoanalytic theories of NDEs have been proposed, but these have been criticized on several grounds, notably the lack of empirical evidence for them and the differences between the symptoms of psychiatric populations and the experiences of NDE subjects.

Counterarguments Against the Neurobiological Critique of NDEs

As mentioned above, the strongest neurobiological critiques of NDEs are based on the well-documented evidence that OBEs can be evoked by brain dysfunction and the somewhat more vague evidence that drugs such as ketamine can mimic some of the other features of NDEs. Believers in the reality of NDEs provide several counterarguments to the neurobiological critiques.

Differences Between True and Artificial NDEs

First, they maintain that there are important differences between true NDEs and artificial ones. For example, it is only in true NDEs that a super-normal visual capacity is reported. Also, people who have experienced a true NDE are usually convinced that their experience was real, and they may claim that it was even more real than normal, which is far from being the case with artificial NDEs. They also maintain that the similarity between different people's NDEs, even from different cultures, is difficult to explain on the basis of the hallucination hypothesis. And they argue that the positive changes in the lives of people who have "come back to life" contrast with the negative emotional effects of most hallucinations.[17]

Not Just the Result of Imagination or Expectation

Even though NDEs are influenced by culture, as we discussed above, it is striking that they have the same overall structure in many different cultures and that some aspects of the experience are largely independent of belief. Thus, in the Western world, an atheist is just as likely to have an NDE as a believer, and to experience a supernatural world with spiritual beings. Famously, atheist philosopher Alfred Ayer had an NDE during which he saw a very bright red light that was "responsible for the government of the universe", but he seems to have remained an atheist.

There is also recent evidence that memories of NDEs are richer (contain more characteristics) than memories of real events or the memories of people who have survived a coma. This suggests that NDEs are not simply the result of imagination.[18]

Veridical Perception During NDEs

Third, and most important, NDE-believers point to reports that many people who "return to life" after an NDE describe not only unverifiable events in the next world, but also eminently verifiable events in this world that they could apparently not have known by natural means. NDE researchers use the term *veridical perception* for such cases as this – observations during an NDE that should not have been possible given the condition and/or location of the subjects' physical bodies and were later corroborated by independent observers. To take a particularly famous example, a woman (the American singer and songwriter Pam Reynolds) underwent an operation to remove an aneurysm under deep hypothermia (temperature below 16 °C) that caused her EEG (electroencephalogram) to go flat. After the operation, she reported having felt herself "pop" outside her body and hover above the operating table watching the surgeons working, and she gave remarkably detailed descriptions of what happened during her surgery that were later verified to be accurate. For example, she described a surgeon sawing into her skull with what looked to her like an electric toothbrush, and she reported precisely what people in the operating room had said as well as many other details of the operation.[19] Pam Reynolds's NDE has been the subject of considerable debate and detailed analyses are available by both NDE-sceptics[20] and NDE-believers.[21]

In a scholarly survey of veridical perception, Janice Holden stated that all reports of it so far have been anecdotal, and that there have only been about 150 of such cases.[22] Of these, several were "strongly evidential", and in a few of the latter alternative explanations had been ruled out. Nevertheless, initial attempts at controlled investigation of veridical perception in NDEs have not so far yielded a positive case: cards or other objects placed so as to be visible only from near the ceiling have not so far been described by people returning from an NDE. This has been attributed to "inattentional blindness",[23] but it seems to me unsurprising in any case, because detailed veridical perception appears to be rare: 150 cases out of the hundreds of millions of NDEs that have occurred is a tiny percentage.

Anecdotal though the evidence is so far for veridical perception, attempts have been made to perform systematic studies. Notably, cardiologist Michael Sabom did a control survey to examine whether the correct descriptions provided by NDEers could be explained by guesswork. In 116 patients who had experienced an NDE, he found that 32 claimed to have observed details of their reanimation procedure. Having access to the files of these patients, Sabom was able to confirm the accuracy of their descriptions, whereas other patients who had been reanimated but without an NDE were hopelessly inaccurate when they tried to guess.[24] This shows that the accuracy of the descriptions by the members of the former group were not the result of guesswork.

Sabom's control survey does not rule out the possibility that veridical perception might result from patients becoming conscious during very light anaesthesia. NDE-believers therefore often emphasize the cases where brain activity was eliminated for a period, as shown by a flat EEG in cases of severe cerebral ischaemia or deep hypothermia. A problem with this line of argument is that it is usually difficult to prove that the NDE occurred during the flat-EEG period, rather than beforehand, or afterwards while the patient's brain activity was recovering. For example, the remarkable veridical descriptions of Pam Reynolds's NDE have been compared with precisely timed independent accounts of her operation, and this indicates that some of the events that she supposedly observed during her NDE (e.g. cannulation of her femoral arteries) occurred well before her brief period of hypothermia and flat EEG, and others after it. Nevertheless, her depth of anaesthesia was monitored in three different ways to ensure that she was deeply anaesthetized throughout the whole operation (including the artery cannulation), and van Lommel has argued that the otherworldly part of her NDE (hyperlucid consciousness, communication with deceased relatives, encounter with the light) did indeed occur during the flat-EEG period.[25]

Further support for the objective reality of NDEs comes from a variety of very unusual experiences. There are occasional (but rare) reports of *group NDEs*, for which it is claimed that several people simultaneously experienced approximately the same near-death episode, and of *shared NDEs*, for which people close to the person who was having an NDE claim that they shared part of the experience.[26] Impressive though this seems, I have not managed to find a report of a group NDE or a shared NDE for which the testimonies of the different people involved were given independently and compared rigorously.

Still further support comes from some very striking reports of blind people, including some who were blind from birth, who had clear vision during an NDE of events that could be verified[27] or of people who had a "flash forward" of future events that did indeed occur.[28] Intriguing though these cases are, I find it difficult to evaluate the precision and reliability of the reports, which were mostly communicated long after the events described.

Finally, the reports of meeting deceased friends or relatives in the kingdom of light take on an evidential status when the experiencer had no means of knowing that the person was dead. For example, van Lommel mentions someone who, during a three-week-long coma at the age of 16, had an NDE in which he met his parents' best friend who told him he must go back because his time had not yet come. Only after his recovery did he learn from his parents that their best friend had died while he was in the coma.[29] There are several striking anecdotes such as this, but I know of no rigorous study on their accuracy.

Overall Evaluation of NDEs

I have to admit to being undecided about the reality of NDEs. On the one hand, attempts so far to explain them away neurobiologically seem to me inconclusive. The fact that ketamine and other drugs can produce several of their features does make it at least conceivable that a disruptive event like cerebral ischaemia could produce an NDE without the need for a soul of the dualist kind, but this fails to explain how NDEs can sometimes occur spontaneously, apparently without any pathological change in brain activity. Moreover, on the hypothesis of a separate soul interacting with the brain, it seems conceivable that brain stimulation or drugs might provoke features of an NDE by virtue of their effects on brain–soul interaction.

On the other hand, the reports of veridical perception, which seem to me to provide the strongest evidence for the reality of NDEs, do not appear to me decisive. Impressive though several of these reports seem, some of them may have been fudged or distorted by selective memory or otherwise exaggerated, especially in cases (the majority!) that were committed to writing long after the event. Also, bearing in mind that many millions of people have had NDEs, I wonder if some of the accounts may have been accurate by sheer chance or guesswork (although Sabom's control experiment mentioned above indicates that this is unlikely to be the main explanation).

I therefore think that the reports of veridical perception need to be confirmed by a more rigorously controlled investigation. Several studies are currently in progress to test the capacity of NDE-experiencers to notice and remember hidden numbers or words, and we must await the results. In view of the rarity of claims of detailed veridical perception, as judged from the anecdotal reports, it may take a long time to settle the question. In the meantime, I remain cautious.

Deathbed Visions

Deathbed visions (also called pre-death visions) resemble NDEs in that a dying person has the impression of meeting angels or other spiritual beings, or deceased friends or relatives, but with the important difference that there is no impression of leaving the body or of entering another world. Instead, he has the vivid impression that the spiritual beings have come to his bedside to prepare him for death. As with NDEs, most deathbed visions are positive, reassuring, and even joyful, but exceptionally they can be frightening and even hellish. Remarkably, deathbed visions are even more frequent than NDEs. The statistics indicate that in terminal care hospices, 75–80 per cent of the patients experience deathbed visions. It is in such situations as hospices that deathbed visions usually occur, to people who have known for many weeks that they were coming to the end of their life, as in terminal cancer. This contrasts with the situations of NDEs, which usually occur in situations of sudden and unexpected stress or threat of death, as in a heart attack, an earthquake, or a fall from a mountain.

Even though deathbed visions are frequent and are mentioned in ancient literature, they have been studied much less than NDEs. The modern literature on them is limited, but a popularly oriented book by Carla Wills-Brandon describes her own visions and 40 others,[30] and hospice physician John Lerma describes 16 cases.[31] Chris Carter's book on NDEs includes three chapters that review the literature on deathbed visions.[32]

The first scientific study of deathbed visions was published in 1926 by Sir William Barrett, a professor of experimental physics at the Royal College of Science in Dublin.[33] He reported that dying patients often saw at their side a deceased friend or relative. He found it striking that the visions were usually experienced by people who seemed rational and clear-minded, and who were surprised by the visions but reacted to them with serenity or joy. Sometimes the patient did not know that the friend or relative had in fact died, but Barrett checked systematically and found that this was always the case. Another detail that impressed Barrett was that dying children were often surprised to see that the angels did not have wings, implying that the visions were not mere projections of the children's presuppositions.

Forty years later, the Irish study of Barrett was confirmed by the publication of a much larger study (as well as a separate pilot study) in the United States based on a survey performed by Karl Osis, who asked thousands of physicians and nurses about the experiences of their patients and received 640 responses concerning over 35,000 dying patients.[34] The results fully confirmed Barrett's study. A minority of the visions appeared to be mere hallucinations, often involving people who were still alive, but most (about two-thirds) were of visitors from beyond the grave, usually deceased relatives. The percentage of people who had visitations was remarkably similar to the high percentages in earlier reports (80 per cent for Barrett, 75 per cent for Osis), and more recent studies have come up with similar figures (e.g. 80 per cent in the study of John Lerma). Interestingly, Osis found a correlation between the duration of the patients' survival after the vision and the purpose that was expressed by the apparition. When the latter said they had come to accompany the patient to the next world, the patients usually died within 60 minutes, but when this purpose was not expressed the patients survived longer.

In order to evaluate the influence of cultural and religious background on the deathbed visions, Osis performed a similar study in India in collaboration with Erlundur Haraldsson, obtaining remarkably similar results.[35] The results were on the whole similar to those in the United States. In both countries, most visions were of deceased relatives, but a few were of religious figures. In both India and the United States a few of the visions were of people who were still alive. But, strikingly, when they came to take the patient to the next world (as was usually the case), the visions were without exception of people who had died. A recent study from India (northern Kerala) largely confirmed the study by Osis and Haraldsson, but mentioned that whereas most socio-demographic factors such as age, gender, and occupation appeared not to be significant, religion did influence the frequency, since Hindu patients reported the visions more frequently than did Muslim patients.[36]

Can these frequent visions be explained psychologically, or as the result of drug or brain dysfunction in the terminal phase before death? I don't know. The "believers" give several arguments for the veridical nature of the visions. Most researchers report that the occurrence of the visions did not correlate with the taking of drugs or with fever and that the mental state of the patients was often good at the time of the visions.

The objective reality of deathbed visions is further supported by occasional reports that the angels or other religious beings, or the deceased friends or relatives witnessed by the patient, were visible and audible to other people in the room. Sir William Barrett's book describes several such cases, and there are two in John Lerma's book. Another case was experienced by psychologist and author Dr Joan Borysenko, who claims that her vision at her mother's deathbed was shared by her son Justin, both Joan and her son seeing the same bright light that transformed the room.[37] Without wishing to dismiss these anecdotal reports, I do feel that they need to be confirmed with a rigorous methodology.

Relevance of NDEs and Deathbed Visions to Christian Belief and to the Monism–Dualism Debate

Relevance to Christian Belief

Some aspects of NDEs and deathbed visions seem to fit in quite well with what would be expected on the basis of Christian beliefs about life after death. Both of these experiences involve angels and deceased friends who had survived death. The NDE experience of leaving behind one's body and travelling without it to a "spiritual" world matches many Christians' conceptions of the soul leaving the body at death. The experience in most Western NDEs of this spiritual world as a place of peace, bliss, and an absence of suffering fits in with Christian expectations of heaven. The presence in this heavenly realm of a supremely loving being of light matches the conception of God, including well-known aphorisms of the New Testament: "God is love" (1 John 4:8); "God is light; in him there is no darkness at all" (1 John 1:5). Also, the life review may match some Christians' conceptions of the last judgment, although in NDEs this review is not usually experienced as judgmental, because the love emanating from the being of light removes any feeling of condemnation. Finally, the experience in some NDEs of the otherworldly realm as hellish and a place of suffering matches the belief of many Christians that some people will be refused entry into heaven and will suffer in hell.

However, in a few cases the hellish experience included being rescued by Jesus; these people subsequently became Christians.[38]

On the other hand, the typical experience of floating out of one's body to the immediate discovery of celestial bliss has more in common with Western folk culture than with biblical teaching. As I pointed out in Chapter 10, biblical scholars consider that the Bible does not teach a Platonic or Cartesian soul that floats out of the body at death. Instead, the New Testament teaches the resurrection of the body, not a disembodied soul floating in the sky.

Another characteristic of NDEs that does not correspond with New Testament teaching is the observation that entry into the kingdom of light does not usually depend on faith in Jesus. In Western NDEs many people of other religions as well as atheists and agnostics enter the heavenly realm, and only a tiny minority experience a hellish NDE. I know of no systematic study on this topic, but base this observation on numerous individual cases that have been published. In both NDEs and deathbed visions, a hellish experience seems to result more from a guilty conscience than from unbelief. One way to resolve this apparent contradiction might be to propose that NDEs are not real experiences of heaven and or hell, but visions given by God to encourage us or warn us. For example, Angie Fenimore relates that after attempting suicide she had a hellish NDE that also involved a vision of Jesus and led her into a deep Christian faith.[39] NDEs after attempted suicide, are not always hellish. Dr Kenneth Ring studied 24 of these attempts and found that most were sad but not hellish.[40] Rarely, NDEs after suicide attempts can even be positive.

Another apparent discrepancy is that many experiencers have claimed to bring back "truths" that contradict biblical teaching. There have been "revelations" during NDEs that have recommended consulting the dead or have taught reincarnation.

Also, the strong influence of culture or expectation on the content of the NDEs raises questions. The fact that Christians often say they have encountered Jesus, whereas Hindus more often report meeting Krishna or Yama, and Buddhists Yama, might perhaps be explained by saying that people of different religions or cultures have the same experiences but interpret them differently. But the cultural differences can be very great, as can be seen by comparing Western NDEs with the example given above of a Thai Buddhist NDE. In cases such as this, it seems to me that the culture affects not only the interpretation, but the experience itself.

Finally, several studies have evaluated the long-term consequences of NDEs, on personal plans, spiritual and religious. These studies show that NDEs have many positive effects on spirituality, increasing, for example, empathy, service to others, feeling the presence of God, and the conviction of the reality of life after death. But they tend to diminish adherence to Christian doctrine and involvement in a Christian community. In the years after the NDE, the experiencers often abandon their organized Christian practice and instead devote themselves to solitary prayer and meditation.[41]

In short, NDEs and deathbed visions match some aspects of Christian belief but clash with others. For this reason, even among Christians there is considerable disagreement about the status of NDEs and deathbed visions.

Relevance to the Mind–Body Relationship

Even if we accept the reality of NDEs and deathbed visions, it still seems to me dubious whether they can be used to support dualistic notions about the mind–body relationship in the here-and-now, such as interactionist dualism or the existence of a disembodied soul. Interactionist dualism affirms that a disembodied soul is continually interacting with the brain as we think, decide, and act, but NDEs say nothing about this, because they usually seem to occur during moments when the body and brain are inert. Also, the spiritual beings encountered in NDEs and deathbed visions are not strictly disembodied, because they can be seen and localized and are often described as beings of light. Furthermore, in NDEs the experiencers describe themselves as having a location, and occasionally as having a body composed of light energy. Thus, these experiences seem to me to be compatible with a modified form of two-aspect monism: the soul/mind is always embodied, but in exceptional circumstances takes on a different body that is perceived to be composed of light.

Can the Debate Be Resolved?

Inevitably, people's attitudes to NDEs and deathbed visions can be strongly influenced by their own experiences and worldview. Those who have had powerful experiences themselves tend to be "believers", but those with a strong commitment to a naturalistic worldview (see

Appendix 2) tend to be sceptics. I have to confess that, personally, I am still sitting on the fence. The fact that many aspects of NDEs can be induced (albeit in a paler, less powerful form) by electrical stimulation of the brain or by drugs does tend to suggest that NDEs are the result of abnormal brain activity. But for the reasons discussed above this argument does not seem to me decisive, and I am reluctant to brush aside the wealth of evidence about NDEs and deathbed visions as mere illusions, when there is certainly no proof that all these experiences are illusory. It's just too easy to dismiss as illusory everything that doesn't fit in with one's worldview. It seems to me that the crucial issue is whether the evidence for veridical perception can be confirmed rigorously by tests of whether people can see hidden numbers or words during OBEs. As was mentioned above, such experiments are still in progress.

Conclusions

- NDEs and deathbed visions are often considered to imply the existence of disembodied souls, but critics argue that these experiences are illusory.
- The reality of the experiences is supported by the fact that they seem much more real than mere illusions, by their widespread occurrence in different cultures, and by claims of "veridical experience".
- Against this must be weighed some important counter-evidence: notably, the details of the experiences are strongly influenced culturally, and many aspects of them can be elicited by drugs or by electrical stimulation of the brain.
- More rigorous data will be required before this debate can be resolved.
- In any case, NDEs and deathbed visions do not strictly contradict the monistic concept of the mind–brain relationship that I advocate in Chapter 10.

12

God in the Brain?

Summary

I have argued in previous chapters that all our mental functions and all our conscious experiences depend on brain processes. Is this true even of religious experience and belief in God? This chapter argues that it is, but that this leaves open the question of whether the experiences reflect a spiritual reality. The main focuses of this chapter are *neurotheology*, which means research on the neural basis of religious or spiritual experiences, and the related question of whether the brain circuits that mediate religious belief and experience are programmed genetically.

> **My work strongly suggests that there is no God "part" or "module", but rather a complex network involving virtually the whole brain when the rich and diverse experiences are elicited. We can point to specific areas of the brain that may be associated with specific components of religious experiences, but since there are numerous ways to perceive, think about or meditate upon God, each method of meditation or prayer will affect the brain's function in slightly different ways.**
> **A. Newberg and M. R. Waldman, *Born to Believe*, 2006**

Religious experiences and beliefs are no exception to the general principle that all our thoughts and experiences and actions are rooted in the activity of the brain. There is now a vast wealth of neuroscientific data showing the implication of different brain regions in religious experience and belief, and I mentioned a small amount of it in Chapter 2. Fascinating though these new advances are, there has been a tendency, especially in the popular press, to extrapolate beyond the facts and to over-interpret the data in order to support extravagant claims for or against belief in God that are in no way justified by neuroscience. My purpose in this chapter is to review this area of research, highlighting real progress while also criticizing excessive claims. More detailed reviews are available.[1]

Neurotheology

The popular term "Neurotheology" was used for the first time by the English author Aldous Huxley in a utopian novel, *Island*, published in 1962. But the term only came into common usage in the 1990s, to describe research focusing on the neural basis of religious or spiritual experiences. This new research field has something of a mixed reputation. It undoubtedly encompasses a great deal of rigorous and sophisticated science, but at its fringes there is also a fair amount of pseudoscience.

The idea that the brain is involved in religious/spiritual experiences is not surprising, because it seems to be involved in all our experiences (see Chapter 2). Nor is this idea new. For centuries, certain groups have used drugs (e.g. "magic mushrooms") to induce experiences that the users consider spiritual, and for many years this has been assumed to result from the action of the drugs on the brain. Also, epilepsy has for many years been associated with religious, mystical, or paranormal experiences – and also with many other features having nothing to do with religion, such as *hypergraphy*, the excessive urge to write. There have also been several reports that damage to various brain regions, including the parietal and prefrontal cortex, can make people more or less religious than they were before. But since the 1980s neurobiological research on religious phenomena has been greatly enriched by the ability to use the new techniques of brain imaging and magnetic brain stimulation, and I shall focus on these approaches.

Functional Brain Imaging During Religious Experience and Belief

As was mentioned in Chapter 2, the various methods of functional brain imaging provide extraordinary methods for studying brain activity in humans in various mental states, including religious or mystical experiences. It is thus possible to detect changes in the brain in relation to such experiences. There have been many such investigations since the early 2000s, but I shall here give just a few examples.

One of the first of these studies was published by Andrew Newberg and his colleagues in 2001. They studied the brain states of experienced Buddhist meditators during meditation, finding increased activation in the frontal lobes and decreased activation in the parietal lobes.[2] In additional studies, the Newberg group has shown effects that were broadly similar, though not identical, in inexperienced meditators or in nuns during meditative prayer.

Another study by the same research group investigated changes in brain activation during glossolalia ("speaking in tongues"), which is the fluid vocalizing of strings of speech-like syllables that lack any readily comprehended meaning. In Pentecostal and "charismatic" Christian communities, this is a very widespread practice and is generally interpreted to reflect the influence of the Holy Spirit. In five Christian women, the main changes during glossolalia were found to be decreased activity in the left caudate nucleus and in both prefrontal cortices.[3] Of course, finding out which brain areas change activity in glossolalia does nothing to clarify whether or not it was really due to the inspiration of the Holy Spirit.

Another early functional imaging study was that of Azari and colleagues, who compared the brain activation patterns in religious Protestant Christians reciting psalms with those in non-religious people reciting non-religious poems learned in childhood. The main difference between the two groups was that only the religious subjects activated a frontal-parietal circuit, composed of the dorsolateral prefrontal, dorsomedial frontal, and medial parietal cortices. The authors emphasize that these areas are involved in cognitive function, not just "affect" (emotions).[4]

Another neuroimaging study investigated the brain activation patterns during improvised prayers (those made up on the spot) by highly religious Christians. There was a strong activation in the temporo-polar region, the medial prefrontal cortex, the temporo-parietal junction, and the precuneus (in the parietal lobe), which are all areas of "social cognition" (the mental processes involved in thinking about relationships with other people). This was very different from the activation patterns during more formal prayer (e.g. recitation of the Lord's Prayer).[5] The fact that social cognition areas should be activated during improvised prayer makes sense, because in this kind of prayer the subjective impression is that one is talking with God as a person, just as one might talk with somebody else.

But what about brain activation during religious *belief*? This is more difficult to study than activation during meditation or prayer. The latter occur during a limited period, so you can study how the brain activity is changed during this period. In contrast, religious beliefs are often almost constant over many years. It is thus very difficult to study the changes in brain activity as the beliefs change, but you can study the changes in activity as people relate their beliefs to particular questions. Several studies have adopted this approach, but for simplicity, I shall mention just one of them, whose first author was none other than new atheist Sam Harris. Harris and colleagues asked committed Christians and nonbelievers to evaluate the truth or falsity of religious and non-religious propositions. Functional imaging was carried out while the evaluations were being performed. In all cases, the judgments were associated with activity changes in broad regions of the frontal, parietal, and medial temporal lobes, and the most striking change was an enhancement in the ventromedial prefrontal cortex, which is known to be involved in various forms of cognition (thought), including the representation of self and emotionality. The fact that similar changes were found for both groups (Christians and nonbelievers) and for both categories of proposition suggests that roughly the same brain areas are involved in religious and non-religious beliefs. Nevertheless, detailed analysis of the results suggested that religious thinking is somewhat more associated with brain regions involved in emotion, self-representation, and cognitive conflict.[6] This seems to me unsurprising.

The present brief review is of course simplified and fails to give a complete account of the many brain regions that are involved in religious experience and belief. A detailed review published in 2009 lists no fewer than 40 distinct brain regions that are activated during religious activities such as prayer and meditation.[7]

Overall, my evaluation of these numerous functional imaging studies is that still more are needed. They have opened the way to address fascinating new questions, and they show that many different brain regions are involved in different aspects of religious experience and belief, but there is still a long way to go. Part of the problem is that there are enormous differences between individuals and their religiosity, even if we limit the field of interest to a single religion. Another is that most people's religious experiences and beliefs and practice involve many different components, ranging from abstract theorizing to powerful emotionality, and it is difficult to disentangle the different components.

Mystical Experiences and Temporal Lobe Stimulation

The Temporal Lobe and Mystical Experience

In the light of the above reports, showing religion-related activity in many parts of the brain, it may seem surprising that a single region, the temporal lobe, is sometimes touted as containing a "god spot" or "god module". These terms were taken up by the media following a lecture at the Society for Neuroscience (USA) in 1997 by Vilayanur Ramachandran, an eminent neurologist and well-known author, who found an unusually strong galvanic skin response (a sign of emotional arousal) in two patients (only two!) with temporal lobe epilepsy when they were presented with religious stimuli. Ramachandran's findings are described in detail and discussed in a popular book that he published the following year.[8] Ramachandran appears not to have followed up these preliminary findings, but the idea caught on, and since then there has been abundant speculation in the media and on the web about whether atheists lack faith because they lack the god spot in the temporal lobe, or whether believers have an excessively active god spot. At about the same time, cognitive science researcher Michael Persinger and his colleagues began to publish numerous papers claiming that very weak magnetic stimulation of the temporal lobe (especially the *right* temporal lobe) evoked mystical or paranormal experiences, and this has become a major subject of controversy, as we shall discuss below. Then, in 2000, Melvin Morse, who is known for his research on NDEs in children, published a popular book entitled *Where God Lives*. Drawing on his knowledge of NDEs, Morse maintained that God (and spiritual experience etc.) reside in the right temporal lobe.[9] We therefore need to take a look at whether there are good reasons to think there is a god spot in the temporal lobe.

The temporal lobe has many functions. Large parts of it are dedicated to the analysis of visual forms or auditory information, and its lower medial part, including the hippocampus, is particularly involved in the storage of memories. Still other parts, at the front of the temporal lobe, are involved in smell. But there is also the widespread idea that somewhere in this lobe there is a region that is key for religious (or mystical or paranormal etc.) experiences. Much of the evidence for this comes from the experiences of people with temporal lobe epilepsy.

Temporal Lobe Epilepsy (TLE) and Religious Experiences

An epileptic seizure is a transient burst of excessive neuronal activity occurring somewhere in the brain. Some seizures are mild and cause only minimal symptoms, for example a brief "absence" (minor impairment of consciousness) or a brief sensory disturbance (e.g. a flash of light) or a muscle contraction, but at the other extreme "tonic clonic" (or "grand mal") seizures involve intense activity that spreads throughout the entire brain and leads to loss of consciousness for several minutes.

Temporal lobe epilepsy (TLE) is of course epilepsy originating somewhere in the temporal lobe. It is one of the commonest types of epilepsy. The symptoms vary according to the precise place of origin within the temporal lobe, but TLE typically begins with partial seizures (limited to parts of the temporal lobe) involving the experience of smells, tastes, voices, music, memories, or unusually intense emotions. Sometimes (but rarely) the intense feelings are interpreted in religious terms.

The religious connotations of epilepsy are very old, going back to 400 BC, when Hippocrates wrote his book *The Sacred Disease*, with its main message that epilepsy is a disease of the brain and not, as was widely believed at that time, a sacred condition sent by the gods. There have been widespread speculations that the mystical experiences of many famous figures from St Paul to Joan of Arc to Thérèse of Lisieux were due to epilepsy. Such views are of course sheer guesswork, since we have no scientific evidence on the matter, and neurologist John Hughes and psychiatrist Peter Fenwick have both criticized these speculations as implausible. Hughes points out that hallucinations are actually not very common in epilepsy.[10] Nevertheless, some epileptics have reported mystical experiences at the beginning of seizures, including Dostoyevsky, who in his novel *The Idiot* famously described his own experience via the mouth of one of his characters, the epileptic Prince Myshkin:

> *I have really touched God. He came into me, myself; yes, God exists, I cried. You all, healthy people can't imagine the happiness we epileptics feel during the second before our attack.*

In many of his letters and other writings, Dostoyevsky described his own experiences during seizures, which sometimes resembled closely those of Prince Myshkin. Specialists all agree that Dostoyevsky was epileptic, but there is disagreement about whether he had TLE.

But there is little doubt that some more recent religious/mystical experiences were due to temporal lobe seizures. In a few cases this was confirmed by electroencephalographic recordings, as in the case of a Japanese lady who had seizures that caused joyous visions of God and of the sun.[11] However, explicitly religious experiences seem to be quite rare during TLE, and it is more common to encounter experiences that are *ecstatic*, with a sense of joy, harmony, and unity but without being explicitly religious.[12]

The Debate About "Temporal Lobe Personality"

The striking, if somewhat rare, religious/mystical experiences of epileptics occur just at the start of their seizures, but there have also been widespread claims that TLE patients are hyper-religious even when they are not having seizures. This idea goes back to the nineteenth century, but became widely accepted as a result of a series of five papers by published in 1963 by Eliot Slater and A. W. Beard, describing their major study of a group of epileptics who had schizophrenia-like symptoms. Slater and Beard focused on the proportions of patients who had had religious or mystical experiences at some time in their lives (not necessarily during a seizure). Three-quarters of the patients in this study had TLE, and more than a third of these claimed to have had religious or mystical experiences, which was considered a high proportion. On the basis of this study and others, Harvard neurologist Norman Geschwind proposed in the 1970s a constellation of many characteristics often displayed by patients with TLE including hypergraphia (overwhelming urge to write), altered sexuality, emotionality, aggressiveness, intensified mental life, hyper-religiosity, and hyper-morality. This set of symptoms came to be referred to as the *Geschwind syndrome* or *temporal lobe personality*, and this became a standard notion for teaching to medical students, although the status of the syndrome is currently debated.

What should we make of the hyper-religiosity claim? First, it is only one of many features in the Geschwind syndrome. Moreover, several authors including Craig Aaen-Stockdale[13] have argued that the evidence for hyper-religiosity as a regular feature of TLE is not compelling. He points out that the widely cited study by Slater and Beard is biased, because the authors deliberately selected unusual cases. Moreover, the proportion of their patients reporting religious experiences was no higher for TLE than for other kinds of epilepsy, and several studies over the last 20 years have found that the proportion of TLE patients who had had religious experiences was actually lower than in the general population. Most modern specialists consider that only a subset of TLE patients present with features of the Geschwind syndrome and that hyper-religiosity is not typical of TLE patients.

To summarize about TLE, it does occasionally provoke religious/ mystical experiences, but TLE patients are not in general hyper-religious.

The role of the temporal lobe in religious (or mystical etc.) experience is thus controversial, but we need to consider another notorious line of experimentation that has further stoked the controversy.

Transcranial Magnetic Stimulation of the Temporal Lobe

Michael Persinger reached celebrity status among the general public by reporting that quasi-mystical experiences could be evoked by stimulating the temporal lobe (and part of the parietal lobe) with very weak, but complex, fluctuating magnetic fields. Stimulation of the brain by *transcranial magnetic stimulation* (TMS) is a widely used technique for studying the human brain, having the advantage of being usable without surgery and with little danger to the person stimulated. Persinger employed an unusual version of TMS involving the use of a specially constructed helmet called the "Koren helmet" (after its designer) or, in the tabloid press, the "God helmet". According to Persinger, during weak TMS of the temporal lobe at least 80 per cent of his test subjects felt a "presence" beside them, resembling God or a deceased relative. Several well-known authors subjected themselves to Persinger's TMS including psychologist Susan Blackmore, who felt powerful emotions (especially anger), and Richard Dawkins, who only felt his leg twitch.

Persinger's research has frequently been invoked to support the idea that most or all religious (and mystical and paranormal etc.) experiences are illusions caused by abnormal brain activity in the temporal lobe, and it is apparent from his 1987 book[14] that this was his fervent conviction even before he started performing his magnetic stimulation experiments. I consider this conclusion to be illogical, but before arguing why, I should mention that Persinger's experimental results with the "God helmet" are controversial for several reasons. One of the problems is that it is difficult to exclude the possibility that the "felt presence" was due to suggestion rather than to the magnetic stimulation. Persinger's test subjects often felt an extraordinary presence *even without magnetic stimulation*. For example, in one study,[15] the subjects (local students who probably knew the expected result of stimulation) remained seated for 20 minutes, with or without magnetic stimulation, in a quiet room, wearing opaque glasses. They were thus under conditions of mild sensory deprivation, which is well known to induce hallucinations, and *even without magnetic stimulation* 33 per cent of the subjects reported a "sensed presence". According to this paper, weak TMS of the right temporal lobe or both temporal lobes more than doubled this frequency, but the only independent attempt (by a Swedish group) to replicate the results failed to confirm them.[16] The Swedish group attempted to reproduce the conditions used by Persinger as closely as possible, using a precise copy of the Koren helmet, but they found no effects of the magnetic stimulation on mystical experiences, although a minority of the participants did report spontaneous mystical experiences. They concluded that the effects attributed to the stimulation in Persinger's experiments were due to suggestion and to errors in the experimental protocol. They also pointed out that the fields used in these experiments were more than a thousand times weaker than those that are generally considered necessary to affect the brain by TMS, casting further doubt on the plausibility of the experiments. The controversy is not yet resolved, but an American group did test the ability of a commercial version of the Koren helmet's weak fields to affect emotions, as claimed by Persinger's associate Todd Murphy, who sells it. The conclusion was that the device had no effect.[17]

But even if the experiences of Persinger were to be validated, they would still not show that religious and mystical experiences occurring *in normal situations* (without TMS or epilepsy) were due to abnormal brain activity. Such a claim would simply be illogical. Brain stimulation can produce all kinds of experience: visual, auditory, olfactory, and even complex organized experiences. Should we conclude that our everyday visual, auditory experiences etc. are all illusory? Of course not! Nobody would make such a mistake! But why then should we apply to religious experience a conclusion that we refuse to all others?

Indeed, Ramachandran, the originator of the term "god spot", has made a related point on several occasions. For example, in a footnote to his book *The Tell-Tale Brain* he writes:

> *I do not wish to imply that God doesn't exist; the fact that some patients develop such delusions doesn't disprove God... I would argue, like Erwin Schrödinger and Stephen Jay Gould, that science and religion (in the nondoctrinaire philosophical sense) belong to different realms of discourse and one cannot negate the other.*[18]

To explain away religious and mystical experiences occurring in normal situations would require a demonstration that these too were due to abnormal events in the brain. Persinger did in fact try to argue this in his 1987 book, where he claimed they were all due to "microseizures", but there is no evidence for this. He has since proposed that paranormal phenomena occurring in natural settings are due to the effects on the brain of geomagnetic (natural) magnetic fields,[19] but this is not generally accepted, and there are several reasons to be sceptical. First, there is no direct evidence for this claim, only indirect arguments based on supposed correlations between geomagnetic phenomena and brain events. Second, other researchers have failed to confirm these correlations.[20] Third, natural magnetic field changes are about a million times smaller than the fields that are needed to stimulate the brain in standard TMS experiments.[21]

Despite all the above reasons to be dubious about Persinger's claims, I remain cautiously open to the possibility that some paranormal and mystical experiences may be due to aberrant brain activity. However, we just don't know what was happening in the brain of St Paul or Joan of Arc or Thérèse of Lisieux when they had their unusual experiences. In any case, for many (most?) religious believers, mystical experiences are not the basis of our faith. Many of us have never had one (I have not), and our main religious experiences are of other kinds, including the everyday one of living in a relationship of trust and obedience with our Creator, in openness to the Holy Spirit, and in fellowship (friendship) with other believers, while enjoying the satisfaction of putting into practice what we believe. In my own case, my Christian faith is based on a wide range of arguments including the evidence for the resurrection of Jesus, fulfilled prophecies, ancient and modern miracles, and answered prayer. Intuition comes in too. It is generally accepted, both by Christians and by members of other religions, that God's existence and other tenets of our faiths cannot be validly inferred from religious experience *alone*. The experience can only be interpreted in the full context of divine revelation. Moreover, the same principle applies also to other kinds of experience. We always need a conceptual framework to make sense of our experiences.

Nothing-buttery and Neurotheology

Despite the above considerations, authors do sometimes draw unwarranted reductionistic conclusions from neurotheological research. For example, Matthew Alper describes the experiments of Persinger in his book *The "God" Part of the Brain*,[22] and goes on to discuss "perceptions, sensations and cognitions" resulting from religious acts such as meditation and prayer that we "tend to interpret as evidence of some divine, sacred or transcendental reality". To Alper we are faced with an either/or dichotomy. He writes, "Nevertheless, recent discoveries in the neurosciences contradict such notions by suggesting that religious/spiritual/sacred/transcendental experiences are not manifestations of contact with God but rather the manner in which our brain interprets certain neurochemical processes." This seems to me a blatant case of the *nothing-buttery* that we discussed in Chapter 4. *All* our experiences, even the most mundane, are, to use Alper's words, "manifestations of... the manner in which our brain interprets certain neurochemical processes". This does not invalidate them! The fact that our brains function by neurochemical processes in no way implies that our experiences (of God, or of anyone or anything else) are illusory. Thus, neuroscientific studies of religious experience may tell us which parts of the brain are involved, but they leave entirely open the question of whether the experiences reflect a spiritual reality.

God, the Brain, and Genetics

Belief in God is Not Programmed in Our Genes

The titles of several articles and even a book give the impression that belief in God is *genetically programmed*. This is a gross exaggeration, as we shall see.

A notable case of misinformation in this sense was the publication in 2004 of a book entitled *The God Gene: How Faith Is Hardwired into Our Genes* by American geneticist Dean Hamer. Shortly after the book's publication, *Time* Magazine, which had a circulation of more than 3 million copies, mentioned "THE GOD GENE" in large letters on its cover and added the words: "Does our DNA compel us to seek a higher power? Believe it or not, some scientists say yes." This was undoubtedly a good message for sales purposes! However, this claim was almost universally ridiculed by scientists. To understand why, it is sufficient to read the book instead of just its title.

First, the book is not even about belief in God! It reports a genetic study by the author on the influence of a gene called VMAT2 (vesicular monoamine transporter-2) not on belief in God, but on a personality trait called *self-transcendence*. VMAT2 is involved in packaging several different emotionality-related neurotransmitters into vesicles ready for their release into the synaptic cleft (Figure 3.3). Self-transcendence is related to spirituality, but is much broader and includes self-forgetfulness, the tendency to feel connected to the universe and an openness to believe things not literally provable. It is evaluated as the score obtained by people who answer a questionnaire containing a variety of questions like: "Do you feel a sense of unity with all the things around you?" or "Do you sometimes feel a spiritual connection to other people that can't be explained in words?" Psycho-geneticists are interested in self-transcendence because studies on twins indicate that it is more strongly influenced genetically than other religious/spiritual measures such as churchgoing or belief in God.

Second, even for self-transcendence, no one imagines that just a single gene is involved, and the author admits in his book that the title is wrong for this reason.

Third, changes in VMAT2 explain only a tiny part of the genetic influence on self-transcendence. Many other genes must be involved.

Finally, no scientific journal agreed to publish this work of Hamer, and it has never been confirmed by another research group.

Science writer Carl Zimmer wrote in *Scientific American* that a better title for the book would have been: "A Gene That Accounts for Less Than One Percent of the Variance Found in Scores on Psychological Questionnaires Designed to Measure a Factor Called Self-Transcendence, Which Can Signify Everything from Belonging to the Green Party to Believing in ESP, According to One Unpublished, Unreplicated Study."

What is the Genetic Contribution to Faith and Religion?

Having refuted Hamer's abusively simplistic title claim that "faith is hardwired into our genes", I must now try to cast a more constructive light on this complex issue. To begin with, it is worth bearing in mind that there are important distinctions between *personality traits* (religiosity, spirituality, etc.), *religious practice* (participation in church services, prayer, etc.), and *religious belief* (in the existence of God, angels, etc.). Even within these categories, experts use many different measures. It should also be noted that the genetic studies are actually studies of the genetic contribution to *variability* between people. If there were a country where everyone had identical genes (of course no such country exists), the studies there would show no genetic influence on anything.

Several approaches are used to separate out the genetic influence from other influences (notably that of the environment). One can study, for example, whether adopted children resemble more their biological parents or the ones who adopted them. But I shall focus on the commonest approach, which is to compare monozygotic twins (from a single egg, so genetically identical) with dizygotic twins (from separate eggs, so genetically non-identical). Numerous "twin studies" have been conducted on various measures of religiosity, spirituality, religious practice, belief, etc. As an identical twin myself, who came to a deep personal faith in Christ at the same time as my twin brother, I thought for many years that genetics must be a key factor in faith. Now, having studied the academic literature, I think this was an overstatement, although genetics does play a role.

As far as religious practice and belief are concerned, most twin studies have shown that genes and environment (especially culture and family) play a more important role than genetic make-up. In all cases, independently of whether the twins are monozygotic or dizygotic, there is some correlation between them. For example, if one of the twins attends a church, it is likely that the other does too. But in most studies, the correlation is only slightly greater in monozygotic twins than in dizygotic twins. For example, an Australian study on the frequency of church attendance found a correlation of about 63 per cent in monozygotic female twins and about 53 per cent in dizygotic female twins. The 10 per cent difference implies that there is indeed a genetic influence on church attendance but that it is rather small. That's just one example, but to summarize a vast area of research in a few words, the environmental influence predominates over the genetic influence in many measures such as church attendance, membership of a particular denomination, and belief in God, although there is in each case also a moderate genetic influence.

On the other hand, the genetic component seems to be more important for the intimate and personal aspects of religion and spirituality, those more directly related to the personality and emotions. This is hardly surprising, since it is well known that emotions and other personality traits are quite strongly influenced genetically. Genetics seems to play an important role in the intimate aspects of spirituality such as the feeling of being in touch with God and guided by God, and in some religious experiences such as being born again.[24] Thus, even though the genetic influence on whether someone will believe in God or go to church is only moderate, the genetic influence on the strength and emotionality of the believer's faith is greater. But even for the factors where the role of genetics is the most important, it is only an *influence*, never *determinative*.

Conclusions

- Abundant experimental data show that religious experience, like all other kinds of experience, involves brain activity.
- This leaves open the questions of whether the experiences reflect a spiritual reality and whether or not God may communicate with us.
- Some notorious reports about the brain basis of religious experience are probably false. These include the claim that there is a single god spot in the temporal lobe, because at least 40 brain regions are activated during prayer and meditation. Likewise, Michael Persinger's assertion that mystical experiences result from abnormal activity in the temporal lobe is not well supported.
- Mystical experiences are important to some people, but for most believers they are not the main basis for faith.
- Reports of a neurogenetic determination of religious practice and belief in God are grossly exaggerated. The intimate and personal aspects of religiosity (like feeling in touch with God) are more genetically influenced than are the institutional aspects (like church attendance), but in all cases the influence falls far short of determinism.

13

Is Religion Just a Side Effect of Brain Evolution?

Summary

The ubiquity of religion has stimulated several researchers to try to explain it in terms of neuropsychological tendencies that are rooted in our genes, presumably as a result of evolution. Some opponents of religion go on to argue that religions are *illusory* products of evolution. I here review the current status of this debate. In particular, I emphasize the difference between religion and the psychological trait of *religiosity*. Evolution may perhaps help to explain religiosity, although attempts to do this are recent and still speculative, but a religion is more than the religiosity of its adherents. A religion has to be evaluated on a much broader basis, including the credibility of its truth claims.

**The predisposition to religious belief is the most complex
and powerful force in the human mind and in all probability
an ineradicable part of human nature. It certainly is one
of the universals of social behavior, taking recognizable form
in every society from hunter-gatherer bands to
socialist republics.**
Edward O. Wilson, *On Human Nature*, 1978

The Omnipresence and Resilience of Religion Calls for an Explanation

There are enormous differences between religions, and even within individual religions. For example, not all religions involve belief in God (or gods), and some Buddhists believe in God (or gods) whereas others do not. But, despite the considerable differences, several features are common to most or all religions. All of them impose rules of conduct and encourage prayer or meditation, and most involve various rituals as well as belief in supernatural agents (not necessarily God or gods) and in an afterlife. Thus, we can use the word "religion" without being impossibly vague, and the omnipresence of religion calls for an explanation.

Religions of one kind or another exist in all cultures throughout the world, and palaeontological evidence indicates that some aspects of ritual have existed from at least 40,000 years ago when humans apparently first became religious. The appearance of large numbers of non-religious people is a relatively new phenomenon, and even today they are a tiny minority in most cultures. They are growing in number in the Western world, where society is becoming increasingly secularized, but even here people continue to have religious or spiritual experiences. For example, a survey in the United Kingdom showed that the percentage of respondents who reported having had religious/spiritual experiences actually *increased* from about 48 per cent in 1987 to more than 76 per cent in 2000.[1]

The *resilience* of religion is also remarkable. Even the most determined attempts by powerful states to repress and extinguish religion (for example in Soviet Russia, China, Albania, and North Korea) have failed. In post-revolutionary France, members of the intellectual elite such as Baron von Holbach confidently predicted the disappearance of Christianity by the end of the eighteenth century, but it survived, even though France did become one of the world's most atheistic countries. What made religion so resilient?

The commonest explanation proposed by scientists is that Darwinian evolution somehow modelled our brains in such a way that we have natural religious or spiritual tendencies, and the aim of this chapter is to look at the different attempts to explain how this could have happened. By "Darwinian evolution" I mean the standard view that all the multifarious life forms on the earth evolved from a single ancestor, and that the mechanism by which they became so varied was the one proposed by Charles Darwin, *natural selection*: random variation followed by the preferential survival of those best adapted to a particular environment. More details are provided in Appendix 2.

This whole research area on the Darwinian evolution of religion is rather controversial and is characterized by several battles: social scientists versus biologists, atheists versus theists, creationists versus Darwinists. The biggest challenge for a Christian such as myself is the implication, favoured by atheists such as Daniel Dennett and Richard Dawkins, that religion is just an evolutionary by-product, and therefore has no validity when it talks about God, truth, or the natural world. I of course disagree!

Evolutionary Psychology, a Recent Discipline

Our main field of concern in this chapter – evolutionary attempts to explain religion – is a branch of a larger discipline known as *evolutionary psychology*, the attempt to explain mental traits and behaviour in terms of evolution. Over the last 20–30 years, advocates of evolutionary psychology have been trying to explain a tremendous range of phenomena from consciousness to gender differences and from three-dimensional vision to language. This larger discipline is itself a hive of controversy, so we need to take a look at it before narrowing down our focus to the evolution of religion.

The development of evolutionary psychology was predicted by Charles Darwin in *The Origin of Species*:

In the distant future I see open fields for far more important researches. Psychology will be based on a new foundation, that of the necessary acquirement of each mental power and capacity by gradation.[2]

However, it was only in the last two decades of the twentieth century that this discipline came to be recognized as a field in its own right. The main assumption underlying evolutionary psychology is that natural selection generated *psychological traits* just as it generated our anatomical characteristics. This assumption is underlain by at least two controversial hypotheses that we need to examine.

Did Our Psychological Traits Arise Because of Their Survival Value?

The first of these is that our psychological traits have arisen because they somehow promote the survival and proliferation of those who possess them and/or their descendants. If this were not the case, the traits could not be produced by natural selection. In some cases, this seems very plausible. It is reasonable, for example, to suppose that the progressive increase in the ability to conceptualize and plan ahead (reflected in the increased size of the frontal lobes) that occurred throughout the evolution of our pre-human ancestors would favour survival. But for other traits this is far less clear. One of these, that troubled Darwin, is altruism, involving the willingness to sacrifice one's own interests, even one's own life, for others. One might expect that altruistic individuals would tend to lose out in competition with others, so that their contribution to the gene pool would only diminish. Darwin favoured an explanation now known as "group selection", the idea being that groups with many altruistic members would tend to survive because of the greater cohesion at the level of the social group; hence genes promoting altruism would tend to be conserved during evolution. There is currently some rather intense debate between those favouring "group selection" and those favouring the rival view of "kin selection", according to which altruism is supposed to have arisen through evolution working at the level not of social groups, but of networks of genetically related individuals.

Are Psychological Traits Genetically Based?

The second hypothesis underlying evolutionary psychology is that psychological traits are to a great extent genetically based. This is by no means universally accepted. While many psychologists and most biologists accept this hypothesis, social scientists often reject it outright. Take *gender identity*, for example. At the time of writing there is a violent controversy in France because the National Assembly (parliament) accepted a proposal to modify the law to require the teaching of "gender theory" in state schools, from the age of six. "Gender theory" in this context refers to the theories of a prominent group of feminist sociologists according to which "gender role attributes" (women being expressive, cooperative, and sensitive to the needs of others, men being aggressive, dominant, and ambitious) are "socially constructed" and not genetically based. At the same time, some evolutionary psychologists write learned papers purporting to explain these differences between men and women in terms of genetic differences due to natural selection. They can't both be right!

The current debate about the genetic basis of psychological traits is linked to the classical debate about whether we have "innate ideas" and "innate knowledge", which goes back to Plato and Aristotle. In the seventeenth and eighteenth centuries, this became something of a battle between Brits and Continentals. British philosophers such as Locke, Berkeley, and Hume held to the Aristotelian view that all understanding arises from sensation. In contrast, most Continental philosophers including Descartes, Spinoza, and Leibniz held to the opposite, Platonic, view of *innate ideas*. Immanuel Kant then built a bridge over the English Channel, so to speak, by arguing for a compromise in the Introduction to his *A Critique of Pure Reason*.

There is still plenty of controversy about this even today, and only a decade ago Steven Pinker felt it necessary to write a book entitled *The Blank Slate* attacking the view, widespread among social scientists, that the mind has no innate traits. Nevertheless, many people now accept an in-between position that accepts innate traits while at the same time acknowledging the importance of environmental factors on the development of brain and mind. There is plenty of evidence, for example, that several phobias, including extreme fear of snakes or of spiders, are partly innate but involve learning as well. Another well-researched area is the attraction of human babies to faces. Judging from the time they spend looking at different images, it has been deduced that they prefer looking at human faces than at other images. This is true in babies of all ages, even ones only a few days old, so this early tendency appears to be innate, not learned, although their skill at face recognition improves enormously over the first six months of life, and learning is thought to be involved in this development. It has also been reported that very young babies spend more time looking at an attractive female face (of a fashion model) than an unattractive one (a plain-looking woman).[3] Good taste begins in the cradle! But before we get too enthusiastic about developing an evolutionary psychology of face preferences, it is worth bearing in mind an observation that (slightly older) babies spend more time looking at attractive tiger faces than unattractive tiger faces![4]

Effects of Genes and Environment on the Development of Neural Circuitry

The above studies involved only behavioural observations, but in several cases it has been possible to analyse the development of the neural circuitry underlying cognitive abilities, and this too has been shown to be due partly to innate mechanisms and partly to experience-dependent changes in neural connections (i.e. learning).

To take an example on which I have personally worked, there has been a great deal of research on the question of whether the response properties of neurons in the visual cortex (described in Chapter 3) are produced by innate developmental mechanisms, or whether they are somehow imposed by visual experience. Some experiments on kittens in the 1960s and early 1970s showed that during the first few months of life visual experience has a tremendous power to model, or re-model, the cortical connections. For example, when one eye was deprived of patterned vision for a few days, the kitten became blind in the deprived eye because the neurons normally activated by it withdrew their connections within the visual cortex. In contrast, the neurons activated by the normal eye extended their territories and dominated the whole of the visual cortex.[5] Also, kittens reared in an environment where they only saw lines of a single orientation became almost blind to other orientations and their visual cortical neurons tended to respond best to the orientation to which the kitten had been exposed. The authors argued that adaptive changes such as this help the brain to match itself to the sensory environment.[6] Because of results such as this, the international zeitgeist became strongly empiricist for a few years, emphasizing the importance of sensory experience in controlling the development of brain and mind. John Locke would have been delighted! However the pendulum soon swung back when it became clear at the end of the 1970s that the specificity of neurons in the visual cortex for lines of a particular orientation can develop in the absence of visual experience in monkeys,[7] and is present even at the moment of birth in some mammalian species,[8] implying that our cognitive strategy of recognizing visual forms by analysing their contours is partly innate. The current view is that the response properties of the visual cortical neurons (and of cortical neurons serving audition, touch, etc.) are specified approximately by innate mechanisms, but are refined in response to experience during the first months of life in kittens or young monkeys, or the first years of life in human babies.

Implications for Evolutionary Psychology

The above examples show that the development of cognitive abilities is due partly to innate (hence genetic) mechanisms and partly to changes in brain connections due to experience. In most cases, however, the relative importance of innate developmental mechanisms versus experience-dependent brain reorganization is unclear and a subject of debate.

Thus, as we turn to the evolution of religion, that it is worth bearing in mind that this is by no means the only branch of evolutionary psychology that is controversial. The whole discipline is rife with disagreement! But that's not unusual in new scientific disciplines.

The Evolutionary Psychology of Religion

Just as in every branch of evolutionary psychology, theories of the evolution of religion are attempts to explain their subject matter in Darwinian terms. The idea is that the psychological traits underlying religious experience and belief arose due to the action of Darwinian selection processes on the genome. This is a new field, and the first *International Conference on the Evolution of Religion* was held (in Hawaii) as recently as 2007, although the underlying idea goes back to the 1960s.

One of the earliest proposers of this view was biologist Sir Alister Hardy, who in his Gifford Lectures (1963–65) proposed an account of the origin of religion in terms of natural selection. Another early advocate was Edward O. Wilson, who, in his 1978 book *On Human Nature*, devoted a chapter to religion and to his idea that religion is rooted in our genes. Hardy was a Unitarian Christian, whereas Wilson has described his position as "provisional deism", but they agreed about the origins of religion.

We looked at the possible genetic basis of religious belief in the previous chapter, where I argued that there is a moderate genetic component to religion and spirituality, and that it is strongest for the intimate and personal aspects, those more directly related to the personality and emotions. However, I was there referring to the genetic contribution to the *differences* between people, the question of whether genetic factors account for the tendency of one person to be religious and another not. The present question is not about differences between people, but about their *similarity*, about what it is that makes most or all people potentially religious (albeit to various extents). This is a subtle question, because if you ask it in the wrong way it becomes almost trivial. You could say, "Genetics explains why humans are more religious than frogs, because no amount of education will make a frog religious, so it is quite obvious that human religion must be genetically based." In a sense, this is correct. Genetics gives us our larger brains, our language, our ability to conceive of a higher power, and our emotionality, all of which are essential for religion, so genetics must be involved somehow. But we shall need to come back to this question when we discuss the two main views about the evolution of religion, known as the *adaptationist* and *by-product* views.

But first, we need to look at the religious tendencies in young children. Just as the innateness of orientation selectivity in visual cortical neurons was supported by the fact that it can be found in newborn animals, so the innateness of religious tendencies would be supported if they could be shown very early in life.

Religious Tendencies Early in Life

In his book *Born Believers: The Science of Children's Religious Belief,* Justin Barrett summarizes a considerable amount of research, by himself and others, on the beliefs of young children. He concludes that belief in God or gods appears to be a naturally occurring human phenomenon, because independently of whether their parents are believers or atheists/agnostics, young children regularly hold beliefs that can be called religious. He writes that children "have strong propensities to believe in gods because gods occupy a sweet-spot in their natural way of thinking: gods are readily and easily accommodated by children's minds and fill some naturally occurring conceptual gaps rather nicely".[9] In other words, the "God-shaped gap" in the human heart is there from infancy.

The Need for an Explanation

This raises the immediate question of why these traits arose. This is particularly a problem for atheists. If God (or gods) and other spiritual beings such as angels and demons do not exist, why do so many people all over the world believe in them and even claim to have experienced them? If there is a genetic component to all this, why did natural selection promote it? Do false beliefs have survival value? Thus, some writings in this area – including Daniel Dennett's *Breaking the Spell: Religion as a Natural Phenomenon*[10] – are attempts by atheists to justify their position by explaining religion within an evolutionary framework. I think it would be wrong, however, to dismiss the evolutionary psychology of religion as an atheistic tool for bashing religion. Whatever one's religious beliefs or lack of them, it seems reasonable to investigate whether science can contribute to an understanding of how religion arose. The field is necessarily speculative, because it is much harder to test ideas about the evolution of religion than, say, ideas about the evolution of running ability, but it should nonetheless be taken seriously.

Religion During Prehistory

Before making theories about the mechanisms that gave rise to religion tendencies, we need to look at the evidence about *when* they first appeared. Evolution is slow, and any genetic basis that there may be for our religious tendencies must have been accumulating over many tens or hundreds of thousands of years. So what are the earliest signs of religious tendencies? Figure 13.1 is a timeline that summarizes the discussion that follows.

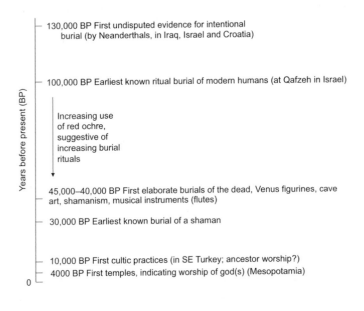

Fig. 13.1. *Timeline of Stone-Age religion (BP means "before present").*

The earliest place of worship to have been discovered is an archaeological site at the top of a mountain ridge at Göbekli Tepe (which means "potbelly hill" in Turkish) in south-east Turkey. The site contains many massive carved standing stones arranged in circles, and is thought by most specialists to have been used for some sort of religious ceremony, perhaps a cult of the dead, around 8000 BC (New Stone Age). It appears also to have been a place of pilgrimage, because pieces of obsidian rock (resembling glass) have been found there that must have been brought from volcanic sites hundreds of miles away. However, archaeological signs of the worship of gods are later, in Mesopotamia, associated with the building of temples there about 4000 BC. By evolutionary standards, this was only yesterday.

Religious tendencies may, however, have been present long before anyone constructed places of worship, but our understanding of these has to be deduced from less direct clues, and conclusions are inevitably somewhat speculative. One fascinating and famous line of evidence is constituted by the extraordinary cave paintings of animals in various parts of Europe, and most notably at Lascaux (Dordogne, France, 17,000 BP, i.e. before the present), at Chauvet (Ardèche, France, c. 30,000 BP), and at El Castillo (Cantabria, Spain, c. 40,000 BP). The paintings at Lascaux include strange creatures that are half-human and half-bird or half-human and half-lion The significance of all these paintings is a matter of debate, but several specialists, including the French prehistorian Jean Clottes, consider that many of them represent different stages of shamanic trances. This view is not universally accepted, but the fact that early humans felt the desire to represent animals and half-humans, and made the effort to venture into dark and inaccessible caves to do so, does seem to indicate that the paintings were important to them and probably had symbolic significance.

Another useful line of evidence is from burials of the dead. Some specialists consider that these began several hundred thousand years ago, and there is even a cave at Atapuerca, in the north of Spain, containing the bones of no fewer than 28 individuals of *Homo heidelbergensis*, which according to some researchers may reflect a burial practice as early as 400,000 BP. This is an isolated case, however, and its significance is disputed. The earliest uncontested intentional burials were by Neanderthals, at about 130,000 BP, at various sites at Krapina in Croatia. The earliest uncontested *ritual* burials were performed by our own ancestors at about 100,000 BP. In one such case, at the Skhul cave at Qafzeh, Israel, human bones were stained with red ochre, a natural earth pigment that appears to have had ritual significance, and were accompanied by various grave goods including the mandible of a wild boar in the arms of one of the skeletons. The grave goods may have been gifts to the deceased person. Similar burial sites from the same period, containing bones stained with red ochre, have been identified at various African locations. The fact that mobile groups of humans should take the trouble to bury their dead and leave grave goods with them suggests that they attached particular significance to death and may have been wondering about the possibility of an afterlife.

Then, between 45,000 and 40,000 BP (the start of the Upper Palaeolithic period in Europe), there seems to have been a tremendous explosion of religiosity and artistic creativity, especially in Europe. The human burials became much more elaborate, and the grave goods included Venus figurines, thought to represent fertility goddesses, as well as various ornaments. This corresponds to the time of the earliest cave paintings, the earliest musical instruments – flutes (43,000 BP) – and the first animal sculpture, a humanoid form with a lion's head. This has been interpreted as implying an important change in symbolic thought at about this time, although some authors argue that the change occurred earlier and more gradually, and that the apparent cultural "explosion" was due to migration into Europe.

To summarize about early religious (or pre-religious) practices, the available evidence is inconclusive, but burial practices suggest that our ancestors may have begun to think about the significance of death, and perhaps even an afterlife, around 100,000 BP. Then, more elaborate burial practices and the appearance of cave art around 40,000 BP suggest that there was an increase in symbolic thought and a beginning of shamanic practices at this time. The first cultic practices may have begun about 10,000 BP, but the earliest organized worship of gods may have been as late as 6000 BP.

Thus, the earliest religious practices began long after the human lineage separated from that of our nearest cousins (Neanderthals and Denisovans), which was some time between 800,000 and 400,000 BP. Nevertheless, *pre-religious* cognitive tendencies such as wondering about an afterlife may have begun much earlier, so the question needs to be asked whether there is any evidence of religious or pre-religious behaviour among other species.

Adam and Eve and the Development of Religion

My main purpose in writing the above section was to give an idea of the timescale over which the biological evolution of our religious tendencies would have had to take place, but in doing so I may have touched on a sensitive issue. How does this timeline fit in with the biblical account? The above description indicates that the earliest religious practices arose around 40,000 BP and were polytheistic (fertility goddesses) or shamanistic. Also, many anthropologists assume that monotheism was a late development from previous animism via polytheism as an intermediate step.

In contrast, the Book of Genesis describes Adam and Eve as having a relationship with a single God. So does the above account contradict the Bible? We can only look very briefly at this controversial question. The accounts in Genesis Chapters 2 and 3 are full of symbolism, and the Hebrew word "adam" means "man", so many biblical scholars think Adam and Eve should be considered as representatives of humankind, rather like "Everyman" in medieval plays, and not literal historical individuals. I tend to favour the non-literal view, but for those who interpret Adam and Eve as "historical", let us look briefly at how this could fit in with the account given above. The description in Genesis 4 of their children Cain and Abel as a crop farmer and a shepherd, and of Cain as building a city, place them in the Neolithic period, perhaps 7,000–9,000 years ago. Clearly, there were human beings long before this, with the artistic ability to produce the extraordinary cave paintings at Lascaux, and Chauvet and El Castillo, but some people interpret Adam and Eve as being the first humans in another sense, that of being the first who were able to communicate fully with the one true God.[11] There is no evidence for monotheistic worship at this time, but nor is there proof that it did not occur. Moreover, some anthropologists consider that animism and polytheism were preceded by an earlier monotheism. This interpretation of Adam and Eve may be defensible, but Neolithic humans living in the Middle East cannot have been the literal ancestors of all humankind; for example, the aborigines of Australia separated from other humans much earlier, at about 60,000 BP.

The above interpretation is just one of many that are possible, but it would be beyond my scope to go into more details. My point is simply that the timeline I gave for the development of religious tendencies in humans is compatible with several interpretations of the early chapters of Genesis.

Proto-Religious Behaviour Among Other Species?

Before coming to grips with the modern debate about the evolution of religion, we need to look at one more line of evidence: the behaviour of other species. The question here is not whether other species are or were religious in the full sense that modern humans are, because they are not and probably never have been. The question rather is whether there is any evidence of behaviour in non-humans that has something in common with human religiosity. I shall call this *proto-religious* behaviour. There is some evidence for this, but it is very limited and ambiguous.

The only palaeontological evidence is in the burial customs of our cousin, *Homo sapiens neanderthalensis*. They deliberately buried their dead, as is mentioned above. Their burials were less elaborate than those of anatomically modern humans, but they occasionally included grave goods, such as bones from bison and aurochs (ancestor of domestic cattle), tools, and the pigment ochre. There is also an indication from Shanidar in Iraq that the Neanderthal burials there included flowers, suggesting ritual burials, but this conclusion is contested, because the flower remains may be due to contamination. Another popular notion, which appears in novels and Hollywood films, is that Neanderthals practised a cult of bears. This view was based on the finding of large collections of the bones of bears in caves, but it is universally rejected by modern specialists. Thus, any glimmerings of religiosity that Neanderthals may have had appear to have been very limited.

The only other evidence for anything resembling religious awareness in animals comes from modern observations. Much of this, again, concerns death. There is plenty of evidence that the higher species such as apes and dolphins grieve for their dead. For example, the death in 2009 of the chimpanzee "Dorothy" in a refuge in Cameroon caused intense emotion and a most unusual silence among the other chimpanzees. It is also a common observation among all the great apes that mothers will cling to the bodies of their dead offspring for several weeks. Elephants likewise are very disturbed by the presence of a dead elephant and may try to lift the cadaver or cover it with branches. All this is in stark contrast to the behaviour of lower species, such as lizards, that walk over the bodies of their dead cousins as if they were mere obstacles.

Other data is very limited, but the psychologist Wolfgang Köhler interpreted reports of communal dancing in apes as possibly representing religious ritual, and J. Malan interpreted the behaviour of baboons and other species in response to sunrise or sunset as religious.[12] Also, Alister Hardy speculated about whether the rather devotional behaviour of dogs toward their owners had a religious quality.[13]

In short, there are some hints that Neanderthals had, and modern higher species have, cognitive functions that might be considered proto-religious, but this falls very far short of what would normally be considered religious or spiritual in humans.

The Adaptationist and By-Product Views

How, then, did religion arise? For those who accept that evolution played an important role, there are two main views. One, the *adaptationist* view, maintains that natural selection favoured the evolution of religious traits because they were adaptive, i.e. directly conducive to survival and reproduction. The other, called the *by-product* view, maintains that religious traits were not adaptive and that natural selection did not favour them as such, but that they emerged as a by-product of other cognitive mechanisms that evolved for reasons not directly related to religion. Let us look at these two views in more detail.

The Adaptationist View

This view maintains that religious behaviour was adaptive during long periods of evolution. It is important to remember that evolutionary changes take a long time (typically hundreds of thousands of years), so the question is not whether religions are *nowadays* adaptive, but whether they were adaptive during very long periods while our ancestors were evolving. Adaptationists such as evolutionary biologist David Sloan Wilson,[14] social anthropologist Richard Sosis, and cognitive psychologist Jesse Bering argue that this was the case. They consider religion to be an adaptive complex of psychological traits derived from "pre-human ritual systems" that were adaptive because they bound the members of a group together, making them more cooperative and fraternal, and hence more able to hunt in teams or to fight off foes.

This view is contested by many scholars who think it more likely that religious traits are *by-products* of traits that arose for reasons having little to do with religion.

The By-Product View

The by-product view is currently the dominant position, and is represented by many of the leading scholars including Justin Barrett, Pascal Boyer, and Harvey Whitehouse. It is favoured also by well-known science writer such as Richard Dawkins. According to this view, religion was not in itself adaptive during evolution, but is an expression of emotional and cognitive mechanisms that evolved because they were indeed adaptive, but in ways that had little to do with religion.

The by-product approach goes back to a famous paper by Steven J. Gould and Richard C. Lewontin, which was not concerned with religion, but with evolution more generally.[15] The authors of this paper criticize the whole adaptationist programme in evolutionary theory, on the grounds that it is based on "faith in the power of natural selection as an optimizing agent". They argue in contrast that some features of organisms were not selected directly, but arose only as by-products. For example, the redness of blood is not in itself adaptive, but the colour is a by-product of selection for an oxygen-carrying molecule, haemoglobin, which just happens to be red when linked to oxygen.

What sort of the non-religious adaptations might have led to religion as a by-product? An obvious example is our large, sophisticated brains with their ability to give rise to sophisticated thought. True though this is, it is rather vague, and by-product theorists have tried to be more specific about non-religious traits that gave rise to religion. I mention just two of these.

One of these has been called the *"hyperactive (or hypersensitive) agency detection device"* (HADD), a term coined by Justin Barrett. The idea here is that we see faces in clouds or imagine ghosts in a dark room, because our brains contain a HADD, and that this evolved because it was essential for our ancestors to detect active agents such as predators or prey. If one of our ancestors assumed that a rustling in the long grass was caused by the wind, when it was in fact caused by a lion, this could be fatal. But the converse error of thinking there was a lion, when the rustling was in fact due to the wind, would be far less costly. Thus, it was adaptive for the detection device to be hypersensitive.

Richard Dawkins argues for another non-religious trait that might, according to him, favour religion: the tendency of children to believe what their parents and tribal elders tell them (*The God Delusion*, Chapter 5). This tendency is indeed explicable in terms of natural selection, because believing the parents when they said that playing with snakes is dangerous would presumably favour survival. But how would it favour the evolution of religion? It would be expected to favour the tendency of religion – and irreligion – to run in families: the children of Christian parents are often Christians, and the children of atheist parents are often atheists. But I fail to see how such a mechanism would favour religion rather than irreligion. Nor could religion initially arise by such a mechanism, because before it arose there would be no religious parents to pass on the tenets (or rituals etc.).

Challenges Raised by the Evolutionary Psychology of Religion

Both theists and atheists may feel challenged by evolutionary theories of religion. Theists may wonder if these theories somehow explain away our faith as nothing but a product of evolution, but I shall argue against this view. Even if our religious tendencies did arise by evolution, we should beware of the "nothing but" in the previous sentence (see the discussion of "nothing-buttery" in Chapter 4). If we accept, as I do, that God chose to use evolution to produce humankind and other species, it seems reasonable to think he would use evolution to give us the psychological capacity necessary for believing in him and communicating with him.

But some atheists have felt uncomfortable with the notion that religion could be a fundamental aspect of human nature, rooted in the genes of most or all human beings. After all, if God exists and is interested in a relationship with human beings, we might expect him/ her to somehow arrange for people to have an innate religious sense. Therefore, a genetically based tendency to believe in God might be considered a confirmation of what theism predicts, and this all seems uncomfortably close to being an evolutionary-genetic version of St Augustine's famous assertion (in *Confessions*, I, 1): "You have made us for yourself, O Lord, and our hearts are restless until they rest in you." Leading Christian thinkers have in fact frequently claimed that people have a natural knowledge of God (the *sensus dei* of St Thomas Aquinas) or a natural religious sense (the *sensus divinitatis* of Calvin – a slightly weaker claim), and eminent philosophers from Descartes to Plantinga have supported such views. Some atheists have therefore sought arguments *against* evolutionary theories of religion, maintaining that they are contradicted by the recent rise in atheistic secularism in the Western world or by the uneven distribution of theism throughout the world. If religion is in our genes, they argue, how is it that, in 2011, 25 per cent of the British population (2011 census) and 35 per cent of the French population (Ipsos/MORI poll) claimed to have no religion?

But other atheists, including Dawkins and Dennett, have favoured evolutionary theories of religion as being necessary for the coherence of their materialistic worldview. They need some such theory to explain why religion is so widespread, even though not absolutely universal. Furthermore, they have attempted to use this approach as a weapon against religion, to undermine religious truth claims as being just an irrational consequence of our inherited religious tendencies. We therefore need to examine their arguments.

Does the Evolutionary Psychology of Religion Undermine Religious Faith?

This whole field of the evolutionary psychology of religion is recent, speculative, and controversial. As we saw above, the specialists can't even agree on whether religion has been adaptive during evolution. Therefore, even if this new field did have anti-religious implications, it would be premature to give these much weight in the current state of knowledge.

But in my opinion the implications of evolutionary psychology for the truth of religion(s) are mostly neutral. Those who use the theories to attack religion or belief in God, such as Richard Dawkins, Daniel Dennett, and Jesse Bering, all (I know of no exception) reject religion for other reasons and then bring in evolutionary psychology to try to explain how it is that so many people make the strange mistake of believing in God (or gods, etc.).

Religion Versus Religiosity

The important point to bear in mind is that the evolutionary psychological theories, whether adaptationist or by-product, do not attempt to explain *religion* in the full sense of that word, but only our psychological tendency to be religious – in other words our *religiosity*. The theories do not address the truth claims of religion, which is far more than the psychology of its adherents.

To understand this, let us consider as an example what would be the implications of an evolutionary psychology of *physics*. Suppose it could be shown that the scientific curiosity of physicists, and their pleasure in measuring, in calculating, in understanding, and in meeting together to discuss each others' ideas were all deeply rooted in their genetic constitutions, which resulted from evolution. Would this undermine physics? Not really. Psychological tendencies may perhaps bias the choice of research topics. I am not claiming that they have no effect at all. But it would be far-fetched to suggest that an evolutionary psychological theory about physicists could sweep away the edifice of physics. Why, then, should it undermine religion? Just as physicists give rational arguments for their beliefs, so do religious adherents, and non-religious people are sometimes convinced by the arguments. Atheists may argue that theists are biased by irrational tendencies programmed into their brains as a result of evolution, but theists can riposte that the atheists are the ones who are biased. Perhaps their brains are not sufficiently evolved? After all, chimpanzees are not renowned for their religious zeal! Or perhaps some brain region(s) important to belief have failed to develop normally? I hasten to add that I am not supporting the latter tongue-in-cheek arguments. My point is that evolutionary arguments can be press-ganged into service by both camps, but only by special pleading. My personal view is that to an unbiased mind, evolutionary psychology is mostly neutral about the truth of theistic or atheistic claims.

But let us look in more detail at two of the more prominent attempts to discredit religious belief by appealing to evolutionary psychology.

Is Religion a By-Product Due to Illusions About the Presence of Living Agents?

I have already mentioned the hypothesis that our brain may contain a *"hyperactive (or hypersensitive) agency detection device"* (HADD), which causes us to imagine that we see faces in clouds or ghosts in a dark room, and that this evolved because it was essential for our ancestors to detect active agents such as predators or prey. Several atheists, including Richard Dawkins and Daniel Dennett, have argued from this that religious beliefs are just a trick played on us by evolution. The idea is that the hypersensitivity of the HADD causes it to produce many false positives (illusory experiences of ghosts, spirits, gods, God), giving us reason to doubt the reliability of beliefs involving such entities. Some specialists in the cognitive science of religion do accept this view, but by no means all. Among them, Justin Barrett, who promotes the notion of a HADD and invented the term, is a Christian. Philosopher Michael J. Murray has analysed different versions of these anti-religion arguments and shows that they do not stand up.[16] My arguments below are simplified versions of some of his.

First, even though the HADD, being hypersensitive, is prone to false positives in certain situations, many of the beliefs that it triggers are in fact true. When we hear footsteps in the hall or a whistled tune, we form the belief that they were generated by a living agent, and we are right to do so. To sustain the claim that religious beliefs generated by the HADD are false, it would be necessary to show that they are generated in situations where false positives were likely, and this has not been shown.

Second, anti-religion arguments based on the HADD assume that religious beliefs are based primarily on the experience of an agent or agents. This is simply untrue. At least among Christians, religious experience is generally considered to be just one among many pointers to God. Christian defenders of the faith usually give a whole range of reasons for believing, ranging from cosmological fine-tuning to the resurrection of Jesus, fulfilled prophecies, and answered prayer. For reasons such as these, the HADD hypothesis does not seem to me to provide a serious basis from which to attack Christian (or other religious) belief.

But some defenders of Christianity have gone further than Murray and have argued that the HADD actually *supports* some versions of Christian belief. Thus, philosopher Kelly Clark and cognitive scientist Justin Barrett teamed up to produce an article arguing that the HADD hypothesis is very much in harmony with *reformed epistemology*, a philosophical position developed by Alvin Plantinga and others, based on John Calvin's doctrine that God has planted in us a *sensus divinitatis* (sense of divinity). Reformed epistemology maintains that belief in God is "properly basic", being produced naturally and directly by a God-implanted cognitive faculty, without any need for reasoning. I would, however, emphasize that in arguing that this direct sense of God is a rational ground for belief in him, the advocates of reformed epistemology are not saying that other arguments for God's existence are useless, only that they are not essential. Clark and Barrett's point is that the HADD hypothesis, when applied to religion, predicts exactly what the reformed epistemologists have been saying all along, that belief in God is a natural and direct product of the brain. They argue that these points of convergence between reformed epistemology and the cognitive science of religion support Christian belief.[17]

All in all, whatever we may think about Reformed epistemology (I'm cautious about it), the HADD hypothesis does not seem to me to pose major problems for religious belief in general, and certainly not for Christianity, whose truth claims are supported (not proved) by a wide variety of arguments.

God as "Adaptive Illusion" (Jesse Bering)

The second of the attempts to discredit religious belief by evolutionary psychology is argued in a provocative book entitled *The God Instinct: The Psychology of Souls, Destiny, and the Meaning of Life* (or *The Belief Instinct...* in the American version), by research psychologist and columnist Jesse Bering.[18] He adopts an adaptationist approach for attacking belief in God, arguing that this evolved as an "adaptive illusion", and that it was adaptive for the rather peculiar reason that it helped our ancestors deal with the problem of reputation-harming gossip. Some of his arguments resemble those discussed above under the title of hyperactive agency detection. Thus, he begins by proposing an account of how our ability to attribute mental states, such as convictions and intentions, to others ("theory of mind" – ToM) arose by evolution, and argues that evolution made our ToM hyperactive. As evidence for the hyperactivity of our ToM, even today, he points out that people sometimes treat inanimate objects or animals as persons. Bering goes on to argue that the hyperactivity of our ToM makes religious beliefs almost inevitable, because it makes it difficult to imagine complete psychological extinction at death, generates perceptions of meaning or purpose (since we attribute these to others), and makes belief in supernatural agents possible, even plausible. But Bering's own rather particular slant is his emphasis on gossip. He argues that this is relevant to evolution, because, by damaging reputations, malevolent gossip would in turn have affected the ability to secure mates and produce offspring. For this reason, he argues, evolution would have conserved any tendency to be on the lookout for observers, who might gossip, and this would have led in turn to a sensitivity to a divine observer. After developing all these ideas in some detail, he reaches the conclusion that beliefs in a "morally invested reactive Other" provided a reproductive advantage among our ancestors, explaining the evolution of such beliefs.

These ideas are interesting but very speculative and controversial. Bering's thesis is at odds with most current theorists because it assumes adaptationism and group selection, and even among adaptationists his focus on gossip is eccentric. To claim that selection against gossip gave us the genes that make us religious assumes that reputation-harming gossip had important effects on reproductive success over a very long period of time. Of course, we actually know nothing at all about gossip in the prehistorical period. We don't even know precisely when language began. The earliest physical representations of language that have been discovered are as recent as 5200 BP, but indirect arguments suggest that rudimentary language may have begun much earlier, at some time between 300,000 BP and 50,000 BP. Genetic changes useful for language development, including changes in the gene called "FoxP2", were occurring several hundred thousand years ago. We have no idea when language reached the level of sophistication necessary for gossip.

But even if Bering's gossip theory were true (and the "if" is rather a big one in this case), this would still be a long way from justifying his anti-God conclusions. The most it could possibly explain would be our psychological openness to the God concept. It might therefore be a challenge to somebody whose sole reason for believing in God was an inner feeling that God was there. But, as I pointed out above, Christians, at least, do not generally justify their faith on the basis of feelings alone, but on a variety of reasons.

Conclusions

- The ubiquity of religion and its resilience even in the face of persecution have stimulated a new field of research based on the assumption that our religious sense, or religiosity, is innate and rooted in our genetic constitution as a result of Darwinian evolution.
- This claim is controversial, but it has been co-opted by some anti-religion polemists such as Dawkins, Dennett, and Bering in their attempt to argue that religions are *illusory* products of evolution.
- I have argued in this chapter that even if the scientific assumptions of these authors were to be validated, this would not justify their anti-religion conclusions. At the most, evolution may help to explain the psychological trait of religiosity, but a religion is more than the religiosity of its adherents and has to be evaluated on a much broader basis.
- Moreover, if human religiosity turned out to be innate, this would be a striking confirmation of the Christian claim that we are made for God, to know him and love him.

V

Drawing the Threads Together

14

Brain, Mind, and Worldview

Summary

This chapter draws the threads together and then considers how to approach the onward march of science, which will inevitably bring surprises and may lead to further changes in worldview.

Only the unknown frightens men. But once a man has faced the unknown, that terror becomes the known.
Antoine de Saint-Exupéry, *Wind, Sand, and Stars*,
1939

Throughout this book I have focused rather single-mindedly on problem areas where advances in neuroscience (and sometimes related fields that impinge on neuroscience such as psychology and genetics) might be thought to undermine the Christian (or other theistic) worldview. Only a small part of neuroscience research is *directly* relevant to the questions discussed (e.g. brain imaging during prayer, or the Libet experiment, or research on the brains of criminals). But, *indirectly*, a much larger part of neuroscience is relevant, because its main thrust – the attempt to understand all thought and behaviour as resulting from brain processes – encourages a mechanistic way of thinking, which, as we saw in Chapter 1, is very different from the way of thinking of the biblical writers or the early church fathers or the great Christian philosophers of the Middle Ages.

It is not surprising, therefore, that incongruities arise when we attempt to fit together biblical teaching or traditional Christian philosophy with modern neuroscience. I have argued, however, that the problems are not insoluble and that mechanistic neuroscience does not require us to abandon a theistic worldview or traditional human values. As science advances, difficulties do indeed arise, but others dissolve. And all worldviews, not just theistic ones, are challenged and indeed changed as new discoveries impose new scientific paradigms.

I have not, however, dealt with all the problems raised by neuroscience. In this last chapter, I recapitulate very briefly the answers that I have given to the problems addressed, and explain also why I left others aside.

Problems Addressed

As we saw in Chapter 1, the abandoning of teleology and the rise of mechanistic thinking at the time of the scientific revolution have raised serious questions for philosophers ever since. But the resulting challenges are for everyone, not just theists, and the need for complementary non-mechanistic approaches has been emphasized by atheists (e.g. Jacques Monod's insistence that living beings are endowed with a purpose or project) almost as much as by theists. Again in Chapter 4, the dangers of naïve or "greedy" reductionism have been signalled by atheists (e.g. Dennett and Pinker) as well as by Christians (e.g. MacKay and Ayala), and the same is true about the need for emergent concepts.

When we come to the question of free will, the debate has become particularly heated in recent years. While it is true that many of those who deny free will are atheists, here again a line of battle cannot be drawn neatly between theists on the one side and atheists on the other. Thus, in defending what I consider to be a Christian approach to free will and moral responsibility in Chapters 5–9, I found myself on the same side as new atheist Daniel Dennett, who is one of the world's leading philosophers of free will and a staunch defender of it. On the other hand, I found myself opposed to Sam Harris (another new atheist) but also to Derk Pereboom (a Christian).

When we come to the question of the soul, one might think the divide between theists and atheists would be more clear-cut, because most theists (including me) believe in the continued existence of some kind of soul after death whereas almost all atheists deny this. Indeed, neuroscience-based attacks on theistic belief have generally focused on the notion of soul. For example, atheistic Buddhist philosopher Owen Flanagan and atheist neuroscientist José Musacchio both attack the Cartesian concept of the soul and assume (wrongly) that this is the standard Christian concept.[1] But, as I explain in Chapter 10, the dualistic assumptions underlying the Cartesian concept of soul are not from the Bible, but were imported into Christianity (and into some forms of Judaism and Islam) through the influence of Platonism. Flanagan and Musacchio seem to be oblivious of this, and completely neglect the major and longstanding Christian tradition strongly critical of Platonism, stemming from St Thomas Aquinas. In fact, most Christian neuroscientists and philosophers accept the biblical view that life after death will not be as disembodied souls (as Plato believed), but as souls (or beings) who are *embodied* in what St Paul calls a "spiritual body", very different from our physical bodies but a body nonetheless. So far as understanding the brain–mind (or brain–soul) relationship in this life, I have argued in favour of two-aspect (or dual-aspect) monism, which avoids the difficulties of interactionist dualism while at the same time accepting that there is a real *duality* (not dualism) between our own first-person account of our inner life and neuroscience's third-person account of our brain's activity.

But despite my preference for two-aspect monism, in Chapter 11 ("Near-Death Experiences and Deathbed Visions") I felt it necessary to "sit on the fence". It seems to me that these powerful and real-seeming experiences have to be taken seriously, not dismissed out of hand, but at the same time I do not think that they have yet been investigated with sufficient rigour to establish a radically dualistic worldview.

Of all the chapters in this book, the one that comes closest to dealing with the neuroscience of belief in God is Chapter 12. Religious experience, like all other kinds of experience, clearly involves brain activity. It is also true that differences between brains, caused by genetic or other factors, are responsible for differences in religiosity. But I was critical in this chapter of extreme claims that are sometimes propagated by the media, such as the notion of a god spot in the temporal lobe or a rigid neurogenetic determination of belief in God.

Finally, Chapter 13 dealt with one of the most controversial areas at the science–religion interface: the idea that religious beliefs and behaviours have a genetic basis that was generated by natural selection during the last tens or hundreds of millennia of evolution. Opponents of religion have an ambivalent attitude to these ideas. Some, including Dawkins and Dennett, adopt them eagerly, because they hope this branch of evolutionary psychology will provide a way of explaining the ubiquity of religion within a naturalistic framework. But other opponents are more hesitant, because they are reluctant to admit that religion is a basic human need or that it can do anything as positive as promoting survival. Along with many Christians, my own approach has been very cautious, partly because of the lack of solid data in this area. Speculative though it is, I don't think the evolutionary psychology of religion can be rejected out of hand. But nor can it justify wild claims that religion is an illusion rooted in our genes.

Problems Not Addressed

Having recapitulated my main answers in this book, I must admit to having left aside some very important questions. I would mention just two of these.

First, the *problem of consciousness*, the extraordinary mystery of why anyone is conscious of anything. As we have seen, there is abundant evidence that consciousness is in some sense a product of the brain, but how can this be? How is it even conceivable that a lump of matter such as the brain can be conscious? Many philosophers nowadays follow David Chalmers in dividing this problem into two: the "easy" and the "hard" problems of consciousness.[2] The (relatively) "easy" problem is the one of explaining how our brains enable us to perform different tasks like recognizing visual forms or sounds or smells, or describing our feelings, or focusing our attention, or performing voluntary movements, or making plans. Of course, this is not really an easy problem at all. It is very complex and challenging, and has been the subject of hundreds of thousands of papers by neuroscientists. But the important point is that we do at least have an idea of what we would have to do to be able to solve the so-called "easy" problem. We can design neuroscience experiments that will get us a little further along the road to understanding.

In contrast, the "hard" problem is the one of explaining why we have experiences at all. How is it that any brain, even the most sophisticated, can give rise to an inner life? Chapter 2 addresses the "easy" problem, but nowadays when philosophers talk about the problem of consciousness they are usually talking about the "hard" problem. I have not attempted to address this, because, important though it is, it does not seem to me central to the main theme of this book – the challenges raised by neuroscience for religion and faith and for a theistic worldview.

Furthermore, the subject is enormous and, well… hard! It is the central question underlying most of the philosophy of mind, and many complete books have been devoted to it, and yet nobody really has an answer (although some think they do). It seemed better to leave this subject aside rather than to address it superficially in a few pages.

But, having said that, I would mention that the "hard problem" seems to me even more problematic for atheistic materialists than for others. If you believe that nothing else exists but matter, you have a very big problem explaining how consciousness (or mind etc.) can possibly exist. But if you believe that a Mind, God, is the "ground of being" (to quote theologian Paul Tillich), then it makes more sense that the universe should be pregnant with consciousness.

A second question that I have steadfastly ignored is the one of *how God communicates with us*. It is standard Christian doctrine that God's Holy Spirit guides us and inspires us. But how? Does he modify the firing of brain neurons? I can think of no other way, but if this is the case, we find ourselves with a problem analogous to the one that Descartes raised about the soul. Would not, then, my arguments in Appendix 1, criticizing the Beck–Eccles model of soul–brain interaction, apply equally to any model of God–brain interaction? I have avoided this question because we know nothing about it from the scientific angle, and I know of no attempt by philosophers or theologians to tackle it. What they have attempted to consider is the more general problem of how God interacts with the world (not just the brain). For example, theologian Wolfhart Pannenberg speculated that the Holy Spirit might in some ways be analogous to a physical force field. Should we then extend this to the idea of a divine force field acting on the brain? There is also considerable scholarship on the relevance of quantum theoretical considerations to the question of God's action in the world, but to have delved into this broad and very speculative field would have taken us too far from neuroscience. I admit the problem, but the moment does not seem ripe for tackling it.

The Future

I am not perturbed by the fact that we cannot now answer questions such as the two mentioned above. We would not expect to be able to answer them, because our current ignorance is too great. But what about the future? It seems safe to bet that new discoveries will raise profoundly difficult questions that we cannot currently even imagine. This may, perhaps, lead to revolutions in thought as profound as those due to the scientific revolution. Who knows? How then should we face this unknown future?

As a Christian, I think we can look ahead to new discoveries with a mixture of enthusiasm and caution. Enthusiasm, because every discovery about God's world shows us something more of God's extraordinary artistry. But caution, too, because not every claim is correct.

Critical caution is essential to science. In my early years of doctoral and postdoctoral research, I was unpleasantly surprised to discover that I was naïve, accepting new scientific results and interpretations too easily, without enough criticism. Every scientist has to learn to think critically, to be on the lookout for experimental difficulties and ambiguities of interpretation. This attitude has to be learned, but in the long run the critical attitude becomes instinctive for all good scientists. One day, after attending a neuroscience lecture that seemed to me excellent, I heard a Nobel Prize laureate say, "I don't believe it!" When asked why, he replied, "I don't believe my own results, so why should I believe his?" Taken literally, his answer was of course illogical, but what he meant was that he wanted first to think about the data, analyse the details, and wait for experimental confirmation from other research groups before accepting the new results. Good scientists are very cautious about accepting new claims.

But critical caution does not mean a closed mind. As a Christian, I believe that worship of the God of truth should make me open to new and unexpected conclusions. Each scientific claim is about God's creation. This leads me to be cautious about accepting premature claims, but also open and even serene in the face of scientific progress. At the time of the scientific revolution in the sixteenth and seventeenth centuries, many people feared that the new experimental science would call into question the traditional faith. But leading scientists including Galileo argued that Scripture and scientific discoveries could never contradict each other, because God is the author of both. I believe that too.

Quantitative Problems with Quantum Libertarianism and Quantum Dualism

This appendix deals with some technical issues relevant to Chapter 5 (where I discuss *quantum libertarianism* – the claim that the fuzziness of quantum theory may provide the indeterminism required by libertarianism) and Chapter 10 (where I discuss *quantum dualism* – the claim that this same fuzziness provides a tiny gap in the causal chain allowing soulish influences to affect the brain). I here focus on *quantum dualism*, but the main arguments and calculations are relevant to quantum libertarianism as well.

The reason why people invoke quantum dualism is to try to solve the problem that soul–brain interaction would require a violation of the laws of physics. The only way of solving this problem that has any modern support is the suggestion that the fuzziness (indeterminacy) of quantum physics (see below) provides a kind of leeway within which very small soul-induced perturbations would be possible (*quantum dualism*). Numerous objections to it have been advanced by many people including me. In this appendix, I discuss just one of the objections: the problem that the indeterminacy is too small to allow significant effects on neurons.

Quantum Physics

Quantum physics (also called quantum mechanics or wave mechanics) is the branch of physics that deals with atomic and subatomic (micro-scale) phenomena. It was founded during the first 30 years of the twentieth century because classical physics was unable to account for certain micro-scale phenomena. One of its important claims is that very small particles such as electrons should be thought of not as miniature billiard balls but as semi-localized waves. If you find this counterintuitive, you are not alone. In fact, one of the great founders of quantum physics, Niels Bohr, once said, "Anyone who is not shocked by quantum theory has not understood it." It would be beyond our present scope to go into the details, so I shall jump rather abruptly to the part of it that tends to be invoked by quantum dualists wanting to solve the problems of soul–brain interaction.

Heisenberg's Uncertainty Principle*

The fact that small particles are semi-localized waves implies that their position, energy, momentum (mass × velocity), and so on are defined only approximately. In other words, they are "indeterminate". There are various forms of this quantum fuzziness, but we here focus on its best-known expression in Heisenberg's famous uncertainty principle, which states that there is a limit to the precision with which the momentum (p) and position (x) of a small particle could be simultaneously measured, given by $\Delta p.\Delta x \geq h/4\Pi$ where Δp and Δx express the indeterminacy of the momentum (p) and distance (x), and h (Planck's constant) = 6.63 × 10^{-34} joule seconds (Js). Thus, the precision limit applies to the product of the two variables. The more precisely one is measured, the greater the imprecision for the other. Other versions exist, applying to different pairs of variables, for example energy (E) and time (t): $\Delta E.\Delta t \geq h/4\Pi$. Since h is very small indeed, Heisenbergian uncertainty is of no relevance to macroscopic objects such as golf balls; but it is very relevant to submicroscopic entities such as electrons and photons.

Thus, there is an inevitable trade-off between the measurement precisions for position and momentum, or for time and energy. For this to serve the needs of quantum dualists, they need to make the further claim that this is not just a problem about the practical difficulties of precise measurement, but is a fundamental statement about the nature of reality. Reality itself is fuzzy. This claim was hotly disputed by Einstein, but it is currently accepted by most physicists and philosophers, although still debated. Let us accept it provisionally, to see how the quantum dualists try to use it.

Quantum Uncertainty at Synapses

The relevance of this to our present concerns stems from the idea that quantum fuzziness might undermine the determinism of brain function. This has been seized on by advocates of libertarian free will, who believe that brain indeterminacy is required for free will (see Chapter 5), and by quantum dualists (our present concern). I shall focus on the publications of Sir John Eccles in collaboration with physicist Friedrich Beck, because these are generally recognized to provide the most plausible (or least implausible) version of quantum dualism.

The synapse is the cellular location for mind–brain interaction most commonly proposed by quantum dualists, including their most eminent advocate, the late Sir John Eccles. One reason for this is that they think the soul/self/mind would need to influence conscious decision-making directly and immediately. Another is that Eccles thought the synaptic vesicles (the tiny – about 50 nanometres – membranous sacs that contain the neurotransmitter) were small enough to be subject to quantum effects, although this is now known to be untrue.

Eccles published numerous versions of his interactionist model, refining them in the light of criticisms, and the best is considered to be the version he published in collaboration with physicist Beck, involving quantum tunnelling of unspecified "quasiparticles" between the thin membrane surrounding the synaptic vesicle and the presynaptic membrane.[1] Since this model was first proposed, some of its biological details have turned out to be incorrect, and its quantitative aspects were criticized by neurophysiologist David Wilson.[2] Wilson further argued that it would be less implausible to postulate Heisenbergian effects on the control of presynaptic calcium concentration rather than on the movement of synaptic vesicles. However, the following argument, which I have adapted from Wilson and elaborated in more detail elsewhere,[3] indicates that Heisenbergian effects are still much too small.

As a specific example, we consider whether a fluctuation within the limits of Heisenbergian uncertainty could affect the presynaptic calcium concentration by changing calcium flow through ion channels in the presynaptic membrane. For this, it would need to modify chemical bonds in the channels. According to Heisenberg's principle, the precision limit to the energy (E) and time (t) is given by $\Delta E.\Delta t \geq h/4\Pi$ where $h = 6.63 \times 10^{-34}$ J.s. To have even a minimal effect on the presynaptic calcium concentration, the ion flow would need to be changed for at least 10 microseconds, probably much more. Substituting this value of Δt gives a ΔE of about 5.2×10^{-30} joules (J), which is about 200,000 times too small to disrupt even a van der Waals interaction, the weakest kind of chemical bond ($E = 1 \times 10^{-24}$ J).

Another problem is that the energy uncertainty (ΔE) is about a thousand million times smaller than the energy of *thermal noise*. Owing to the non-zero temperature of the body, every molecule (and every part of every molecule) is constantly moving in a way that is not controlled by the cellular control mechanisms. The problem of this for quantum dualism is that any soul-mediating effect of Heisenbergian uncertainty would be swamped by the far greater energy of the thermal noise. Furthermore, to be able to cope with the thermal noise, all cells (including neurons) and all organs (including the brain) have noise-resistance mechanisms, as I have discussed in detail elsewhere.[4] If these can make the cells resistant to thermal noise, they should be more than sufficient to ensure resistance to Heisenbergian uncertainty.

It is sometimes argued that the effects of Heisenbergian uncertainty might be amplified. There are many problems with this, not least that the amplification mechanism would have to increase the effects of the Heisenbergian uncertainty but not those of the thermal noise, which seems implausible. There are other problems as well, beyond our present scope, and I have argued in more detail elsewhere that amplification is unlikely to provide the indeterminacy required for quantum dualism.[5]

These are not the only quantitative problems with quantum dualism. Others have been discussed by Smith.[6] All in all, the quantitative case against quantum dualism seems to me strong, and I can only see one possible opening for counterarguments. This is that indeterminate quantum fluctuations much greater than those predicted by Heisenbergian uncertainty are theoretically possible.[7] The warm, wet environment of a biological organism tends to make such events exceedingly brief, but recent evidence indicates that they can have significant effects in certain biological situations, notably photosynthesis and magnetic field sensitivity.[8] Such effects have never been shown in neuron-to-neuron communication or in any aspect of brain function, but this is a new field, so we must wait to see what the future reveals.

In conclusion, apart from a faint flicker of hope offered by new data on quantum indeterminism above Heisenbergian levels, quantum fuzziness seems to be too limited to provide a plausible leeway within which a separate Cartesian soul might influence the brain. This is not where I would lay my bets![9]

Neo-Darwinism and Why I Accept It

The overwhelming majority of biologists accept the current version of Darwinian evolution, known as *neo-Darwinism*, which is by definition the "modern synthesis" of Darwinian evolutionary theory with genetics. I here explain briefly the main tenets of neo-Darwinism and why I accept them. It would be beyond our present scope to tackle the subject in depth, and I do not expect by the following few words to convince opponents of neo-Darwinism to change their minds. But I think I owe it to sceptics about evolution to address briefly current evolutionary theory and explain why I accept it, since I assume its truth in Chapter 13 on *religion*, because the entire scientific literature on the latter takes for granted the truth of neo-Darwinism.

The Two Components of Darwinian Evolution

Darwin's theory of evolution involves two separate claims: *evolution by common descent* and *natural selection* (Figure A2.1).

Evolution by Common Descent

This is the claim that the vast multitude of diverse life forms on this planet are all descended from a few initial forms, or just one. Most modern biologists think that all modern organisms are in fact derived from one single "initial form", a single-celled organism. The question of how that first organism arose is not dealt with in Darwinian theory. The *common descent* claim is that after the first organism(s) had appeared, its descendants gave rise to the diversity of life. This leaves open the question of what *caused* the diversification to happen and does not necessarily deny the role of a creator or an "intelligent designer". Those who deny common descent are nowadays called *creationists*, even though many theists who accept common descent insist that they too believe in creation. Most creationists object to common descent at least partly because they consider it contradicts the accounts of creation in certain religious texts, notably the Old Testament (Hebrew Bible) or the Koran. As a Christian, I do not find this a major worry, because many (probably most) Old Testament scholars (both Jewish and Christian, ranging from liberals to moderate conservatives) argue that the creation accounts in Genesis are complex literary constructions that were never intended to be interpreted in scientific terms.[1]

	Common descent	Natural selection
Main claim	All life forms descended from a few initial ones (probably just one).	The diversity of life forms arose mainly by a particular mechanism: random variation followed by the preferential survival of the fittest.
Main challenge to religious belief	Seems to contradict the descriptions of creation in certain sacred texts	Is sometimes taken to imply metaphysical naturalism

Fig. A2.1. *The two components of neo-Darwinism and their implications for religion*

Natural Selection

This is the theory that attempts to explain what caused the diversification, the *mechanism* of how the enormous diversity of life forms arose by descent from a single life form (or a few). The theory of natural selection postulates that random mutations (modifications) produce variation and that certain variations persist because they are better adapted to their environment and therefore tend to survive and produce more offspring. Since the foundation of genetics at the beginning of the twentieth century, the variations referred to above have been understood to be changes in genes, which are (roughly) the parts of the DNA that encode proteins. *Intelligent design* proponents are those who deny that natural events such as natural selection can account for all the sophistication of living creatures and argue that there must have been an *intelligent designer*. They mostly accept evolution by common descent and may accept a partial role for natural selection, but they claim that an intelligent designer needs to be invoked in order to explain the many complex features of living beings that are so suggestive of design. *Intelligent design* proponents give scientific arguments for their views, but the main philosophical/religious issue at stake is the question of *naturalism*, which we shall discuss below.

Why I Accept Neo-Darwinism

I here give only very briefly some of my reasons for accepting neo-Darwinism. For those who want to examine the evidence in more detail, many excellent accounts are available, written by biologists from many different religious and philosophical viewpoints. Among those written by Christians, I would recommend two well-known books by Francis Collins[2] and Denis Alexander.[3] I find it useful to deal separately with neo-Darwinism's two claims of common descent and natural selection.

The *common descent claim* is very strongly supported by numerous converging lines of evidence. As a young scientist in the 1970s, I felt uncertain. I was aware that most specialists accepted common descent, but the vast array of biological, palaeontological, and geological data that they adduced was very difficult to evaluate for a neuroscientist such as myself, with no training in palaeontology or geology. For me, the truth of common descent became crystal clear in the 1980s and 1990s when the application of molecular biological techniques provided a striking confirmation of the mainstream view. The evolutionary trees established from the study of genetic sequences matched beautifully the trees that had long before been proposed on the grounds of anatomical comparisons.

Still more recently, molecular genetic techniques have provided superbly convincing evidence for common descent. To take just one example, when retroviruses infect a sperm or egg cell, they insert identifiable pieces of DNA into the DNA of the infected cell, and these insertions are then passed down to the offspring where they can be identified at exactly the right place in the chain of small molecules that make up the DNA. The study of these *retroviral insertions* is a very powerful method for establishing evolutionary trees, because we can be sure that organisms with exactly the same insertion in exactly the same location in the DNA must have a common ancestor. This approach has, for example, provided totally convincing confirmation of the standard view that humans, chimps, and gorillas are descended from a common ancestor, that these and orangutans and gibbons are descended from an earlier ancestor, and that all these and Old World monkeys and New World monkeys are descended from a still earlier ancestor.[4]

In contrast, the evidence for *natural selection* as the main mechanism of species diversification seems to me somewhat less strong, but still sufficient to be accepted as the best available theory. The problem is that natural selection works on such a long timescale that it is difficult to study experimentally, except in rapidly dividing species such as bacteria or fruit flies. Thus, a famous experiment by Dobzhansky showed that selection of fruit flies over 20 generations on the basis of their attraction to light caused changes in the genes. It has also been clearly shown that bacterial populations exposed to antibiotics develop resistance due to genetic changes and that these are conserved and spread by natural selection (and by the direct transfer of genetic material between bacteria, which does not happen in higher species). There is thus little doubt that natural selection can occur, but this does not prove that it is the *main* mechanism of diversification *in all life forms*. Furthermore, there are indications that mechanisms other than natural selection can contribute to evolution, although the importance of these is still somewhat controversial. For reasons such as these, I am not quite so confident about *natural selection* being the main mechanism of species diversification as I am about the truth of common descent, but I accept it as the best available theory.

Natural Selection and Naturalism

The main reason why opponents of natural selection feel strongly about it is that it is linked to *naturalism*, which is the philosophical claim that only natural (as opposed to supernatural) laws and forces operate in the world. To accept this would be to deny any role for God within his universe except perhaps (in some versions of naturalism) as the upholder of the laws of nature.

Now the idea that God continually upholds the universe and everything in it, including the laws of nature, is perfectly compatible with Christian (and Jewish and Islamic) doctrine and is even an important part of it. This relates to the Christian doctrine of *general providence*. If the laws of nature only worked some of the time, living beings could not exist, so God's upholding of natural law is an expression of his love for his creatures. But a Christian wants to affirm not only *general providence* but *special providence* as well. In the words of John Calvin:

> *The carnal mind, when once it has perceived the power of God in the creation, stops there... It imagines that all things are sufficiently sustained by the energy divinely infused into them at first. But faith must penetrate deeper. After learning that there is a Creator, it must forthwith infer that he is also a Governor and Preserver, and that, not by producing a kind of general motion in the machine of the globe as well as in each of its parts, but by a special providence sustaining, cherishing, superintending, all the things which he has made, to the very minutest, even to a sparrow.*[5]

We notice here that Calvin was already, almost a century before the discoveries of Galileo, giving thought to the implications of a mechanistic approach to the world. He realized that a God who merely produced "a kind of general motion in the machine of the globe" would not be the God of the Bible who loves and cherishes his creatures, so Calvin emphasized the doctrine of *special providence*. But moving on now to the modern era, how can we square special providence – including miracles and answers to prayer – with the deterministic regularities of modern science? I would like to suggest that a solution can be found in the distinction between naturalism in the original sense (sometimes called *ontological* or *metaphysical naturalism*) and *methodological naturalism* (also called *scientific naturalism* or *methodological materialism*).

Methodological Naturalism

The term *methodological naturalism* cropped up occasionally as early as the 1930s, but its modern usage dates from its reintroduction in the 1980s by Paul de Vries, an evangelical philosopher at Wheaton College (a Christian liberal arts college near Chicago). De Vries defined methodological naturalism as the working assumption, necessary for the practice of science, that the events we study are explicable in terms of natural processes. This says nothing about God's existence. In explaining methodological naturalism, de Vries wrote:

If I put two charged electrodes in water, the hydrogen and oxygen will begin to separate. If I were writing a lab report (even at a Christian College!), it would be unacceptable to write that God stepped in and made these elements separate. A "God Hypothesis" is both unnecessary and out of place within natural scientific explanations.[6]

The term has caught on and is now used by philosophers and scientists of all religions or none. I think most of us can agree with de Vries that it would be inappropriate to bring in God as part of our scientific explanations. That is not to deny that God might decide to override his own laws. He can do anything, and he could perform a miracle right there in the laboratory if he wanted to! I believe that miracles can occur. But if today's experiment failed to confirm yesterday's, I would assume I had made a mistake and would not invoke an intervention by God. In science, our aim is to understand as much as possible in terms of natural laws, and for our scientific practice we accept *methodological naturalism* as a working assumption – not a dogmatic conviction, just a working assumption. In the words of Christian de Duve, a Nobel Prize-winning cell biologist with no religious commitment:

Science is based on naturalism, the notion that all manifestations in the universe are explainable in terms of the known laws of physics and chemistry. This notion represents the cornerstone of the scientific enterprise... Contrary to the view expressed by some scientists, this... does not imply that naturalism is to be accepted as an a priori philosophical stand, a doctrine or belief. As used in science, it is a postulate, a working hypothesis often qualified as "methodological naturalism" by philosophers, which we should be ready to abandon if faced with facts or events that defy every attempt at a naturalistic explanation. But we should only accept the intervention of "something else" as a last resort after all possibility of explaining a given phenomenon in naturalistic terms has been exhausted.[7]

That's the approach that I adopt in Chapter 13. In trying to evaluate attempts to explain religious tendencies through natural selection, I adopt the provisional postulate of methodological naturalism, but this does not imply commitment to the a priori doctrine of metaphysical naturalism.

Glossary

Terms explained in this glossary are marked by an asterisk at their first mention in the main text and at any mention in the glossary.

Amygdala: Brain region situated deep in the front part of the temporal lobe. Parts of it are involved in emotions.

Action potential: Electrical impulse that travels along *axons** (and sometimes along *dendrites**). Muscle fibres also produce action potentials.

Axon: A *neuron's** "output wire". A long, slender projection from the neuronal cell body that typically conducts *action potentials** to the next cells.

Basal ganglia: A group of brain nuclei, situated mainly in the forebrain, that are involed primarily in the control of volutary movements.

Bouton: See *synaptic bouton**.

Cartesian: Adjective for Descartes.

Cartesian dualism: Interactionist (or interactive) dualism or interactionism. The view according to which souls and brains are two separate, and radically different, entities that interact.

Cognition, cognitive: *Cognition* (from *cognitio*, Latin for knowledge, judgment, idea) refers to thought processes such as knowing, thinking, understanding, planning, perceiving, or imagining.

Cortex: Brain tissue arranged in layers. The brain contains several cortices, including the cerebral cortex and the cerebellar cortex. In this book, as in popular usage, the single word cortex refers to the cerebral cortex, the large, outermost layer of brain tissue that covers the frontal, parietal, temporal, and occipital lobes (Figure 2.1). The cerebral cortex is particularly developed in humans.

Compatibilism: The view that free will and *determinism** are compatible.

Dendrites: Branched protrusions from the cell body of *neurons**. They receive information from other neurons and transmit electrical stimulation to the soma.

Determinism: The view that every event or state of affairs is the necessary consequence of previous events or states of affairs.

Dualism: The philosophical doctrine according to which everything that exists can be explained in terms of two realities or *substances** but not in terms of just one. In the context of brain and mind (or soul), the term dualism is used in various ways. Some people use it to mean that the mind is not the brain, but others use it to imply the much stronger claim that the mind is not, or not wholly, a product of the brain. See *Cartesian dualism** and *monism**.

Duality: Some biblical scholars use the word *duality*, rather than *dualism**, to avoid the philosophical implications of the latter.

Emergence: In philosophy and science, emergence is the way higher orders of organization arise out of multiple simple interactions.

Epiphenomenalism: The philosophical position that mental events are mere *epiphenomena* (side effects), being caused by physical events in the brain but having no effects on physical events. The modern debate about epiphenomenalism goes back to various nineteenth-century authors including Shadworth Hodgson (1870) and Thomas Huxley (1874). Epiphenomenalism is currently a minority view among philosophers. Its supporters all invoke the Libet experiment.

fMRI: See *functional magnetic resonance imaging**.

Functional brain imaging: Any method of brain imaging, including *fMRI** and *positron emission topography**, that indicates the level of brain activity in different areas.

Functional magnetic resonance imaging (fMRI): This technique measures the activity in different brain regions, by detecting the changes in blood oxygenation that occur in response to neural activity. fMRI can be used to produce three-dimensional "activation maps" showing which brain regions are involved in a particular mental process.

Hebbian synapse: A *synapse** that is strengthened when it succeeds in activating the next *neuron**.

Heisenberg's uncertainty principle: A statement of the "uncertainty relation" between the position and the *momentum** (or the energy and the time etc.) of a subatomic particle, such as an electron.

Hippocampus: Brain region shaped like a *hippocampus* (Greek for sea horse) lying deep in the temporal lobe. It plays an important role in the memory of events.

Hylomorphism: From Greek *hylē* (matter) and *morphē* (form). The metaphysical view that every natural body (even if inanimate) consists of two intrinsic principles: matter and form. It was central to Aristotle's philosophy of nature and was adapted by St Thomas Aquinas.

Hypothalamus: Brain region situated at the base of the brain and containing nuclei involved in the control of vital functions (eating, drinking, sleep, aggression, sex, etc.).

Interactionism: Interactionist dualism. See *Cartesian dualism**.

Ion: Electrically charged atom or molecule. In cells, the ions of sodium, potassium, calcium, and chloride are particularly important.

Ion channels: Narrow pores (holes) in a biological membrane formed by complexes of proteins. They allow only *ions** of a certain size and/or charge to pass through. In most cases their opening is controlled by chemical or electrical signals.

Ischaemia: A restriction in blood supply, causing a lack of oxygen and of chemicals such as glucose that are needed for the cells to be able to function. Heart failure causes ischaemia throughout the whole body, including the brain. Ischaemia in a given body part, such as

the brain, can be caused when an artery in that part of the body gets blocked.

Lateral geniculate body: Small structure deep in the brain that receives the main output of the retina and projects to the primary visual *cortex**. "Geniculate" means "knee-shaped".

Libertarianism: In the philosophy of mind, libertarianism is the view that free will is incompatible with *determinism** but that we are nevertheless free.

LTP (long-term potentiation): Long-lasting increases in *synaptic strength**, considered to be an important means of memory storage.

Materialism (or physicalism): The philosophical doctrine that everything in the universe is material (matter) or physical, and that there are no immaterial forces such as a *Cartesian** soul. Extreme versions of materialism deny the existence of mind.

Mechanism, mechanistic: In everyday usage, a mechanism is a mechanical contrivance with moving parts; a machine or a part of one. In modern biology, the term has a more abstract meaning, referring to a network of causes. The adjective *mechanical* refers to mechanism in the everyday sense, whereas *mechanistic* refers to mechanism in the modern biological sense.

Monism: The philosophical doctrine according to which everything that exists, including mental events, can be explained in terms of a single reality or *substance**. See also *two-aspect monism** and *dualism**.

Neuron (nerve cell): Cell within the nervous system capable of producing *action potentials**.

Neurotransmitter: Chemical substance released from nerve endings (*synapses**) that mediates communication between the nerve ending and its target cell.

Nucleus accumbens: Large cluster of *neurons** at the base of the frontal lobe that are involved in motivation and pleasure.

Orbito-frontal cortex: A part of the *prefrontal cortex** situated just above each eye socket and known to play a role in moral behaviour.

Positron emission tomography (PET): An imaging technique that can measure the amount of radioactive material taken up by different body regions, for example, the regions of the brain. For technical reasons, the radioactivity employed is of a special kind that produces positrons, each of which immediately dissociates to give two gamma rays that travel in opposite directions. By detection of the gamma rays, the location of the radioactive material can be deduced. PET can be used for *functional brain imaging*.

Prefrontal cortex: The front part of the frontal lobe, lying in front of the motricity-related regions (i.e. the motor cortex and premotor cortex). The prefrontal cortex is particularly involved in the so-called *executive functions*, an umbrella term that refers to refers to the higher-level *cognitive* (thinking) skills that we use to control and coordinate our other cognitive abilities and behaviours. Executive functions include planning, problem-solving, working memory, abstract thinking, self-control, and moral decision-making. See *cortex*.

Rational soul: See *soul*.

Reductionism (also called reduction): The view that the behaviours of complex systems can be explained in terms of their parts and the interactions between them. Most philosophers consider that some forms of reduction are valid whereas others are not. See Chapter 4.

Religiosity: In this book, this word refers to the personality trait of having a tendency to be religious. In popular usage, the term can refer to *excessive* involvement in religious activities, but in this book no such implication is intended.

Soul: Principle of life. Medieval philosophy assumed the existence of three soul functions (or three souls): the vegetative soul, present in all living creatures; the animal soul, present in animals and man; and the rational soul, present only in man. The soul has variously been considered a principle integrated in the body (Aristotelian tradition) or a separate entity interacting with the body (Platonic–*Cartesian* tradition). When Descartes used the word "soul", he was referring to the "rational soul", which was virtually synonymous with "mind".

Substance: In philosophy, a basic entity of being or a particular kind of basic entity.

Synapse: From Greek *synaptein* "to clasp". A functional connection between two *neurons*.

Synaptic bouton: From the French *bouton* (button), referring to the button-like terminal enlargement of an *axon* that ends in relation to another *neuron* (or other cell) at a *synapse* (see Figures 3.1, 3.2, and 3.3).

Synaptic strength: The power of an *action potential*, arriving in a *synapse*, to affect its *postsynaptic neuron*.

Synaptic vesicle: A very small membranous bag that contains *neurotransmitter* molecules.

Synaptotagmin: A class of calcium-sensitive proteins that are involved in *neurotransmitter* release. They are attached both to *synaptic vesicles* and to the cell membrane. When a calcium *ion* binds to the synaptotagmin molecule, this causes it to change shape and to pull the vesicle against the membrane so that they fuse together. The neurotransmitter molecules can then spill out of the vesicle into the synaptic cleft.

Teleonomy: Apparent teleology. The apparent purposefulness and goal-directedness of living organisms or of their parts.

Teleology: Philosophical account that recognizes the presence of *purpose* in nature.

Thomistic: Related to Thomism, the philosophical school originating in the thought of St Thomas Aquinas.

Two-aspect monism (also called *dual-aspect monism, double-aspect theory*, etc.): The view that our subjective, first-person, account of our inner life and neuroscience's objective, third-person account of our brain's activity refer to complementary aspects of a single entity. Two-aspect monism is virtually identical to *neutral monism*.

Utilitarianism: The view that the morality of an action depends on the extent to which it maximizes some "utility" such as happiness or lack of suffering.

Vitalism: The belief, now abandoned, that living organisms possess a vital element or force (or *élan vital* or *entelechy*) not present in dead matter.

Notes

Introduction

1. J.M. Musacchio, *Contradictions: Neuroscience and Religion*, New York: Springer, 2012.
2. Terms explained in the Glossary are marked by an asterisk at their first mention in the main text.
3. F. Crick, *The Astonishing Hypothesis: The Scientific Search for the Soul*, New York: Scribner, 1994, p. 3.
4. S. Harris, *Free Will*, New York: Free Press, 2012.
5. O. Flanagan, *The Problem of the Soul: Two Visions of Mind and How to Reconcile Them*, New York: Basic Books, 2002.
6. C. Carter, *Science and the Near Death Experience: How Consciousness Survives Death*, Rochester, VT: Inner Traditions International, 2010.

1. How We Came to Think of Humans as Complex Machines

1. F.A. Schaeffer, *Escape from Reason*, London: Inter-Varsity Press, 1968, p. 37.
2. C.S. Lewis, *English Literature in the Sixteenth Century, Excluding Drama*, Oxford: Clarendon Press, 1954, pp. 3–4.
3. A.R. Damasio, *Descartes' Error: Emotion, Reason, and the Human Brain*, New York: Putnam, 1994.
4. J. Monod, *Chance and Necessity: An Essay on the Natural Philosophy of Modern Biology*, 1st American edn, New York: Knopf, 1971, p. 9.

2. Brain Makes Mind

1. P. Broca, "Remarques sur le siège de la faculté du langage articulé, suivies d'une observation d'aphémie", *Bulletin de la Société Anatomique* 36 (1861): 330–57.
2. M.A. Preis, C. Schmidt-Samoa, P. Dechent, and B. Kroener-Herwig, "The Effects of Prior Pain Experience on Neural Correlates of Empathy for Pain: An fMRI Study", *Pain* 154 (2013): 411–18.
3. S. Ortigue, F. Bianchi-Demicheli, N. Patel, C. Frum, and J.W. Lewis, "Neuroimaging of Love: fMRI Meta-Analysis Evidence Toward New Perspectives in Sexual Medicine", *The Journal of Sexual Medicine* 7 (2010): 3541–52.
4. H.R. Heekeren, I. Wartenburger, H. Schmidt, H.P. Schwintowski, and A. Villringer, "An fMRI Study of Simple Ethical Decision-Making", *Neuroreport* 14 (2003): 1215–19.
5. J.D. Greene, R.B. Sommerville, L.E. Nystrom, J.M. Darley, and J.D. Cohen, "An fMRI Investigation of Emotional Engagement in Moral Judgment", *Science* 293 (2001): 2105–08.
6. M. Beauregard and V. Paquette, "Neural Correlates of a Mystical Experience in Carmelite Nuns", *Neuroscience Letters* 405 (2006): 186–90.
7. A.B. Newberg, N.A. Wintering, D. Morgan, and W.R. Waldman, "The Measurement of Regional Cerebral Blood Flow During Glossolalia: A Preliminary SPECT Study", *Psychiatry Research* 148 (2006): 67–71.

8. E. Halgren and K. Marinkovic, "Neurophysiological Networks Integrating Human Emotions", in M. Gazzaniga (ed.), *The Cognitive Neurosciences*, Cambridge, MA: MIT Press, 1995, pp. 1137–51.

9. W. Penfield and T. Rasmussen, *The Cerebral Cortex of Man*, New York: Macmillan, 1950.

10. W. Penfield, "The Twenty-Ninth Maudsley Lecture: The Role of the Temporal Cortex in Certain Psychical Phenomena", *Journal of Mental Science* 101 (1955): 451–65.

11. O. Sacks, *The Man Who Mistook His Wife for a Hat and Other Clinical Tales*, New York: Summit Books, 1985.

12. V.D. Costa, P.J. Lang, D. Sabatinelli, F. Versace, and M.M. Bradley, "Emotional Imagery: Assessing Pleasure and Arousal in the Brain's Reward Circuitry", *Human Brain Mapping* 31 (2010): 1446–57.

13. I. Boileau, J.M. Assaad, R.O. Pihl, et al., "Alcohol Promotes Dopamine Release in the Human Nucleus Accumbens", *Synapse* 49 (2003): 226–31.

14. N.M. Fisk, R. Gitau, J.M. Teixeira, X. Giannakoulopoulos, A.D. Cameron, and V.A. Glover, "Effect of Direct Fetal Opioid Analgesia on Fetal Hormonal and Hemodynamic Stress Response to Intrauterine Needling", *Anesthesiology* 95 (2001): 828–35.

15. S. Kouider, C. Stahlhut, S.V. Gelskov, et al., "A Neural Marker of Perceptual Consciousness in Infants", *Science* 340 (2013): 376–80.

16. J.A. Reggia, "The Rise of Machine Consciousness: Studying Consciousness with Computational Models", *Neural Networks* 44C (2013): 112–31.

17. K.R. Popper and J.C. Eccles, *The Self and Its Brain*, New York: Springer International, 1977.

18. R.W. Sperry, E. Zaidel, and D. Zaidel, "Self Recognition and Social Awareness in the Deconnected Minor Hemisphere", *Neuropsychologia* 17 (1979): 153–66.

19. F. Crick and C. Koch, "Consciousness and Neuroscience", *Cerebral Cortex* 8 (1998): 97–107; C. Koch and F. Mormann, "The Neurobiology of Consciousness", in A.H. Zewail (ed.), *Physical Biology: From Atoms to Medicine*, London and Hackensack, NJ: Imperial College Press, 2008, pp. 367–99.

3. How the Brain Works

1. J.A. Hirsch and L.M. Martinez, "Circuits That Build Visual Cortical Receptive Fields", *Trends in Neurosciences* 29 (2006): 30–39.

2. J.C. Meadows, "Disturbed Perception of Colours Associated with Localized Cerebral Lesions", *Brain: A Journal of Neurology* 97 (1974): 615–32.

3. A.J. Parker and W.T. Newsome, "Sense and the Single Neuron: Probing the Physiology of Perception", *Annual Review of Neuroscience* 21 (1998): 227–77.

4. J.J. DiCarlo, D. Zoccolan, and N.C. Rust, "How Does the Brain Solve Visual Object Recognition?" *Neuron* 73 (2012): 415–34.

5. C. Carter, *Science and the Near Death Experience: How Consciousness Survives Death*, Rochester: Inner Traditions, 2010.

6. D.A. Jirenhed, F. Bengtsson, and G. Hesslow, "Acquisition, Extinction, and Reacquisition of a Cerebellar Cortical Memory Trace", *The Journal of Neuroscience* 27 (2007): 2493–502.

7. C.N. Smith and L.R. Squire, "Medial Temporal Lobe Activity During Retrieval of Semantic Memory is Related to the Age of the Memory", *The Journal of Neuroscience* 29 (2009): 930–38.

8. J. O'Keefe and J. Dostrovsky, "The Hippocampus As a Spatial Map: Preliminary Evidence from Unit Activity in the Freely-Moving Rat", *Brain Research* 34 (1971): 171–75.

9. E.I. Moser, E. Kropff, and M.B. Moser, "Place Cells, Grid Cells, and the Brain's Spatial Representation System", *Annual Review of Neuroscience* 31 (2008): 69–89.
10. N.A. Suthana, A.D. Ekstrom, S. Moshirvaziri, B. Knowlton, and S.Y. Bookheimer, "Human Hippocampal CA1 Involvement during Allocentric Encoding of Spatial Information", *The Journal of Neuroscience* 29 (2009): 10512–19.
11. R.Q. Quiroga, "Concept Cells: The Building Blocks of Declarative Memory Functions", *Nature Reviews Neuroscience* 13 (2012): 587–97.
12. T. Lomo, "The Discovery of Long-Term Potentiation", *Philosophical Transactions of the Royal Society. B: Biological Sciences* 358 (2003): 617–20.
13. S. Ramón y Cajal, "The Croonian Lecture: La fine structure des centres nerveux", *Proceedings of the Royal Society of London* 55 (1894): 444–68.
14. D.O. Hebb, *The Organization of Behavior*, New York: Wiley and Sons, 1949.
15. F. Rosenblatt, "The Perceptron: A Probabilistic Model for Information Storage and Organization in the Brain", *Psychological Review* 65 (1958): 386–408.
16. D. Marr, "A Theory of Cerebellar Cortex", *Journal of Physiology (London)* 202 (1969): 437–70; J.S. Albus, "A Theory of Cerebellar Function", *Mathematical Biosciences* 10 (1971): 25–61.
17. D. Marr, "Simple Memory: A Theory for Archicortex", *Philosophical Transactions of the Royal Society of London. Series B, Biological Sciences* 262 (1971): 23–81; K. Kaneki, O. Araki, and M. Tsukada, "Dual Synaptic Plasticity in the Hippocampus: Hebbian and Spatiotemporal Learning Dynamics", *Cognitive Neurodynamics* 3 (2009): 153–63.
18. D. Marr, "A Theory for Cerebral Neocortex", *Philosophical Transactions of the Royal Society. B: Biological Sciences* 176 (1970): 161–234.
19. J. Lisman, R. Yasuda, and S. Raghavachari, "Mechanisms of CaMKII Action in Long-Term Potentiation", *Nature Reviews Neuroscience* 13 (2012): 169–82.
20. R.G. Morris, E. Anderson, G.S. Lynch, and M. Baudry, "Selective Impairment of Learning and Blockade of Long-Term Potentiation by an N-methyl-D-aspartate Receptor Antagonist, AP5", *Nature* 319 (1986): 774–76.
21. J.Z. Tsien, P.T. Huerta, and S. Tonegawa, "The Essential Role of Hippocampal CA1 NMDA Receptor-Dependent Synaptic Plasticity in Spatial Memory", *Cell* 87 (1996): 1327–38.
22. X. Liu, S. Ramirez, P.T. Pang, et al., "Optogenetic Stimulation of a Hippocampal Engram Activates Fear Memory Recall", *Nature* 484 (2012): 381–85.

4. Nothing but a Pack of Neurons?

1. This chapter includes (or adapts) some material, written by the present author, taken from the chapter "Humanity and Humanness" in R.J. Berry (ed.), *The Lion Handbook of Science and Christianity*, Oxford: Lion Hudson, 2012.
2. S. Pinker, *The Blank Slate: The Modern Denial of Human Nature*, New York: Viking, 2002, p. 69.
3. F. Crick, *The Astonishing Hypothesis: The Scientific Search for the Soul*, New York: Scribner, 1994, p. 3.
4. K.R. Popper, "Scientific Reductionism and the Essential Incompleteness of All Science", in F.J. Ayala and T. Dobzhansky (eds.), *Studies in the Philosophy of Biology: Reduction and Related Problems*, London: Macmillan, 1974, pp. 259–84.
5. N.C. Murphy and W.S. Brown, *Did My Neurons Make Me Do It? Philosophical and Neurobiological Perspectives on Moral Responsibility and Free Will*, Oxford and New York: Oxford University Press, 2007.
6. F.J. Ayala, "Introduction", in F.J. Ayala and T. Dobzhansky (eds.), *Studies in the Philosophy of Biology: Reduction and Related Problems*, London: Macmillan, 1974, pp. vii–xvi.

7. Murphy and Brown, *Did My Neurons Make Me Do it?*
8. Ayala, "Introduction", p. viii.
9. P.W. Anderson, "More is Different", *Science* 177 (1972): 393–6 (pp. 393, 395).

5. Are We Robots Without Free Will?

1. R. Doyle, *Free Will: The Scandal in Philosophy*, Cambridge, MA: I-Phi Press, 2011.
2. T. Honderich, *A Theory of Determinism: The Mind, Neuroscience, and Life-Hopes*, Oxford: Clarendon Press, 1988.
3. A. Einstein quoted in M. Planck, *Where Is Science Going?* New York: W.W. Norton & Co., 1932, p. 201.
4. The Free Dictionary, http://www.thefreedictionary.com/free+will; italics are mine.
5. P.L. Harriman, *Handbook of Psychological Terms*, Paterson, NJ: Littlefield, Adams, 1963.
6. More precisely, Honderich accepts determinism but thinks he has strong arguments against both compatibilism and incompatibilism! Pereboom is undecided about determinism, but rejects free will anyway because he thinks it is incompatible with both determinism and indeterminism.
7. For simplicity, I here focus on compatibilist arguments related to the definition of free will. Other lines of argument exist, however, including Donald MacKay's argument that even a brain that is physically determinate must be "logically indeterminate" when it makes a choice (D.M. MacKay, *Freedom of Action in a Mechanistic Universe*, Cambridge: Cambridge University Press, 1967).
8. Some compatibilists include also internal constraints if they are compulsive, as in obsessive–compulsive disorder, but for simplicity I limit the present discussion to normal situations.
9. D. Hume, *An Enquiry Concerning Human Understanding*, ed. L.A. Selby-Bigge, Oxford: Clarendon Press, 1963 (1748), pp. 97–98.
10. M.S. Gazzaniga, *Who's in Charge? Free Will and the Science of the Brain*, New York: HarperCollins, 2011.
11. P. van Inwagen, *An Essay on Free Will*, Oxford and New York: Clarendon Press, 1983, p. 16.
12. R. Kane, *The Oxford Handbook of Free Will*, 2nd edn, Oxford and New York: Oxford University Press, 2011.
13. R. Swinburne, *Mind, Brain, and Free Will*, Oxford: Oxford University Press, 2013.
14. R. Kane, *A Contemporary Introduction to Free Will*, New York and Oxford: Oxford University Press, 2005.
15. R. Kane, *The Significance of Free Will*, New York and Oxford: Oxford University Press, 1996.
16. P.G.H. Clarke, "Determinism, Brain Function and Free Will", *Science & Christian Belief* 22 (2010): 133–49.
17. P.G.H. Clarke, "The Limits of Brain Determinacy", *Proceedings of the Royal Society. B: Biological Sciences* 279 (2012): 1665–74.
18. Clarke, "The Limits of Brain Determinacy".
19. M. Brownnutt, "Response to Peter Clarke on 'Determinism, Brain Function and Free Will'", *Science & Christian Belief* 24 (2012): 81–86.
20. E.R. Lewis and R.J. MacGregor, "On Indeterminism, Chaos, and Small Number Particle Systems in the Brain", *Journal of Integrative Neuroscience* 5 (2006): 223–47.
21. R.F. Baumeister, A.W. Crescioni, and J.L. Alquist, "Free Will as Advanced Action Control for Human Social Life and Culture", *Neuroethics* (Netherlands) 4 (2011): 1–11.
22. S. Harris, *Free Will*, New York: Free Press, 2012.

23. Harris, *Free Will*, p. 5.
24. Harris, *Free Will*, p. 6.
25. Harris, *Free Will*, p. 16.
26. R. Blackford (2012) book review http://www.abc.net.au/religion/ articles/2012/04/26/3489758.htm (accessed 3 March 2015).
27. A. Plantinga (2013) book review http://www.booksandculture.com/articles/2013/ janfeb/bait-and-switch.html?paging=off (accessed 3 March 2015).

6. Electrophysiology-Based Attempts to Refute the Efficacy of Conscious Will

1. Much of the material in this chapter is derived from the author's recent article "Neuroscientific and Psychological Attacks on the Efficacy of Conscious Will" (*Science & Christian Belief* 26 (2014): 5–24) and from his "The Libet Experiment and its Implications for Conscious Will" (Faraday Paper No. 17 (2013), available from https://www.faraday.st-edmunds.cam.ac.uk/Papers.php).
2. B. Libet, C.A. Gleason, E.W. Wright, and D.K. Pearl, "Time of Conscious Intention to Act in Relation to Onset of Cerebral Activity (Readiness-Potential). The Unconscious Initiation of a Freely Voluntary Act", *Brain: A Journal of Neurology* 106 (Pt 3) (1983): 623–42.
3. W. Sinnott-Armstrong and L. Nadel, *Conscious Will and Responsibility*, Oxford and New York: Oxford University Press, 2011.
4. I. Fried, A. Katz, G. McCarthy, et al., "Functional Organization of Human Supplementary Motor Cortex Studied by Electrical Stimulation", *Journal of Neuroscience* 11 (1991): 3656–66.
5. M. Desmurget, K.T. Reilly, N. Richard, A. Szathmari, C. Mottolese, and A. Sirigu, "Movement Intention After Parietal Cortex Stimulation in Humans", *Science* 324 (2009): 811–13.
6. H.H. Kornhuber and L. Deecke, "Hirnpotentialänderungen bei Willkürbewegungen und passiven Bewegungen des Menschen: Bereitschaftspotential und reafferente Potentiale", *Pflugers Archiv fur die gesamte Physiologie des Menschen und der Tiere* 284 (1965): 1–17.
7. I. Fried, R. Mukamel, and G. Kreiman, "Internally Generated Preactivation of Single Neurons in Human Medial Frontal Cortex Predicts Volition", *Neuron* 69 (2011): 548–62.
8. A.R. Mele, *Effective Intentions: The Power of Conscious Will*, Oxford and New York: Oxford University Press, 2009.
9. There is a suitable clock at http://www.informationphilosopher.com/freedom/ libet_experiments.html.
10. A.N. Danquah, M.J. Farrell, and D.J. O'Boyle, "Biases in the Subjective Timing of Perceptual Events: Libet et al. (1983) Revisited", *Consciousness and Cognition* 17 (2008): 616–27.
11. D.C. Dennett and M. Kinsbourne, "Time and the Observer: The Where and When of Consciousness in the Brain", *Behavioral and Brain Sciences* 15 (1992): 183–201.
12. H.C. Lau, R.D. Rogers, and R.E. Passingham, "Manipulating the Experienced Onset of Intention After Action Execution", *Journal of Cognitive Neuroscience* 19 (2007): 81–90.
13. M. Matsuhashi and M. Hallett, "The Timing of the Conscious Intention to Move", *The European Journal of Neuroscience* 28 (2008): 2344–51.
14. C.S. Soon, M. Brass, H.J. Heinze, and J.D. Haynes, "Unconscious Determinants of Free Decisions in the Human Brain", *Nature Neuroscience* 11 (2008): 543–45.
15. M. Lages and K. Jaworska, "How Predictable are 'Spontaneous Decisions' and 'Hidden Intentions'? Comparing Classification Results Based on Previous

Responses with Multivariate Pattern Analysis of fMRI BOLD Signals", *Frontiers in Psychology* 3 (2012): 56.

16. P.E. Roland, B. Larsen, N.A. Lassen, and E. Skinhoj, "Supplementary Motor Area and Other Cortical Areas in Organization of Voluntary Movements in Man", *Journal of Neurophysiology* 43 (1980): 118–36.

17. P. Haggard and M. Eimer, "On the Relation Between Brain Potentials and the Awareness of Voluntary Movements", *Experimental Brain Research* 126 (1999): 128–33.

18. A. Schlegel, P. Alexander, W. Sinnott-Armstrong, A. Roskies, P.U. Tse, and T. Wheatley, "Barking Up the Wrong Free: Readiness Potentials Reflect Processes Independent of Conscious Will", *Experimental Brain Research* 229 (2013): 329–35.

19. C.S. Herrmann, M. Pauen, B.K. Min, N.A. Busch, and J.W. Rieger, "Analysis of a Choice-Reaction Task Yields a New Interpretation of Libet's Experiments", *International Journal of Psychophysiology* 67 (2008): 151–57.

20. J. Trevena and J. Miller, "Brain Preparation Before a Voluntary Action: Evidence Against Unconscious Movement Initiation", *Consciousness and Cognition* 19 (2010): 447–56.

21. A. Schurger, J.D. Sitt, and S. Dehaene, "An Accumulator Model for Spontaneous Neural Activity Prior to Self-Initiated Movement", *Proceedings of the National Academy of Sciences of the United States of America* 109 (2012): E2904–13.

22. B. Libet, *Mind Time: The Temporal Factor in Consciousness*, Cambridge, MA: Harvard University Press, 2004.

23. P. Haggard, "Human Volition: Towards a Neuroscience of Will", *Nature Reviews Neuroscience* 9 (2008): 934–46.

7. Psychology-Based Attempts to Refute the Efficacy of Conscious Will

1. Parts of this chapter are taken from, or based on, the author's article "Neuroscientific and Psychological Attacks on the Efficacy of Conscious Will", *Science & Christian Belief* 26 (2014): 5–24.

2. K.R. Popper and J.C. Eccles, *The Self and Its Brain*, New York: Springer International, 1977.

3. R. Sperry, "Consciousness, Personal Identity and the Divided Brain", *Neuropsychologia* 22 (1984): 661–73.

4. D.G. Myers, *Intuition: Its Powers and Perils*, New Haven, CT: Yale University Press, 2002.

5. B.J. Baars, "The Conscious Access Hypothesis: Origins and Recent Evidence", *Trends in Cognitive Sciences* 6 (2002): 47–52.

6. B.J. Baars, S. Franklin, T.Z. Ramsoy, "Global Workspace Dynamics: Cortical 'Binding and Propagation' Enables Conscious Contents", *Frontiers in Psychology* 4 (2013): 200.

7. D. Kahneman, *Thinking, Fast and Slow*, New York: Farrar, Straus and Giroux, 2011.

8. R.E. Nisbett and T.D. Wilson, "Telling More Than We Can Know: Verbal Reports on Mental Processes", *Psychological Review* 84 (1977): 231–59.

9. R. Custers and H. Aarts, "The Unconscious Will: How the Pursuit of Goals Operates Outside of Conscious Awareness", *Science* 329 (2010): 47–50.

10. B.R. Newell and D.R. Shanks, "Unconscious Influences on Decision Making: A Critical Review", *Behavioral and Brain Sciences* 37 (2014): 1–19 (p. 19).

11. D.M. Wegner, *The Illusion of Conscious Will*, Cambridge, MA: MIT Press, 2002, p. 336.

12. A.R. Mele, *Effective Intentions: The Power of Conscious Will*, Oxford and New York: Oxford University Press, 2009.

13. S. Pockett, W.P. Banks, and S. Gallagher, *Does Consciousness Cause Behavior?* 1st MIT Press pbk edn, Cambridge, MA: MIT Press, 2009.
14. G.D. Caruso, *Free Will and Consciousness: A Determinist Account of the Illusion of Free Will*, Lanham, MD: Lexington Books, 2012, pp 210–11.
15. Wegner, *The Illusion of Conscious Will*, pp. 15, 327.
16. Wegner, *The Illusion of Conscious Will*, pp. 171–84.
17. E.F. Kelly, "[Review of] The Illusion of Conscious Will by D. Wegner", *Journal of Scientific Exploration* 17 (2003): 166–71.
18. M. Faraday, "Experimental Investigation of Table Turning", *Athenaeum* (July 1853): 801–03.

8. Ethics and the Brain

1. L. Young and J. Dungan, "Where in the Brain Is Morality? Everywhere and Maybe Nowhere", *Social Neuroscience* 7 (2012): 1–10.
2. J.D. Greene and J.M. Paxton, "Patterns of Neural Activity Associated with Honest and Dishonest Moral Decisions", *Proceedings of the National Academy of Sciences of the United States of America* 106 (2009): 12506–11.
3. O. Feldmanhall, D. Mobbs, and T. Dalgleish, "Deconstructing the Brain's Moral Network: Dissociable Functionality Between the Temporoparietal Junction and Ventro-Medial Prefrontal Cortex", *Social Cognitive and Affective Neuroscience* 9 (2014): 297–306.
4. J.M. Burns and R.H. Swerdlow, "Right Orbitofrontal Tumor with Pedophilia Symptom and Constructional Apraxia Sign", *Archives of Neurology* 60 (2003): 437–40.
5. S. Harris, *The Moral Landscape: How Science Can Determine Human Values*, New York: Free Press, 2010.
6. Harris, *The Moral Landscape*, p. 1.

9. Bio-Environmental Determinism and Criminal Liability

1. A. Raine, *The Anatomy of Violence: The Biological Roots of Crime*, London: Allen Lane, 2013.
2. Y. Yang and A. Raine, "Prefrontal Structural and Functional Brain Imaging Findings in Antisocial, Violent, and Psychopathic Individuals: A Meta-Analysis", *Psychiatry Research* 174 (2009): 81–88.
3. R. de Oliveira-Souza, R.D. Hare, I.E. Bramati, et al., "Psychopathy as a Disorder of the Moral Brain: Fronto-Temporo-Limbic Grey Matter Reductions Demonstrated by Voxel-Based Morphometry", *NeuroImage* 40 (2008): 1202–13.
4. P.F. Goyer, P.J. Andreason, W.E. Semple, et al., "Positron-Emission Tomography and Personality Disorders", *Neuropsychopharmacology* 10 (1994): 21–28.
5. A. Raine, J.R. Meloy, S. Bihrle, J. Stoddard, L. LaCasse, and M.S. Buchsbaum, "Reduced Prefrontal and Increased Subcortical Brain Functioning Assessed Using Positron Emission Tomography in Predatory and Affective Murderers", *Behavioral Sciences & the Law* 16 (1998): 319–32.
6. Brief of the American Medical Association et al. as Amici Curiae in Support of Respondent, at 4-5, Roper v. Simmons, 543 U.S. 551 (2005) (No. 03-633), 2004 WL 1633549.
7. C. Lombroso, *L'uomo delinquente studiato in rapporto alla antropologia, alla medicina legale, ed alle discipline carcerarie [The criminal man studied in relationship to anthropology, forensic medicine and prison doctrines]*, Milan: Ulrico Hoepli, 1876.
8. F. Forzano, P. Borry, A. Cambon-Thomsen, et al., "Italian Appeal Court: A Genetic

Predisposition to Commit Murder?", *European Journal of Human Genetics* 18 (2010): 519–21.

9. M.L. Baum, "The Monoamine Oxidase A (MAOA) Genetic Predisposition to Impulsive Violence: Is It Relevant to Criminal Trials?", *Neuroethics* (Netherlands) 6 (2013): 287–306.

10. J. Greene and J. Cohen, "For the Law, Neuroscience Changes Nothing and Everything", *Philosophical Transactions of the Royal Society. B: Biological Sciences* 359 (2004): 1775–85.

11. Greene and Cohen, "For the Law", p. 1780; italics are mine.

12. P.G.H. Clarke, "The Limits of Brain Determinacy", *Proceedings of the Royal Society. B: Biological Sciences* 279 (2012): 1665–74.

13. J. Bentham, *A Fragment on Government*, London, 1776, Preface. Available online at http://www.constitution.org/jb/frag_gov.htm.

14. J.S. Mill, *Utilitarianism*, London: Parker, Son, and Bourn, 1863, p. 24.

15. I. Kant, *Metaphysical Elements of Justice: Part I of The Metaphysics of Morals*, translated by J. Ladd, Indianapolis: Hackett, 1999 (1797), §49.E.I (p. 138).

16. C.S. Lewis, *The Problem of Pain*, London: Fontana, 1957, pp. 81–82.

17. S. Harris, *Free Will*, New York: Free Press, 2012, p. 57.

18. T. Grimsrud and H. Zehr, "Rethinking God, Justice and Treatment of Offenders", *Journal of Offender Rehabilitation* 35 (2002): 253–79.

10. Does Neuroscience Debunk the Soul?

1. F. Crick, *The Astonishing Hypothesis: The Scientific Search for the Soul*, New York: Scribner, 1994; O. Flanagan, *The Problem of the Soul: Two Visions of Mind and How to Reconcile Them*, New York: Basic Books, 2002.

2. C.G. Gross, "Aristotle on the Brain", *The Neuroscientist* 1 (1995): 245–50.

3. There were some differences. Aquinas extended the notion of "form" to immaterial beings such as God or angels and was not so strictly monistic as Aristotle. Some scholars even refer to Aquinas's view as "substance dualism", but everyone agrees it is not interactionist dualism. He maintained that a disembodied soul was possible (after death but before the resurrection of the body), but that this would not be a human being. For our present neurobiological interests, we are not concerned with angels but with human beings in this present life on earth, and for this context it is a fair approximation to consider Aquinas as a monist.

4. S. Gaukroger, *Descartes: An Intellectual Biography*, New York: Oxford University Press, 1995.

5. L. Shapiro, *The Correspondence Between Princess Elisabeth of Bohemia and Rene Descartes*, Chicago: University of Chicago Press, 2007, p. 68.

6. B.A.W. Russell, *What is the Soul?*, Raleigh, NC: Hayes Barton Press, 2006 (1928), p. 2.

7. D. MacDougall, "Hypothesis Concerning Soul Substance Together with Experimental Evidence of the Existence of Such Substance", *Journal of the American Society for Psychical Research* 1 (1907): 237–44.

8. L.E. Hollander, "Unexplained Weight Gain Transients at the Moment of Death", *Journal of Scientific Exploration* 15 (2001): 495–500.

9. J. Turl, "Substance Dualism or Body-Soul Duality?", *Science & Christian Belief* 22 (2010): 57–80 (78).

10. J.B. Green, *Body, Soul and Human Life: The Nature of Humanity in the Bible*, Carlisle: Paternoster, 2008.

11. A. Farrer, *The Freedom of the Will*, London: A. & C. Black, 1958, p. 87.

12. J.W. Cooper, *Body, Soul, and Life Everlasting: Biblical Anthropology and the Monism–Dualism Debate*, Grand Rapids, MI: Eerdmans, 2000.

13. W. Hasker, *The Emergent Self*, Ithaca, NY: Cornell University Press, 1999.

14. M.A. Jeeves and W.S. Brown, *Neuroscience, Psychology, and Religion*, West Conshohocken, PA: Templeton Foundation Press, 2009.

15. J.P. Moreland and W.L. Craig, *Philosophical Foundations for a Christian Worldview*, Downers Grove, IL: InterVarsity Press, 2003; S. Goetz and C. Taliaferro, *A Brief History of the Soul*, Chichester: Wiley-Blackwell, 2011.

11. Near-Death Experiences and Deathbed Visions

1. D. Mobbs and C. Watt, "There Is Nothing Paranormal About Near-Death Experiences: How Neuroscience Can Explain Seeing Bright Lights, Meeting the Dead, or Being Convinced You Are One of Them", *Trends in Cognitive Sciences* 15 (2011): 447–49.

2. E. Alexander, *Proof of Heaven: A Neurosurgeon's Journey into the Afterlife*, New York, London, and Delhi: Simon & Schuster, 2012.

3. M. Nahm, B. Greyson, E.W. Kelly, and E. Haraldsson, "Terminal Lucidity: A Review and a Case Collection", *Archives of Gerontology and Geriatrics* 55 (2012): 138–42.

4. M.B. Sabom, *Recollections of Death: A Medical Investigation*, New York: Harper and Row, 1982.

5. R. Moody, *Life After Life: The Investigation of a Phenomenon – Survival of Bodily Death*, New York: Bantam, 1975.

6. N.A. Bush, "Distressing Western Near-Death Experiences: Finding a Way through the Abyss", in J.M. Holden, B. Greyson, and D. James (eds.), *The Handbook of Near-Death Experiences*, Santa Barbara, CA: Praeger, 2009, pp. 63–86.

7. A. Kellehear, "Census of Non-Western Near-Death Experiences to 2005: Observations and Critical Reflections", in J.M. Holden, B. Greyson, and D. James (eds.), *The Handbook of Near-Death Experiences*, Santa Barbara, CA: Praeger, 2009, pp. 135–58.

8. T.T. Suwannathat cited by T. Murphy, "Near-Death Experiences in Thailand", *Journal of Near Death Studies* 19 (2001): 161–78 (167).

9. Mobbs and Watt, "There is Nothing Paranormal about Near-Death Experiences".

10. O. Blanke and S. Dieguez, "Leaving Body and Life Behind: Out-of-Body and Near-Death Experience", in S. Laureys and G. Tononi (eds.), *The Neurology of Consciousness*, London: Academic Press, 2009, pp. 303–25.

11. E. Facco and C. Agrillo, "Near-Death Experiences Between Science and Prejudice", *Frontiers in Human Neuroscience* 6 (2012): 209.

12. J.A. Cheyne and T.A. Girard, "The Body Unbound: Vestibular-Motor Hallucinations and Out-of-Body Experiences", *Cortex* 45 (2009): 201–15.

13. O. Blanke, S. Ortigue, T. Landis, and M. Seeck, "Stimulating Illusory Own-Body Perceptions", *Nature* 419 (2002): 269–70.

14. A. Guterstam and H.H. Ehrsson, "Disowning One's Seen Real Body During an Out-of-Body Illusion", *Consciousness and Cognition* 21 (2012): 1037–42.

15. R. Strassman, *DMT: The Spirit Molecule: A Doctor's Revolutionary Research into the Biology of Near-Death and Mystical Experiences*, South Paris, ME: Park Street Press, 2001.

16. O.W. Sacks, *Hallucinations*, New York: Alfred A. Knopf, 2012, pp. 101–02.

17. P. van Lommel, *Consciousness Beyond Life: The Science of the Near-Death Experience*, New York: HarperOne, 2010.

18. M. Thonnard, V. Charland-Verville, S. Bredart, et al., "Characteristics of Near-Death Experiences Memories as Compared to Real and Imagined Events Memories", *PLOS ONE* 8 (2013): e57620.

19. M. Sabom, *Light and Death: One Doctor's Fascinating Account of Near-Death Experiences*, Grand Rapids, MI: Zondervan, 1998.

20. G.M. Woerlee, *Mortal Minds: The Biology of Near-Death Experiences*, Amherst, NY: Prometheus Books, 2005.
21. Van Lommel, *Consciousness Beyond Life*, pp. 171–78.
22. J.M. Holden, "Veridical Perception in Near-Death Experiences", in J.M. Holden, B. Greyson, and D. James (eds.), *The Handbook of Near-Death Experiences*, Santa Barbara, CA: Praeger, 2009, pp. 185–211.
23. P. van Lommel, "Near-Death Experiences: The Experience of the Self as Real and Not as an Illusion", *Annals of the New York Academy of Sciences* 1234 (2011): 19–28.
24. Sabom, *Recollections of Death*, p. 83.
25. Van Lommel, *Consciousness Beyond Life*, p. 177.
26. R.A. Moody and P. Perry, *Glimpses of Eternity: Sharing a Loved One's Passage from This Life to the Next*, New York: Guideposts, 2010.
27. K. Ring and S. Cooper, *Mindsight: Near-Death and Out-of-Body Experiences in the Blind*, 2nd edn, Bloomington, IN: iUniverse, 2008.
28. Van Lommel, *Consciousness Beyond Life*, Chapter 2.
29. Van Lommel, *Consciousness Beyond Life*, p. 33.
30. C. Wills-Brandon, *One Last Hug Before I Go: The Mystery and Meaning of Deathbed Visions*, Deerfield Beach, FL: HCI Books, 2000.
31. J. Lerma, *Into the Light: Real Life Stories About Angelic Visits, Visions of the Afterlife, and Other Pre-Death Experiences*, Franklin Lakes, NJ: Career Press, 2007.
32. C. Carter, *Science and the Near Death Experience: How Consciousness Survives Death*, Rochester, VT: Inner Traditions, 2010.
33. W. Barrett, *Death Bed Visions*, London: Methuen, 1926.
34. K. Osis and E. Haraldsson, *At the Hour of Death*, New York: Avon Books, 1977.
35. K. Osis and E. Haraldsson, "Deathbed Observations by Physicians and Nurses: Cross-Cultural Survey", *Journal of the American Society for Psychical Research* 71 (1977): 237–59.
36. S.P. Muthumana, M. Kumari, A. Kellehear, S. Kumar, and F. Moosa, "Deathbed Visions from India: A Study of Family Observations in Northern Kerala", *Omega* 62 (2010): 97–109.
37. Moody and Perry, *Glimpses of Eternity*, pp. 160–61.
38. H. Storm, *My Descent into Death: A Second Chance at Life*, New York: Doubleday, 2005.
39. A. Fenimore, *Beyond the Darkness: My Near-Death Journey to the Edge of Hell*, New York: Bantam Books, 1995.
40. K. Ring, *Life at Death: A Scientific Investigation of the Near-Death Experience*, New York: Coward, McCann & Geoghegan, 1980.
41. C. Sutherland, *Transformed by the Light: Life After Near-Death Experiences*, Sydney: Bantam Books, 1992.

12. God in the Brain?

1. P. McNamara, *The Neuroscience of Religious Experience*, Cambridge and New York: Cambridge University Press, 2009; M.A. Jeeves and W.S. Brown, *Neuroscience, Psychology, and Religion*, West Conshohocken, PA: Templeton Foundation Press, 2009.
2. A. Newberg, A. Alavi, M. Baime, M. Pourdehnad, J. Santanna, and E. d'Aquili, "The Measurement of Regional Cerebral Blood Flow During the Complex Cognitive Task of Meditation: A Preliminary SPECT Study", *Psychiatry Research* 106 (2001): 113–22.
3. A.B. Newberg, N.A. Wintering, D. Morgan, and M.R. Waldman, "The Measurement of Regional Cerebral Blood Flow During Glossolalia: A Preliminary SPECT Study", *Psychiatry Research: Neuroimaging* 148 (2006): 67–71.

4. N.P. Azari, J. Nickel, G. Wunderlich, et al., "Neural Correlates of Religious Experience", *European Journal of Neuroscience* 13 (2001): 1649–52.
5. U. Schjoedt, H. Stodkilde-Jorgensen, A.W. Geertz, and A. Roepstorff, "Highly Religious Participants Recruit Areas of Social Cognition in Personal Prayer", *Social Cognitive and Affective Neuroscience* 4 (2009): 199–207.
6. S. Harris, J.T. Kaplan, A. Curiel, S.Y. Bookheimer, M. Iacoboni, and M.S. Cohen, "The Neural Correlates of Religious and Nonreligious Belief", *PLOS ONE* 4 (2009): e0007272.
7. A.A. Fingelkurts and A.A. Fingelkurts, "Is Our Brain Hardwired to Produce God, or Is Our Brain Hardwired to Perceive God? A Systematic Review on the Role of the Brain in Mediating Religious Experience", *Cognitive Processing* 10 (2009): 293–326.
8. V.S. Ramachandran and S. Blakeslee, *Phantoms in the Brain: Probing the Mysteries of the Human Mind*, New York: William Morrow, 1998.
9. M. Morse and P. Perry, *Where God Lives: The Science of the Paranormal and How Our Brains Are Linked to the Universe*, New York: Cliff Street Books, 2000.
10. J.R. Hughes, "Did All Those Famous People Really Have Epilepsy?", *Epilepsy & Behavior* 6 (2005): 115–39.
11. H. Naito and N. Matsui, "Temporal Lobe Epilepsy with Ictal Ecstatic State and Interictal Behavior of Hypergraphia", *The Journal of Nervous and Mental Disease* 176 (1988): 123–24.
12. J.L. Saver and J. Rabin, "The Neural Substrates of Religious Experience", *The Journal of Neuropsychiatry and Clinical Neurosciences* 9 (1997): 498–510.
13. C. Aaen-Stockdale, "Neuroscience for the Soul", *Psychologist* 25 (2012): 520–23.
14. M.A. Persinger, *Neuropsychological Bases of God Beliefs*, New York: Praeger, 1987.
15. M.A. Persinger and F. Healey, "Experimental Facilitation of the Sensed Presence: Possible Intercalation Between the Hemispheres Induced by Complex Magnetic Fields", *The Journal of Nervous and Mental Disease* 190 (2002): 533–41.
16. P. Granqvist, M. Fredrikson, P. Unge, et al., "Sensed Presence and Mystical Experiences Are Predicted by Suggestibility, Not by the Application of Transcranial Weak Complex Magnetic Fields", *Neuroscience Letters* 379 (2005): 1–6.
17. M.H. Gendle and M.G. McGrath, "Can the 8-Coil Shakti Alter Subjective Emotional Experience? A Randomized, Placebo-Controlled Study", *Perceptual and Motor Skills* 114 (2012): 217–35.
18. V.S. Ramachandran, *The Tell-Tale Brain: A Neuroscientist's Quest for What Makes Us Human*, New York: W.W. Norton & Co., 2011, p. 323, n. 16.
19. M.A. Persinger, "Geophysical Variables and Behavior: 71. Differential Contribution of Geomagnetic Activity to Paranormal Experiences Concerning Death and Crisis: An Alternative to the ESP Hypothesis", *Perceptual and Motor Skills* 76 (1993): 555–62.
20. R. Schnabel, M. Beblo, and T.W. May, "Is Geomagnetic Activity a Risk Factor for Sudden Unexplained Death in Epilepsies?", *Neurology* 54 (2000): 903–08.
21. The earth's magnetic field ranges from 25 to 65 microtesla, but its changes are much smaller, about 25 nanotesla over a day, and only about 1 nanotesla over a few seconds. (A nanotesla is one thousandth of a microtesla.)
22. M. Alper, *The "God" Part of the Brain*, New York: Rogue Press, 2001.
23. Alper, *The "God" Part of the Brain*, p. 114.
24. M. Bradshaw and C.G. Ellison, "Do Genetic Factors Influence Religious Life? Findings from a Behavior Genetic Analysis of Twin Siblings", *Journal for the Scientific Study of Religion* 47 (2008): 529–44.

13. Is Religion Just a Side Effect of Brain Evolution?

1. D. Hay and P.M. Socha, "Spirituality as a Natural Phenomenon: Bringing Biological and Psychological Perspectives Together", *Zygon* 40 (2005): 589–612.
2. C. Darwin, *On the Origin of Species by Means of Natural Selection*, London: J. Murray, 1859, p, 449.
3. A. Slater, G. Bremner, S.P. Johnson, P. Sherwood, R. Hayes, and E. Brown, "Newborn Infants' Preference for Attractive Faces: The Role of Internal and External Facial Features", *Infancy* 1 (2000): 265–74.
4. P.C. Quinn, D.J. Kelly, K. Lee, O. Pascalis and A.M. Slater, "Preference for Attractive Faces in Human Infants Extends Beyond Conspecifics", *Developmental Science* 11 (2008): 76–83.
5. T.N. Wiesel and D.H. Hubel, "Comparison of the Effects of Unilateral and Bilateral Eye Closure on Cortical Unit Responses in Kittens", *Journal of Neurophysiology* 28 (1965): 1029–40.
6. C. Blakemore and G.F. Cooper, "Development of the Brain Depends on the Visual Environment", *Nature* 228 (1970): 477–78.
7. T.N. Wiesel, "Postnatal Development of the Visual Cortex and the Influence of Environment", *Nature* 299 (1982): 583–91.
8. P.G.H. Clarke, V.S. Ramachandran, and D. Whitteridge, "The Development of the Binocular Depth Cells in the Secondary Visual Cortex of the Lamb", *Proceedings of the Royal Society. B: Biological Sciences* 204 (1979): 455–65.
9. J.L. Barrett, *Born Believers: The Science of Children's Religious Belief*, New York: Free Press, 2012, p. 25.
10. D.C. Dennett, *Breaking the Spell: Religion as a Natural Phenomenon*, New York: Viking, 2006.
11. The Anglican theologian John Stott used the term *Homo divinus* for this idea, which has since been developed by Professor R.J. Berry and others.
12. J. Malan, "The Possible Origin of Religion as a Conditioned Reflex", *American Mercury* 25 (1932): 314–17.
13. A.C. Hardy, *The Biology of God: A Scientist's Study of Man the Religious Animal*, London: J. Cape, 1975.
14. D.S. Wilson, *Darwin's Cathedral: Evolution, Religion, and the Nature of Society*, Chicago: University of Chicago Press, 2002.
15. S.J. Gould and R.C. Lewontin, "The Spandrels of San Marco and the Panglossian Paradigm: A Critique of the Adaptationist Programme", *Proceedings of the Royal Society. B: Biological Sciences* 205 (1979): 581–98.
16. M.J. Murray, "Four Arguments That the Cognitive Psychology of Religion Undermines the Justification of Religious Belief", in J. Bulbulia, R. Sosis, E. Harris, R. Genet, C. Genet, and K. Wyman (eds.), *The Evolution of Religion: Studies, Theories, and Critiques*, Santa Margarita, CA: Collins Foundation Press, 2008, pp. 393–98.
17. K.J. Clark and J. Barrett, "Reformed Epistemology and the Cognitive Science of Religion", *Faith and Philosophy* 27 (2010): 174–89.
18. J. Bering, *The God Instinct: The Psychology of Souls, Destiny, and the Meaning of Life*, London: Nicholas Brealey Publishing, 2011.

14. Brain, Mind, and Worldview

1. J.M. Musacchio, *Contradictions: Neuroscience and Religion*, New York: Springer, 2012; O. Flanagan, *The Problem of the Soul: Two Visions of Mind and How to Reconcile Them*, New York: Basic Books, 2002.
2. D.J. Chalmers, *The Conscious Mind: In Search of a Fundamental Theory*, New York: Oxford University Press, 1996.

Appendix 1. Quantitative Problems with Quantum Libertarianism and Quantum Dualism

1. F. Beck, "Synaptic Quantum Tunnelling in Brain Activity", *NeuroQuantology* 6 (2008): 140–51; F. Beck and J.C. Eccles, "Quantum Aspects of Brain Activity and the Role of Consciousness", *Proceedings of the National Academy of Science, USA* 89 (1992): 11357–61.
2. D.L. Wilson, "Mind–Brain Interaction and Violation of Physical Laws", *Journal of Consciousness Studies* 6 (1999): 185–200.
3. P.G.H. Clarke, "Determinism, Brain Function and Free Will", *Science & Christian Belief* 22 (2010): 133–49; P.G.H. Clarke, "Neuroscience, Quantum Indeterminism and the Cartesian Soul", *Brain and Cognition* 84 (2014): 109–17.
4. P.G.H. Clarke, "The Limits of Brain Determinacy", *Proceedings of the Royal Society. B: Biological Sciences* 279 (2012): 1665–74.
5. Clarke, "Neuroscience, Quantum Indeterminism and the Cartesian Soul".
6. C.U. Smith, "The 'Hard Problem' and the Quantum Physicists. Part 2: Modern Times", *Brain and Cognition* 71 (2009): 54–63.
7. M. Brownnutt, "Response to Peter Clarke on 'Determinism, Brain Function and Free Will'", *Science & Christian Belief* 24 (2012): 81–86.
8. P. Ball, "Physics of Life: The Dawn of Quantum Biology", *Nature* 474 (2011): 272–74.
9. The above arguments deal only with the question of quantum indeterminism and do not exclude other ideas on the relationship between quantum physics and consciousness, e.g. the famous but controversial theory of Penrose and Hameroff on quantum computation in brain microtubules. This vast field is beyond our scope.

Appendix 2. Neo-Darwinism and Why I Accept It

1. E. Lucas, *Can We Believe Genesis Today? The Bible and the Questions of Science*, Nottingham: Inter-Varsity Press, 2005.; H. Blocher, *In the Beginning: The Opening Chapters of Genesis*, Leicester: Inter-Varsity Press, 1984.
2. F.S. Collins, *The Language of God: A Scientist Presents Evidence for Belief*, New York: Free Press, 2006.
3. D. Alexander, *Creation or Evolution: Do We Have to Choose?*, revised edn, Oxford: Monarch Books, 2014.
4. Y.B. Lebedev, O.S. Belonovitch, N.V. Zybrova, et al., "Differences in HERV-K LTR Insertions in Orthologous Loci of Humans and Great Apes", *Gene* 247 (2000): 265–77.
5. J. Calvin, *Institutes of the Christian Religion*, translated by H. Beveridge, Peabody, MA: Hendrickson Publishers, 2008 (1559), I.16.1 (p. 114).
6. P. de Vries, "Naturalism in the Natural Sciences: A Christian Perspective", *Christian Scholars Review* 15 (1986): 388–96 (p. 389).
7. C. de Duve, "Mysteries of Life: Is there 'Something Else'?" *Perspectives in Biology and Medicine* 45 (2002): 1–15 (p. 1).

Recommendations for Further Reading

Neuroscience and the Mind

Stanislas Dehaene, *Consciousness and the Brain: Deciphering How the Brain Codes Our Thoughts*, New York: Viking Penguin, 2014.
Excellent account of recent experiments attempting to understand consciousness and the patterns of brain activity that underlie it, and how these differ from those underlying unconscious processes. Dehaene is a leading authority on this subject. One of his key points is that conscious thought involves the sharing of information between widespread areas of the brain.

Malcolm Jeeves, *Minds, Brains, Souls and Gods: A Conversation on Faith, Psychology and Neuroscience*, Downers Grove, IL: InterVarsity Press, 2013.
This book is aimed at students, and takes the form of a series of imaginary email exchanges between a first-year psychology student with Christian convictions and the author. Thus, the questions to be dealt with in the book are asked by the student (about free will, the soul, neurotheology, evolutionary psychology, NDEs, reductionism, evolutionary theory, etc.), and Jeeves's answers follow. The format is thus rather "popular", but the answers are sound and up-to-date.

Malcolm Jeeves and Warren S. Brown, *Neuroscience, Psychology, and Religion: Illusions, Delusions, and Realities about Human Nature*, West Conshohocken, PA: Templeton Press, 2009.
Written by two eminent neuropsychologists, this excellent book focuses on how the soul/mind relates to the brain, and includes a history of attempts to understand this relationship. It is comprehensible for readers without specialized knowledge. The final chapters include questions in the philosophy of mind, and the authors, who are both Christians, argue for dual-aspect monism/ nonreductive physicalism.

David J. Linden, *The Accidental Mind: How Brain Evolution Has Given Us Love, Memory, Dreams, and God*, Cambridge, MA: Belknap Press of Harvard University Press, 2007.
A fascinating survey, written for the general public, on numerous neuroscience topics including brain development, sensation, memory, human individuality, love, sex, sleep, and dreams. The book includes controversial subjects such as sexual orientation and the religious impulse, claims that the brain is an accidental result of evolution, and makes scathing criticisms of those who oppose Darwinian evolution in the name of religion, but accepts that many forms of religious belief are compatible with evolution.

Vilayanur S. Ramachandran, *The Tell-Tale Brain: A Neuroscientist's Quest for What Makes Us Human*, London: Heinemann, 2011.
Very readable and lively account for the general public, making use of numerous case studies to make deductions about human brain function, and about how this underlies our humanity.

Free Will, Responsibility, and Ethics

Mark Balaguer, *Free Will*, Cambridge, MA: MIT Press, 2014.
This is one of the most accessible books available on free will. The author considers that free will as defined in the compatibilist sense is so obviously true that it does not require detailed treatment. He therefore focuses on libertarian free will, and his main claim is that attempts so far to refute it do not succeed. The book is short, and the arguments intelligible even for those not used to grappling with philosophy.

Bob Doyle, *Free Will: The Scandal in Philosophy*, Cambridge, MA: I-Phi Press, 2011.
This 458-page book is based on Bob Doyle's Information Philosopher website, which is a wonderful resource on free will. The book brims over with insights and ideas, and is surprisingly easy to read given the difficulty of the subjects being dealt with. Doyle favours a two-stage model of libertarian free will, but gives balanced accounts of other views.

Richard Swinburne, *Mind, Brain, and Free Will*, Oxford: Oxford University Press, 2013.
Swinburne is one of the few leading philosophers adopting a substance dualist view of the mind–body relationship. This closely argued account pleads for a form of libertarian free will known as "agent causal free will". Not for novices.

The Soul, Neurotheology, Religion, and the Evolution of the Religious Impulse

All these issues are dealt with briefly in the above books by Jeeves and Brown, and by Jeeves. For more specialized accounts I would recommend:

Justin L. Barrett, *Born Believers: The Science of Children's Religious Belief*, New York: Free Press, 2012.
Summarizes findings of contemporary cognitive and evolutionary psychology indicating that very young children have a natural tendency to believe in God, and in design behind life and the world around us.

Stewart Goetz and Charles Taliaferro, *A Brief History of the Soul*, Chichester: Wiley-Blackwell, 2011.
The first 130 pages provide a concise history of the philosophical concept of soul. The last 80 pages address the modern debate and argue in favour of substance dualism.

Barbara B. Hagerty, *Fingerprints of God: What Science is Learning about the Brain and Spiritual Experience*, New York: Riverhead Books, 2009.
Lively journalistic enquiry into neurotheology, including near-death and other mystical experiences. Reports numerous interviews with specialists in several areas including brain imagery, neurology, and genetics, and also with people who describe their own spiritual experiences.

Patrick McNamara, *The Neuroscience of Religious Experience*, Cambridge: Cambridge University Press, 2009.
Academic level book that draws on neurology, biology, and cognitive science to clarify the relationships between the brain, the self, and religious experience.

Colin Renfrew and Iain Morley (eds.), *Becoming Human: Innovation in Prehistoric Material and Spiritual Culture*, New York: Cambridge University Press, 2009.
Academic level book with chapters by 15 archaeologists and theologians who discuss the early emergence of human qualities including spirituality. The book stems from a conference held in 2004.